'This ambitious book fills a yawning gap in the social scientific literature and will appeal to a readership across the social sciences.' Alan Warde, Professor of Sociology, University of Manchester, UK

'*The Sociology of Elite Distinction* is a superb, balanced and critical synthesis of the major theoretical and comparative works that deal with elite distinction...Daloz's book fills a gap in the literature on elites.' *International Political Anthropology*

'Daloz's book is a most interesting contribution to the sociology of consumption for it draws attention to the perspective of elitist distinction which has been little explored by social scientists, despite its great importance.' *Politica y Sociedad*

'A whirlwind tour of erudition.' *Contemporary Sociology*

'Daloz displays an intimidating knowledge of settings from antiquity to the present. He compares how elites in these myriad settings have used ostentation or austerity to demonstrate distinctiveness. The book is a tour de force in the sociology of elites and the mechanisms used to sustain their prominence.' *Winterthur Portfolio*

'A strength of Daloz's book lies within the richness of the empirical examples he offers: the reader experiences several revelations that indicate her/his own ignorance. It is also refreshing that Daloz does not commit to a single theoretical tradition.' *Sosiologia*

'A thorough investigation of distinction was overdue, and Daloz's insightful and engaging work is a welcome contribution to the literature. Daloz's book is a good first step, and for that it merits distinction.' *Acta Sociologica*

'Daloz identifies and challenges the simplifications and reductions that have marked sociological efforts to investigate the symbolic displays of classes and elites. In his often witty, encyclopaedic exploration of the fantastic variations that actually have marked such displays, he gives the culture of distinction not only an autonomy but an internal structure – for the first time.' Jeffrey C. Alexander, Professor of Sociology, Yale University, USA

'Thanks to its comparative approach and its concern for varieties of social behaviour, this analysis of social distinction by Jean-Pascal Daloz helps us to go beyond Bourdieu's famous study, published thirty years ago.' Peter Burke, Professor of Cultural History, University of Cambridge, UK

The Sociology of Elite Distinction

From Theoretical to Comparative Perspectives

Jean-Pascal Daloz
University of Strasbourg, France
and University of Oxford, UK

First published 2010 by
PALGRAVE MACMILLAN
Paperback edition published 2012

Palgrave Macmillan in the UK is an imprint of Macmillan Publishers Limited, registered in England, company number 785998, of Houndmills, Basingstoke, Hampshire RG21 6XS.

Palgrave Macmillan in the US is a division of St Martin's Press LLC, 175 Fifth Avenue, New York, NY 10010.

Palgrave Macmillan is the global academic imprint of the above companies and has companies and representatives throughout the world.

Palgrave® and Macmillan® are registered trademarks in the United States, the United Kingdom, Europe and other countries.

ISBN: 978–0–230–22027–0 hardback
ISBN: 978–1–137–00365–2 paperback

This book is printed on paper suitable for recycling and made from fully managed and sustained forest sources. Logging, pulping and manufacturing processes are expected to conform to the environmental regulations of the country of origin.

A catalogue record for this book is available from the British Library.

A catalog record for this book is available from the Library of Congress.

10 9 8 7 6 5 4 3 2 1
19 18 17 16 15 14 13 12 11 10

Printed and bound in Great Britain by
CPI Antony Rowe, Chippenham and Eastbourne

For Minä

Contents

Preface and Acknowledgements

One sometimes ends up writing the books for which one has vainly searched. Since I began studying elites in the 1980s and, later, taught on symbolic aspects of social superiority, I have frequently deplored the absence of a volume which would provide an overall picture of the significant theme of 'social distinction'. The present text aims to fill this gap and I hope that it will serve as a useful introduction for readers in search of a thorough presentation of the major analytical frameworks available. It will also offer a detailed discussion on key manifestations and variables.

The main objective of this book, however, is to propose a systematic reflection on the usefulness and limits of the theories concerned when confronted with empirical realities in a large number of environments. As such, it is first and foremost an essay in *comparative sociology*. Comparativists (at least this is the way I experience it) are rather special researchers. They are enthusiastically passionate about anything touching on their favourite subject across time and space, and are usually obsessed by the issue of generalisation versus diversity. As a result, they tend to have an ambiguous relationship with theoretical assumptions. They may be interested in theorisation but are more sceptical than others regarding the universalist pretensions of some explanatory schemes.

My ambition in this volume is not to identify the insights of each and every celebrated approach in order to attempt to erect a new (synthesising) grand theory. I remain extremely doubtful about the possibility of any such attempt. Instead, I examine how a thoughtful deployment of the relevant reading grids, in relation to various contexts, may help to reach convincing explanations.

The Sociology of Elite Distinction, perhaps even more than any of my previous books, has necessitated reading in various scientific fields. For several years, I have received helpful comments from colleagues working in different disciplines. It is not possible to list here those with whom I have been having valued exchanges. However, warm thanks are due to Alan Warde and Jukka Gronow who strongly encouraged me to write this book and to Peter Burke who was kind enough to share his immense historical knowledge with me. I am also truly grateful to Mattei Dogan for having prompted me to develop activities within the domain of comparative sociology and to my other colleagues from the ISA Research Committee 20. I am no less appreciative of the intellectual culture which I have found within the IPSA Research Committee 2 where I can regularly meet renowned specialists of elite studies. In particular, I benefited greatly from working with John Higley. When preparing this book, I was given the invaluable opportunity to present some of my arguments to various audiences. I am chiefly indebted to Fredrik Engelstad, Wendy Griswold, Ursula Hoffmann-Lange, Anne Krogstad and Aagoth Storvik for having invited me to speak and to sharp commentators such as Phil Smith.

I also wish to acknowledge the support of several institutions. In Oxford, it has been a pleasure to work with colleagues, students and staff from the Maison Française, the Department of Politics, St Antony's College and the European Research Group. Thanks are owed to the persons in charge of these establishments or teams for their gratefully received feedback. While completing the typescript, I also productively collaborated with sociologists, principally Tak Wing Chan. At the University of Oslo, I would like to offer collective thanks to all my very good colleagues from the Departments of both Political Science and Sociology for their habitual kindness and generosity. I owe a special debt to the doctoral students who attended my July 2007 course, within the framework of the Summer School in Comparative Social Science Studies, for some interesting testimonies about their respective countries. I must not neglect to mention my former days in Bordeaux and the many exchange visits in which I participated, giving me the opportunity for very pleasant stays (notably at the Universities of Colorado and Washington State).

I would also like to express my gratitude to Philippa Grand and Olivia Middleton from Palgrave for their efficient assistance in the publication of this book, and to Brill Publishers and Routledge for allowing me to reproduce parts of my articles 'Elite Distinction: Grand Theory and Comparative Perspectives' published in *Comparative Sociology* (vol. 6/1–2, 2007, pp. 27–74), and 'Towards the Cultural Contextualization of Social Distinction' published in the *Journal of Cultural Economy* (vol. 1/3, 2008, pp. 305–20). Last, but certainly not least, thanks very much indeed to Rosemary March and Catherine Lowne for proofreading the typescript.

J.-P. D.
Oxford (October 2007–March 2009)

Preface to the Paperback Edition

Two years have now passed since the first edition of this book. Judging from the dozen reviews published in academic journals so far and also from numerous comments received during an international tour of presentation, my impression is that, by and large, it has met with approval. The following discussion will be devoted, however, to addressing some more critical/defensive reactions to my approach that I believe warrant further reflection. I will consider briefly the question of theoretical eclecticism vs. dogmatism, my use of the term elites and, at somewhat greater length, my conception of comparative analysis.

As is stated in the preface of the hardcover edition, my intention was first of all to offer a panorama of the major theoretical frameworks dealing with social distinction – knowing that it is not uncommon to meet students and even scholars who believe that interest in this topic basically started with Pierre Bourdieu. More specifically, however, my main purpose was to emphasise both the virtues and limitations of these frameworks when confronted with diverse empirical realities cutting across a wide spectrum of environments. I argue that while most of the models of interpretation available provide useful insight, more often than not they turn out to be typical products of the societies they derive from. Consequently, from a comparative perspective, they should be seen as tools that are more or less operational depending on the context under analysis.

I was well aware of the fact that such an enterprise would be considered contentious, particularly in the eyes of those of our colleagues who are convinced of the superiority of their own school of thought over all others. As could have been anticipated, scholars strongly wedded to a given sociological tradition have tended to mostly pay attention to the critical remarks levelled against their favoured explanatory scheme, overlooking the fairly balanced view I take toward the lines of thinking considered. Let me add that the three endorsements on the back of the hardcover version (notably Peter Burke's statement that my comparative approach was helping us 'go beyond Bourdieu'), which have undoubtedly contributed to raise the visibility of the book, may also have fostered excessive expectations in some quarters. Indeed, it seems that more than a few readers, browsing through my book, took its main ambition to be nothing less than the production of a new grand theory aimed at replacing existing ones. I would like to reiterate here that my objections never concerned the very real and significant theoretical achievements of key authors, but only reflected a degree of uneasiness with the limited applicability of some of the interpretations they have proposed on the question at hand. In this, my aim was only to argue for a well-considered scientific eclecticism when assessing which of the classical analytical frameworks are best suited to a broad comparative canvas.

I also came across colleagues who queried my approach in terms of 'elites' and I realise now that more space should perhaps have been devoted to the topic in the book's introduction. It is true that my position on this matter is a little bit unorthodox in so far as, unlike several specialists with whom I occasionally collaborate, I do not fully embrace the elitist (chiefly Paretian) paradigm. On the other hand, I find the notion particularly useful as a comparativist as it enables me to encompass a variety of upper groups. Faced with a knotty problem of definition, my opinion is that we should deliberately avoid being too explicit because the varying nature of those who stand at the apex of societies is precisely part of what is at stake when one studies social distinction. Having the opportunity to regularly address the issue of elites in front of very different audiences, I am often struck by the vastly dissimilar inferences the word carries from country to country. In some places, it seems to be taken for granted and in others almost unacceptable; to be imbued with rather positive or altogether negative connotations; to refer to a tiny minority or to be almost synonymous with upper class, and so on. In my view, it is important to avoid an excessively narrow conception of elites, to allow for some flexibility in the use of the notion and, obviously enough, to beware of normative standpoints.

Certain reactions also confirmed my worry that the type of reasoning involved in the comparative perspective I develop remains unfamiliar, even alien, to some. Admittedly, this volume does not easily fall into established academic categories such as the textbook, the theoretical essay, or the monograph study resting on new research. It definitely has a theoretical purpose that is closely related to comparative concerns over the allegedly universalistic suitability of some established readings. And, although I refer to some of my own field research (from sub-Saharan Africa to Scandinavia), it is not an original empirical work as such. Unlike colleagues whose work bears exclusively on one country or period, I often get the feeling that my scientific activity is of an altogether different nature, at once more extensive and more specific, requiring a limitless erudition yet focusing predominantly on a restricted number of select themes. Jeffrey Alexander was of course much too generous in his endorsement when he wrote that I offer an 'encyclopedic exploration' of the variations that have marked the symbolic displays of classes and elites. As a matter of fact, however, compared to 'generalists' in the sociological discipline, I realise that I have developed a considerably wider-ranging body of knowledge, in the pursuit of which I have necessarily straddled the social sciences and cast as broad a net as possible.

Equally, in marked contrast to those authors who passionately seek out the latest signs of social change, this type of comparative perspective entails a very distanced analysis. I mention this because when debating with sociologists who follow a strongly normative research agenda, one is sometimes left with the impression that the identification of variations in elitist forms of symbolic superiority (that are not easily encompassed within a single theory) is perceived as a rather futile art-for-art's-sake kind of comparison. The question of social distinction is a particularly sensitive one, nowhere more so than at the top of societies: occasionally giving rise to impulsive over-generalised statements and, not infrequently, leading to the wholesale dismissal of cross-cultural dissimilarities which are deemed superficial in light of so-called common fundamental structures. In this book, my goal was to challenge the reductive nature of such views. Another risk also beckons, however: that of tackling the question from an essentially teleological standpoint and of casting moral judgements according to one's own contemporary ideals. Comparative analyses that are mindful of the need to enter the realm of meaning cannot afford the luxury of conforming to canons of political correctness, especially as the latter are irredeemably ethnocentric.

This brings me to a final, more complicated comparative issue. Some commentators, who otherwise assessed the book favourably and found my arguments convincing, pointed out that such a demonstration should be followed up with constructive propositions. To highlight variability in the manifestation and logics of elite distinction, along with the dangers of dogmatic reductionism, is one thing. But to do so without giving the opposite impression of a world irreducible to cross-contextual models of interpretation is another. How can we safely navigate the thin line between these twin perils? This question requires a nuanced answer. Empirical evidence indeed reveals that most theories of social distinction have validity. The problem is that these are valid mainly as middle-range theories rather than as the ubiquitous explanatory schemes they usually claim to be. I do not subscribe to the old positivistic view that the only type of comparative research which can be deemed serious is the one that seeks to uncover causal relations between more or less significant variables. On the other hand, I think it is a reasonable goal to seek to identify divergent patterns of social distinction and to formulate hypotheses in order to account for significant variations. Interpreting them requires inductive work aimed at deciphering contextually meaningful codes, not simply applying ready-made deductive reasoning.

This is the task of the succeeding volume I am now completing, entitled: *Rethinking Social Distinction* (also to be published by Palgrave Macmillan). Its purpose is to develop foundations for a comparative analysis avoiding the pitfalls of ethnocentrism and reductionism.

J.-P. D.
Strasbourg
October 2011

Introduction

At the heart of sociological analysis lie the classic theme of stratification and the everlasting issue of inequality, both of which are widely explored. The intention of the present work is to provide a more restricted and complementary angle of attack: a detailed study of the symbolic expressions of social position.

It is quite common to see people judging themselves as socially superior and eager to distinguish themselves from members of lower strata. Tellingly, the word *distinction* refers literally to the objective idea of separation and, in derived meanings, to noticeable eminence as well as to refined manners.[1] Because of the remarkable success of Pierre Bourdieu's book (1984 [1979]) on the topic, perspectives in terms of social distinction have become very much associated with his school of thought. As will quickly become clear, the present volume does not espouse a Bourdieusian line – nor does is aim to refute Bourdieu either. The reading grid of the French author will be presented as one of the possible ways of envisaging the 'problematic' of distinction and (as with all the other models of interpretation discussed here) we shall endeavour to emphasise its merits and demerits from a comparative point of view. However, for the sake of definitional clarity, it is important to mention at this stage that Bourdieu has developed a specific conception of social distinction, denoting the seemingly natural (discreet and mainly embodied) superiority arguably manifested in dominant classes. Therefore, within his analytical framework, distinction is understood as the opposite of conspicuous display. In contrast, the term will be used throughout in a larger sense enabling us to encompass all means of differentiation, including ostentatious ones.

Although we give a general account of theories of social distinction, we essentially focus attention on *elite* distinction. The concept of elite is used here as a convenient way to designate categories standing at the apex of societies. Like many others in the social sciences, it has heuristic advantages and disadvantages. Its principal merit is that it subsumes all sorts of upper groups, including within those contexts where the concept of class would seem inappropriate. However, such a breadth is also liable to be viewed as an inconvenience, in so far as the bringing together of members from disparate sectors potentially entails a relative imprecision. Another difficulty is that this concept is sometimes perceived as connoting elitism.[2] It should be stressed that in the present author's works, it has no evaluative implication whatsoever (such as 'the best' or people of particular excellence) but refers to a research theme. Clearly, the logics of social distinction are not confined to the upper spheres only – they may indeed concern the lowest levels[3] – and we shall occasionally have the opportunity to talk about other echelons. It remains, however, that these logics are perhaps more visible, and crucial, at the top.

As its title indicates, the analytical foundation of this volume is sociological. The objective is to consider concrete manifestations of elite distinction in light of the theoretical arguments developed on this topic by various social scientists. Nonetheless, especially when it comes to empirical research, it goes without saying that contributions by scholars from many other disciplines are essential. Anthropologists and historians have produced quite outstanding works which have led to the formulation of a broad range of highly pertinent questions. Likewise, the comparativist is indebted to geographers (about residential areas, for example), archaeologists (e.g. on 'prestige goods') or linguists (e.g. on 'respect language') and sub-sections of this book will justly be devoted to political, psycho-sociological and socio-economical perspectives.

General theories which have received acclaim are automatically applied, or at least invoked, in case studies by investigators producing field and historical research on elite expressions of social prestige. On their side, the proponents of the competing sociological schools of thought enthusiastically welcome descriptions that bolster their favourite theoretical frameworks. It has to be admitted, however, that the reading grids called upon by some researchers in support of their enquiries are far from always being entirely convincing in certain contexts. Equally, many scholars appear wilfully blinded by the dogmatic assumptions of their favourite model of interpretation and cannot easily accommodate an interest in those cases that might appear to invalidate it. One of the primary tasks of this book is to build bridges between various currents of social analysis and the insightful contributions of the more empirical literature on this subject. The challenge ahead is to prevent excessively reductionist views and to enlighten students of elite distinction as to what is implied when turning to a particular theory, and of the limited applicability of certain concepts.

As has been emphasised in the Preface, the perspective of this volume is deliberately a comparative one. This will lead us to consider not only contemporary 'Western' societies but also non-Western settings and societies of the past. That said, the purpose of a comparative undertaking may be to search first and foremost for invariants (largely thanks to abstract concepts applicable to a wide range of distinct cases), whereas particularisms are merely taken to be surface phenomena, or it may consist in taking observable diversity very seriously. Within the first tradition – so predominant within those paradigms hoping to emulate the physical sciences – the quest for a general 'grammar' underpinning all social relations and for a universal theoretical synthesis is central. Within the second, comparativists pay attention to important cross-societal differences and are cautious of the trend of grand theories toward one-sided explanatory schemes. Our comparative explorations and reasoning will be clearly anchored in the second alternative. From this standpoint, the goal is obviously not to pursue an allusive and superficial approach aimed at cataloguing more or less contingent dissimilarities, but to hint at the reality of what we might call the multifaceted and often contradictory workings of elite distinction throughout the world, mainly in relation to sociological theory and available interpretative grids. What will be advocated is an inductive method that consists in resorting to the theories which appear to be the most convincingly relevant to the cases under consideration.

It should be added that the approach proposed here favours a certain version of cultural analysis, chiefly concerned with examining patterns of meanings and what makes sense, or not, to the social actors studied. Further to pioneering developments in some quarters of anthropology,[4] or history,[5] a cultural contextualisation of some key research topics is currently emerging in sociology. Cultural sociology has gained popularity among researchers during the last 15 years. As it defies the meta-theoretical assumptions of several classical schools of thought, this 'cultural turn' is controversial. Some sociologists now consider culture as an independent variable (Alexander, 2003), which is indeed revolutionary for a discipline which used either to ignore cultural dimensions, to treat them as emanating from social structures or, at best, to view them (like Weber) in terms of 'elective affinities'. Culture will be understood here as a context not necessarily derived from other, allegedly more consequential, processes. Of course, it is liable to be manipulated and it is illusory to assume that it can be studied as a 'neutral' system. Yet, when cultural universes are conceived in terms of 'webs of significance' that people have learned and share with others, some wide differences manifestly appear.[6]

A great deal has been written on social distinction and Part I is intended as an introduction to the major theoretical contributions on this subject. The presentation is intentionally 'reader friendly', perhaps at risk of superfluity for those already very familiar with the topic. Yet, it is true that if some classical frameworks appear ubiquitous, acquaintance with other, equally important, ones is at best sketchy. The principal argument posited in these opening chapters is that most of the explanatory schemes were dominated by efforts at building systematic theories. Such ambitions were not without merit but they also proved detrimental to comparative studies. As we shall see, a typical bias stems from consistent generalisations made from a particular case. However, it will be concluded that many analytical frameworks indeed remain worthy of note when taken not as ultimate models of interpretation but rather as containing elements of truth for some social environments.

In Part II, we shall consider some key manifestations of elite distinction (external, embodied and vicarious signs of superiority) largely in relation with the reading grids previously introduced. Comparativists are sensitive to the risks of extrapolation and one of their concerns, in this respect, is to furnish counter-examples liable to raise doubts about grand theories held to be universally valid. Nevertheless, referring to some empirical data that has some bearing on the question of similarities versus dissimilarities will also allow us to stress how proper recourse to the theories available can prove relevant.

Finally, Part III is specifically designed to give a sense of the variability of elite distinction logics. This section of the book contains three chapters. The first will aim to summarise some significant historical dimensions. The following two will, respectively, discuss some basic alternatives (e.g. quantitative/qualitative emphasis and distinction through antiquity/novelty) and engage with some controversial themes such as the determination of standards of superiority, taste or style.

Part I

Social Theory and Elite Distinction

There is an abundance of theories related to elite distinction. A number of prominent social scientists have, implicitly or explicitly, addressed the topic. Quite evidently, their arguments have been rooted in dissimilar analytical frameworks and have arisen in the context of various fields of studies. Relevant theoretical perspectives can thus be found in the literature focusing on many diverse research objects: status; conspicuous consumption; the leisure class; luxury; fashion; court society; presentation of self; or taste, for example. Despite the pronounced variety of these works, the underlying theme discovered concerns the necessity for dominant groups to display signs of superiority that signal their upper social position.

In keeping with the aims of the volume, it matters to discuss at first the theoretical propositions made by those scholars who have contributed significantly to writings on the subject. A comprehensive coverage of classical or more recent sociological thinkers and their accounts of elite distinction will be offered. Each theory will be situated in reference to the system of thought of their author, as well as with regard to their most influential contemporaries or precursors. This will present an opportunity to critically examine the concepts and tools of analysis developed in the extent literature.

Part I consists of three chapters, the first of which deals with early explanatory endeavours. Chapter 2 pursues the discussion of social theories by considering the major subsequent contributions. Finally, Chapter 3 underlines both the virtues and limitations of each reading grid from a comparative perspective.

1
Classical Approaches to Social Emulation and Distinction

Several founders of the discipline of sociology at the turn of the twentieth century devoted their attention to the question of elite distinction. With the notable exception of Veblen, all, however, tackled it as a subsidiary theme within the ambit of their more general conceptualisations, and not in relation to what might be termed a particular tradition of studies. Consequently, instead of referring to other seminal works, these sociologists were prompted by a desire to provide writings on distinction that were coherent with the key processes or principles underlying their respective approaches. This chapter therefore discusses the rather disjointed enterprises of some pioneers – from Spencer, Tarde and Veblen to Simmel, Weber and Sombart – which are relevant in one way or another to the understanding of elite distinction. Before turning to these, it is appropriate to say a few words about even more ancient views first.

Precursors

Elite distinction is hardly a new topic; the discussion goes back to antiquity. However, it is important to underline at the outset that this earlier literature is largely dominated by normative concerns. Think, for instance, of Sybaris, the Greek colony which surpassed all others in refinement according to Herodotus (and from which the adjective 'sybaritic' – as a description of a person addicted to luxury and pleasurable sensations – is derived) or of Sparta, the city associated with the ideas of military prowess and austerity (hence the adjective 'spartan'). Alternatively, contrast the image of the Roman statesman Cincinnatus, who gained fame because he embodied a model of simplicity, with that of his countryman, Lucullus, who used the vast treasure he had amassed during wars to retire to extravagant leisure, a few centuries later. These illustrations – whether historical or embellished – have travelled down the ages and emphasise the ancients' preoccupation with issues such as dissipation in riotous living and the ethics of renunciation.

Excessive pretension was commonly denounced by philosophers and moralists, where some members of the elite indulged in paroxysms of ostentation (particularly, but not exclusively, during the Hellenistic period and the Roman Empire). Plato and Aristotle had considered this problem to be of prime importance. Plato was especially preoccupied with the fact that gross social disparities among citizens might be disruptive to the harmony of the *polis*. In the *Republic*, for instance, he presented a famous dialogue between Socrates and Glaucon about the 'healthy' versus the 'luxurious' city. The former promotes the restriction of necessities to what is 'natural' and 'basic', together with the related fear that appetite is likely to develop out of control as it surpasses what is sufficient to meet bodily requirements. Glaucon responds that such a description would merely amount to that of a 'city of pigs' and he calls for more sophisticated satisfactions.[1] The central motif of Socrates' diagnosis is that when a city experiences luxury food, clothes or dwellings, it gives way to conflict among the people. Plato contended that the gravest danger was that of social disunity and that the pursuit of unlimited distinction could clearly lead to such a situation. For his part, in *Nichomachean Ethics,* Aristotle discussed the virtues of magnificence and magnanimity.[2] A magnanimous person, according to Aristotle, is capable of the greatest actions and deserving of the greatest honours, but should also be high-minded and an exemplary citizen. A man who falsely claims honour is vain but the underestimation of one's own value amounts to an undesirable pettiness. The magnificent man should know how to deal correctly with great wealth and power. He is expected in particular to spend large amounts of money for civic projects; this stands in marked contrast to those who show off improperly and are more concerned with making a grand impression than with the public welfare. In his *Rhetoric,* where he discusses the questions of envy and emulation, Aristotle again criticises men who boast in order to demonstrate their superiority.[3]

In this democratic setting, where citizens were theoretically political equals but in reality tensions frequently occurred between the opulent elite and the remaining *demos*, several famous orators used their power of speech to combat ostentation. The expert in rhetoric, Isocrates, was known for his defence of rich clients, but he also put forth warnings against the softness engendered by luxury, which made for poor endurance in the campaign against the Persian Empire. Demosthenes, in his *Speech against Meidias,* endeavoured to demonstrate that some men were guilty of *hubris;* that is, they acted in a supercilious manner toward others.[4] Demosthenes' tactic was to isolate his opponent completely by depicting him as someone whose attitude would be irreconcilably at odds from those of the majority of the citizens. Later, the Cynic philosophers, abhorring luxury and full of contempt for anybody claiming social superiority, were to adopt in reaction an extremely ascetic lifestyle. The dominant figure here is Diogenes of Sinope, who propounded a return to animalism and about whom anecdotes abound. In spite of their denunciation of the desire for prominence, a form of inverted conspicuousness was, paradoxically, one of the characteristics of the Cynics. In a far less exhibitionist way, Epicureanism advocated a simple, self-sufficient life avoiding excesses and any form of distinction.

To a large extent, we find in Rome a similar moralistic lament as well as proselytising discourses against vain ostentation. A recurring theme in many classic critiques of insolent luxury is that of degeneration.[5] The allegedly virtuous life of early Rome was continually contrasted with the decadent mores of subsequent times. The vices of the affluent elite would have undermined ancient discipline. Here, one might mention a wide variety of texts treating the extravagant competition for invidious status with opprobrium. Cicero, for example, liked to refer to Cato the Elder (whose stringent regulations against luxury remained famous) as a desirable model for the virtuous life Romans should follow. In his *Catilinarian Orations,* he violently laid the blame on the depraved Lucius Catilina, whom he epitomised as representing all the evils festering in the declining Republic – clearly in sharp opposition to heroes of the third century BC, who had perfectly embodied the virtue of *frugalitas.*[6] In the same vein, the historian Sallust suggested that when one generation no longer puts the consideration of virtue into practice, the succeeding generation is likely to be a decadent one. Another historian, Livy, emphasised that Rome had been able to triumph over her neighbours precisely because of her cult of an austere life, synonymous with superior strength. However, according to Livy, the conquest of Greece and victories in Asia had also led to encounters with much more refined styles and manners, which would have brought about a detrimental feebleness.

With the advent of the Empire and its outburst of outrageous behaviour, thinkers became greatly concerned with what was interpreted as indisputable signs of moral decadence, and several certainly did not refrain from judgemental commentary. For instance, both Pliny the Elder and Martial deplored the fact that so much expense was devoted to the nefarious pursuit of luxury. Unsurprisingly, the never-satiated quest for elite distinction also attracted the scorn of satirists such as Petronius and Juvenal. Last but not least, the Stoics decried a society succumbing to unnecessary frivolous habits. Epictetus wrote that 'shoes are meant to fit the foot, but why should they be gilded, purpled and then studded with jewels?'[7] It is worth noting that some of those authors advocating independence from worldly attachments and warning others against the threat of riches were far from being irreproachable themselves.[8] Moreover, if some Romans loathed personal luxury, most of them were appreciative of public splendour, although the differentiation between private forms of ostentation and public display was then unclear.

During the Middle Ages, with Christianity beginning to pervade all aspects of life, any attempt to place oneself above others would theoretically bring instant disapprobation. Overtly pious discourses readily referred to the sin of pride and to the Christian ideal of humility. The subject of temperance seems to have been almost an obsession for many clerics. Needless to say, the insistence on sins also concerned food (gluttony) and sex (lust). Early 'Church Fathers' such as Tertullian had instigated the practice of fasting as a distinguishing mark for the new Christian elite. For his part, Augustine, who appropriated the Roman anti-luxury argument, was to insist particularly on sexual restraint with, of course, a reference to 'the Fall'. The exemplary figure of the Middle Ages was that of the saint – the perfect incarnation of the virtues advocated by the Church – and, to a lesser extent, that of the monk, who was supposed to banish any sign of distinction (even hair). However, if some mendicant orders really led an ascetic life, not all monastic communities adopted a very austere existence. It is worth recalling here that Christian doctrines held that social inequalities should be considered as natural and indeed as the will of divine providence. This sought to justify high levels of ostentation for the glory of God and that of his intercessors. More precisely, there was a crucial distinction made between a legitimate splendour, which the Church did not associate with sin (in so far as it was organically linked to a sacred transcendence), and the pursuit of luxury (that which was unrelated to the official hierarchy of differentiated estates ordained by God and therefore condemned). In this respect, Thomas Aquinas was to reinterpret in an appropriate Christian manner the above-mentioned Aristotelian category of magnificence.

The world of chivalry was also fairly ambivalent. It could tend toward knightly ascetic honour or involve great vanity and display (brightly coloured clothes, banners, accompanying retainers, etc.). We encounter here contradictory intellectual models carried out by both Christian thought – laying stress on religious exemplarity – and medieval epic literature. With the reinforcement of royal powers and the advent of the first courts (those of the Popes, in Avignon or Rome, and that of Burgundy, which were particularly ostentatious), social distinction was increasingly legitimised by Catholic theologians who knew very well how to preserve the self-interests of the Church. Elites – whether monarchical, aristocratic, religious or bourgeois – could indulge in lavish banquets and many other pleasurable delights, in the knowledge that they could seek redemption for their sins by giving generously to ecclesiastic institutions and thereby secure their salvation.

Prescriptive discourses remained omnipresent during the Renaissance but with a different tone. This period, marked by the rediscovery of antiquity, the Reformation and humanism, notably saw the flowering of what can be called an 'advice literature'. In his famous book, *The Prince* (1995 [1532]), surveying various bold means of acquiring and maintaining power, Machiavelli blamed Christianity for having extolled humility rather than glory, the feeble and not the strong and submissiveness instead of domination. Another influential opus we will meet again is Castiglione's *The Courtier* (1974 [1528]) which was to be translated into many languages and became the bible of many courts (see Burke, 1995). In this work, the speakers describe, through dialogue, ideal elitist manners: emphasising the aristocratic capacity to preserve tight control over the emotions under all circumstances in a dispassionate and calm appearance. 'Proper conduct' was therefore the subject of a specialised literature that circulated among the members of Europe's courtly societies. Because of the subtlety of the advocated codes of behaviour, knowledge of them was an important resource used by the established members to test others' status. However, authors such as the Renaissance humanist, Erasmus – who wrote extensively on the question of civility as an aspect of good citizenship – or, later on, the Spanish Jesuit Balthazar Gracian (1980 [1647]) – who stressed the importance of appearance – produced treatises intended for an audience larger than courtiers. We shall return to some of these texts when we deal with the question of distinguished manners. The sixteenth and seventeenth centuries also witnessed writers who wondered about the superiority of powerful people, sometimes in a sophisticated way, but usually with a critical eye: one can mention the works of Montaigne, La Boétie and Pascal, among others.

Although still mainly framed by normative concerns, some eighteenth-century contributions are of importance for our theme. In what can be considered a prelude to the identification of the 'trickle effect' tendency – which we shall discuss at some length – Swift evoked 'fashions always descending from those of quality to the middle sort, and thence to the vulgar'.[9] Several debates, respectively over luxury, good taste and refinement, are also worth mentioning here. A growing literature addressed the issue of luxury no longer according to the habitual moralistic view which had predominated for centuries, but instead in a positive way, essentially on economic grounds. To give just three illustrations,[10] Mandeville, in his *Fable of the Bees* (1962 [1714]), attempted to show how 'private vices' (luxury being related to pride, envy and vanity) could have 'public benefits' (a wealthy society). Voltaire's poem *Le mondain* [1736]), followed a year later by his *Défense du mondain ou l'apologie du luxe* [1737], declared that luxury is indeed an important element for the happiness of human beings. Hume, in his essay entitled *Of Luxury* [1752], provided a significant link with the notions of civilisation and refinement. He also contributed to the invention of the elitist figure of the 'man of taste'. If Montesquieu can be regarded as perhaps the first 'modern' comparativist – avoiding excessive ethnocentrism – his views on this matter, as mainly expressed in his *Essai sur le goût* [1757], are rather typical of what was written during the eighteenth century, that is the thesis that the sphere of the judgement of taste is a prerogative of an exclusive elite.[11] In diametrical opposition, Rousseau challenged the canon on luxury, good taste and manners. In *The Discourse on the Arts and Sciences* (1992 [1750]) and even more so in his book on children's education, *Emile* (2003 [1762]), Rousseau defended 'authenticity' – as opposed to alienation from oneself, associated with an artificial aspiration to distinction. In context of a rising critique toward aristocratic privilege which was to lead to the 1789 Revolution in France, plenty of other authors and works could be mentioned. The same is true for writings from the beginning of the nineteenth century (those of Tocqueville's or Carlyle's for instance).

It goes without saying that the references given in this all too brief overview are by no means exhaustive. The body of literature is vast and it would be difficult to acknowledge all venerable contributions to the subject discussed here. Furthermore, although instructive in some respects (as regards cultural differences or evolving mentalities), most of these earlier writings may be considered as of limited relevance from a 'scientific' point of view. The analytical ambition of sociology steers us away from moral judgements and toward objectivity; the foregoing discussion has made it clear, however, that these texts are full of normative statements. As already suggested, we shall occasionally return to some of these precursors when they prove to be more than of peripheral interest.

To go back to social theorists proper, it can be stated that the related themes of emulation and distinction have been an object of scholarly attention since the 1880s. The first theoretician to address these concerns systematically was Spencer.

Spencer

Although a dedicated autodidact who largely kept his distance from academic circles, Herbert Spencer (1820–1903) is commonly regarded as one of the classical founders of the discipline. Pivotal to his prolific oeuvre are the ideas of progress and process – which he was to develop in various fields – as well as the concepts of functions, structures, differentiation, integration or complexity, all of which are of importance to the social sciences. Spencer is best known for his attempt to transpose some key aspects of Darwin's evolutionary theories to the study of society, leading to an approach which is sometimes referred to as 'Social Darwinism'. Spencer's work enjoyed a great popularity during his lifetime. He seems to have addressed the preoccupations of some of his contemporaries, particularly those of American businessmen and successful mid-Victorians, through the ideological implications of his expressions such as the 'survival of the fittest'. However, the dire ethical consequences of his contentions that free competition can lead only to increasing progress and that the poor strata of the population should never be given any assistance contributed to the irrevocable rejection of Spencerism by many sociologists. Spencer is also chastised on epistemological and methodological grounds for his speculative scientism, his deterministic philosophy, his generalisations without empirical verification and his teleological views.

Such queries are valid. Many pages from Spencer do indeed have an archaic ring for the present-day reader. Nevertheless, he still remains a fairly interesting author in several respects. Prior to the publication of his three-volume *Principles of Sociology*, Spencer had devoted considerable energy to compiling ethnographic facts about all types of societies. With the help of assistants, he collected material from different sources on extinct or contemporary civilisations, as well as on 'primitive' peoples. Eight volumes about various parts of the world were published between 1873 and 1881 – to be followed by seven others after Spencer's death. His ultimate aim was of course not descriptive but comparative and theoretical, and he was to draw material constantly from these empirical publications (entitled: *Descriptive Sociology*) in order to elaborate his more systematic sociological treatise.

The abstracted data were arranged by themes, and of interest for us are the 12 chapters included in Part IV (Second Volume) of his *Principles of Sociology* (1893) on 'Ceremonial Institutions'. In these 225 pages, as in the rest of the collection, Spencer attempted to demonstrate his general hypothesis, according to which societies can be classified in terms of differentiation and integration, and that an enduring trend toward increasing complexity can be discerned. Following developments on trophies, presents, forms of address, titles, badges and costumes – providing innumerable illustrations about traditional settings – he also discussed other aspects of 'class-distinction' in more 'advanced' societies. Spencer concluded with an important piece on 'Ceremonial Retrospect and Prospect', anticipating Elias on the question of submissive manners, which, by spreading downward, result in ubiquitous politeness. We shall return to this and, more generally, we will have the opportunity to refer to some passages worthy of attention here throughout. Spencer is particularly stimulating on the topics of commendable gaits and expected postures of self-abasement (cf. his chapter on 'Obeisances'). One of the great advantages of his approach is that he has taken into consideration a wide range of cases across time and space. Admittedly, some of his descriptions and deductive interpretations might be deemed outdated by some Africanists or Americanists and it would be unacceptable to give them uncritical credence.[12] However, for the student of, say, ceremonial pomp, prestige goods or distinguished manners and language, this work is often instructive.

Tarde

Gabriel de Tarde (1843–1904) is little read today. It should be recalled that during his lifetime, this French sociologist was as famous as his major competitor, Durkheim. Focusing his attention on the relationship between individuals, Tarde challenged abstract sociologism and was to have a strong influence on American micro-sociology and actor-network theory. Very broadly speaking, Tarde's objectives were similar to those of Spencer in the sense that both firmly believed in the unity of all sciences. They propounded the idea that everything, from the cosmos to living creatures and human societies, is governed by major principles. In their view, the task of the scientist is therefore to discover these principles, to deduct laws from them and to apply the latter to various fields. However, on closer inspection, their respective sociological visions prove to be largely incompatible. For example, according to Spencer, individuals are negligible, whereas for Tarde they constitute the very basis of the social order.[13]

Several of Tarde's books are constructed around a single key process – that of imitation – through the prism of which he tackled many subjects such as psychology, history, sociology, economics, politics or art.[14] In his *magnum opus* on *The Laws of Imitation* (1962 [1890]), he argued that 'society is imitation'. This merits a brief explanation. According to Tarde's social theory, individuals as well as societies are constantly influenced by each other (one important corollary being that, in his analytical framework, there is no difference between basic units and larger groupings). Fathers are likely to be imitated (respect being a kind of imitation) as are heroes and even civilisations. Imitation, acting as a catalyst, eventually leads to harmonisations and standardisation.

In the passages most relevant to our topic, Tarde expressed the idea that people generally seek to imitate those socially superior to them, whom they idealise, by adopting their values and attitudes. These imitation attempts would often be crude, but at times also quite thorough. Tarde's main interest was in exploring why an imitation is not exactly the same thing as the original model. In many respects, his analysis proves to be much more sophisticated than it might at first seem. For instance, he proposed reflections on distance from a sociological point of view, on imitation and proximity, on admiration, on elites who end up doubting themselves and on both rational and unconscious grounds for imitation. Although he did not hold extreme evolutionist beliefs – he regarded Spencer's unilinear teleological theories with scepticism – it should be added that he also devoted some pages to the study of developments from total, close and conformist imitation in 'traditional societies' (i.e. reproduction of ancestors' behaviour, parochial references and fixed etiquette) to partial and more individualistic imitations in 'modern societies'. Tarde considered that the aping of one's superiors occurs in all stratified societies. But he clearly differentiated between contexts in which the chief determinants of status are hereditarily transmitted – such as aristocratic ones where the elite train their children to observe codes, setting the tone for the whole society – and those much more open to 'individual whims' – such as the modern city. This led him to important reflections on the plurality of available models. Tarde can equally be regarded as a pioneering scholar in the sociological study of fashion (along with Spencer, Veblen or Simmel). He certainly viewed imitation as a major factor of repetition and assimilation, constitutive of societies, but also as a dynamic phenomenon aiming toward more variations and higher standards.

The advantage of this type of approach is that it opens a whole field of study on elites as paragons. Moreover, it is useful for the analysis of borrowings from foreign patterns (see Chapter 8 below). Historians, anthropologists and sociologists have long recognised the importance of working on the exportation/importation of means of distinction – and Tarde can undoubtedly be of inspiration here. Yet, from a comparative perspective, what matters is to show that the imitation of upper groups is not necessarily the only possible option, nor is it the only one empirically observable.

The remaining sections focus on the work of four near-contemporaries belonging to the next generation of sociologists. We shall start with a figure who may be considered as most central for our theme.

Veblen

In this chapter as in the following one, it is fitting to give not only an overview of the classic sociologists' major works and theoretical 'problematic' but also some biographical information. In this respect, the life of Thorstein Veblen (1857–1929) particularly deserves to be brought up in so far as it sheds some light on his characterisation of the social system. Of note is the fact that this author was the sixth child of an immigrant Norwegian family which, by the mid-nineteenth century, had encountered serious troubles with land speculators and money lenders in Minnesota. His Scandinavian roots, but also the austerity which shaped the everyday life of this peasant household, made him scornful of any form of ostentation and extremely sensitive to the issue of waste.[15] The environment he experienced when he elaborated his seminal book on *The Theory of the Leisure Class* (1994 [1899]) is that of Chicago in the 1890s with its 200 millionaires and their lavish mansions by Lake Michigan, its nouveaux riches eager to show off, aggressive capitalism and serious class antagonism.[16] Veblen had always been an outsider who described and analysed the universe of elite distinction in a fairly ironic tone. Never really assimilated into American society and eccentric in many respects, Veblen had a patchy academic career, moving from one institution to the other more often than not as a result of scandals. He was an intellectual who despised the university system – a system that felt similarly toward him.

Opinions on Veblen's work remain divided. They range from the claim that he was *the* father of the study of social distinction, who provided key pioneering formulations which many influential theorists subsequently dealing with this topic did no more than translate into their own jargon, without acknowledging their debt, to the idea that he was merely a moralist writing essays which lacked scholarly rigour. Not all commentators, however, share such clear-cut views. Some try to show the ways in which Veblen was 'a genius' and 'a failure', or a very sharp but unsystematic thinker. Appraising Veblen is not a straightforward task. He was sometimes extremely innovative, and provided such subtle analyses in his *Theory of the Leisure Class* that the book inevitably became a standard reference. Nonetheless, this work also proves to be irritating in many ways. Despite the inventiveness of Veblen's model of interpretation, its limitations stem notably from his ahistorical reading of human nature.

In this respect, his grand theory is not especially different to those elaborated by Spencer or Tarde. One can reckon that he has illuminated several important mechanisms, albeit from one specific angle, which led him to a reductionist line of argument. Veblen was also – admittedly to a lesser degree than the above-mentioned authors – a believer in the authority of science and aimed to develop law-based generalisations. On the other hand, it is debatable whether or not he was an evolutionist. Although he reasoned about stages ('peaceful savagery', 'barbarian' and 'civilized'), he was one of the rare sociologists of his generation who rather stressed continuity and persistence instead of change or progress.[17]

Particularly disconcerting about Veblen is that his work resists categorisation, of which his relationship to Marxism may serve as good evidence. Veblen was unquestionably a radical in his condemnation of bourgeois society and may be considered as one of America's early critical social theorists. If (like Marx) he took an interest in economics after having studied philosophy, his theoretical framework differs from a Marxian one in many ways. He rejected dialectical materialism and did not believe in the inevitable decline of capitalism, nor even in class struggles (although he welcomed the 1917 Revolution in Russia). His critical reflections did not prompt him to social involvement or political activism but rather to a detached, individualistic and ironic perspective.[18] To give a second illustration, in his earliest work (i.e. his first articles published in the 1880s on 'The Economic Theory of Women's

Dress' or 'The Barbarian Status of Women'), Veblen depicted women as the eternal victims of masculine domination: criticising their reification and the institution of marriage as a continuation of more ancient forms of subjugation. Although, feminists justifiably consider him as forward-thinking, in his personal life he was far from treating his own companions in a respectful way. Veblen's first wife divorced him because of his notorious lechery and he apparently tried to extract sexual favours from his female students and to seduce his colleagues' spouses. The fact that he was an unconcealed womaniser (together with his marked disrespect for his superiors and his exceedingly unorthodox procedure of marking students' work) largely explains why he was asked to resign from several academic institutions.[19]

Veblen is also vulnerable to more serious criticisms from a methodological point of view and can be reproached for his often vague references[20] and incomplete citations (although this was common practice at the time). From a comparative perspective, it is relatively simple to highlight the limits of his general theses: later chapters will elaborate this argument. Nevertheless, many sociologists, economists and historians have long recognised the importance of Veblen's conceptualisations.

We may begin with the subject of his major book,[21] the 'Leisure Class'. In ancient and aristocratic societies, a life of leisure, or in other words a manifest exemption from productive labour, was one of the best means by which to prove one's social superiority. Dirty, menial occupations were left to servants. A master expected many functions to be fulfilled by the latter in a way that benefited his position in society. In chapter III, entitled 'Conspicuous Leisure', Veblen develops and illustrates his views on this matter. For example, he points out that some attributes show indirectly that their owner is not accustomed to work, or that having much time at one's disposal may lead to a superior sophistication. It might be considered that with the advent of industrial societies, labour has become prestigious and praised – Veblen also mentions the case of (necessarily) hard-working pioneers in America. However, even entrepreneurs may dream of taking over a leisured existence as soon as it may be afforded. Referring to the world of the nouveaux riches of his time, Veblen offers some views in terms of generations. Some captains of industry might have been extremely active in order to enrich themselves but their (grand)sons are likely to be less willing to work assiduously if it can be avoided and when compelled to do so, they have the opportunity to show 'conspicuous leisure' through their wives or children. We are touching on the crucial phenomenon of 'vicarious display' (i.e. showing off via one's entourage), which will deserve much further consideration (Chapter 6 below). Close rereading of *The Theory of the Leisure Class* leads one to realise how sophisticated Veblen's analyses can be. If leisure should obviously be understood as the opposite of labour activities (and, in the Veblenian terminology, as a form of 'waste'), it does not connote idleness or indolence at all. On the contrary, it may mean serious work when it comes to, for instance, being well-groomed or learning how to master language and other skills.

Veblen's most famous concept is probably that of 'conspicuous consumption' (1994 [1899], chapter IV). In 'modern' societies, particularly in large cities, external appearance does not confirm an already known status but pertains to a constant reassertion of self. According to Veblen, the purchase by the affluent of expensive material goods and services is driven primarily by a desire for display. In this respect, conspicuous consumption has to be considered in terms of social perception. It is essential to consume luxuries conspicuously in order to gain recognition. We shall see that this concept, closely related to the issue of visibility, proves to be an operational tool in some – but not all – cases.

Several other concepts, being part of the thesis expanded in *The Theory of the Leisure Class,* are worth mentioning, such as 'pecuniary emulation' and 'invidious distinction'. These clearly refer to comparisons of status measured on the basis of possessions and wealth. What is at work, on the one hand, is a principle of emulation, that is a dynamic force behind people's impulse (especially felt by envious inferiors) to own goods signalling superior status or to copy the styles of the elite.[22] On the other hand, the upper classes are engaged in an invidious struggle for respectability within their own milieu as well as vis-à-vis challenging outsiders. Veblen argued (1994 [1899], chapter V) that the elite constantly differentiates itself from commoners by redefining the fashionable whereas the lower, yet aspiring, social groups continually follow these fashions. This endlessly propels the upper class to resort to further insignia of distinction.

Veblen also initiated a breakthrough in the study of elitist taste. A corollary of his general perspective is that the emulated classes develop ever-more expensive and elaborate patterns of taste in order to guard their position against rising groups (see his chapter VI on 'Pecuniary Canons of Taste'). His argument would seem to imply that a monolithic leisure class effectively monopolises the criteria of reputability, being the ultimate arbiters of taste. This raises the controversial question of hegemony, which we shall discuss in Chapter 9 here. Against traditional laws of economics about supply and demand, Veblen has taught us that decreasing prices may prevent elites from buying high-status commodities because they lose their 'snob' appeal. Through his introduction of sociological dimensions and his taking issue with the rational approach of the *homo oeconomicus*, Veblen may be considered to be a remarkable thinker in economics and an essential initiator of what was to be called the 'institutional approach' in this field.

More than a century after the publication of *The Theory of the Leisure Class,* a number of factors have meant that some of Veblen's perspectives might no longer be convincing. Several authors (e.g. Linder, 1970; J. Brooks, 1981; Rojek, 2000) have drawn attention to the fact that economic elites are not in a position to devote as much time to leisure activities as the workers they employ. Likewise, consumer items have become more widely available and this has most certainly altered the nature of 'pecuniary emulation'. Nevertheless, in assessing the importance of Veblen's model of interpretation, the issue is not so much whether there are still 'leisure classes' in the contemporary world. It is rather to what extent the theoretical model and conceptual apparatus he formulated from the observation of a particular type of society is of any use in deciphering elite distinction in other ones.

Simmel

Most notable, too, among those who indirectly contributed to the theorisation of elite distinction are three German sociologists: Simmel, Weber and Sombart. Georg Simmel (1858–1918) was born in Berlin and spent more than 50 years in that city. After studying philosophy, he became a significant figure in intellectual circles and a very popular lecturer attracting large audiences. Although he was a prolific writer whose publications were translated into various languages, he encountered systematic difficulties when attempting to obtain a full professorship. Partly because of his Jewish ancestry and partly because of his unorthodox position straddling the fields of philosophy, sociology and psychology, Simmel remained an academic outsider. He was eventually able to secure a chair in Strasbourg (at that time a provincial German city), but only at the age of 56 and on the eve of World War I, when university activities were interrupted.

Unlike some other classic thinkers, Simmel has been criticised for his impressionistic tone and for the fact that his 600-page *Soziologie* is a disparate collection of small essays rather than a consistent treatise.[23] Simmel rejected positivism and teleological assumptions (he considered for instance that Comte, Spencer and Marx were dogmatists who had produced mere ideologies, not relevant analyses) and deliberately proposed circumscribed models of interpretation, as opposed to fundamental scientific laws. His micro-sociological approach is a phenomenological one whereby the scholar is expected to pay particular attention to perceptions and meanings. Durkheim was among several sociologists who viewed Simmel's books as overly psychological and generally irrelevant. By contrast, Simmel's work was well received in the United States, notably by members of the Chicago School (carrying ethnographic fieldwork on the urban environment), by inter-actionists such as Goffman and later – less expectedly – by some postmodernists.[24] As a result of his emphasis on relations between individuals, he was close to, and influenced by, Tarde.

Simmel is important for the purposes of this volume principally in two respects: first as the author who formulated a lasting theory of fashion and distinction and second as a brilliant analyst of the modern metropolitan experience. We will therefore focus more specifically on these two aspects. Social distance was a phenomenon of significance for Simmel, who elaborated an emulationist approach to status within his famous article entitled 'Fashion' (1957 [1904]). Emphasising the tension between imitation and differentiation, he offered an enlightening interpretation of the tendency for commodities to pass down through the status hierarchy. In the course of their descent they are 'vulgarised'; they lose their ability to express superior position and soon come to be considered by the upper classes as dispensable, thereby setting the conditions for a new cycle of fashion. As we have seen, this type of mechanism was also observed and analysed by Veblen and, in many respects, the two authors arrived at similar conclusions. However, the Simmelean account of fashionability differs in several important ways from Veblen's model. To begin with, it proposes an original reflection on both collective and individual styles (this theme, crucial to Simmel's work, will occupy us in Chapter 9). There is, effectively, a potential contradiction between the logic of desire for personal conspicuousness and that of class representativeness. All sorts of meanings are envisaged by Simmel, in a very sophisticated way – e.g. distinction through observance or conscious avoidance of conventional formulas, fashion as supplementing a person's lack of importance or as a mask conveying a message of modesty, etc. – sometimes, perhaps, to the detriment of the overall coherence of the thesis. Another dissimilarity between him and Veblen is that new fashions do not systematically emanate from the top, but are possibly formed by the *demi-monde*, thus giving rise to some comments about the middle classes at the end of the article.

With regard to the sociological analysis of metropolis, Simmel showed that 'modern societies' are primarily characterised by the relative impersonality of relationships. Here, his position is quite close to that of Veblen, arguing that in anonymous contexts, social superiority may involve resorting to conspicuousness. Proposing analyses about the urban environment was not very original at this time. What makes Simmel's approach specific is his phenomenological emphasis on perceptions and networks of intersecting spaces. Urban life may certainly be a liberating experience but also entails greater complexities and sometimes boredom or indifference. Importantly for our theme, Simmel posited that interactions within large cities depend very much on 'credit', in the sense that one is permanently confronted with the question of knowing whether one may trust a stranger simply by his appearance.

Finally, it should be emphasised that scattered Simmelean contributions on several other topics – such as adornment or flirtation – are also of relevance for the analysis of elite distinction, and will be considered later.

Weber

Max Weber (1864–1920) is presumably too well known a social theorist to need an introduction. Several of the major Weberian themes – such as domination and order, authority, legitimacy, the protestant ethic and charisma – are indirectly pertinent for our theme. His ideal-typical constructions undoubtedly lead to rigorous analyses and prove most useful when related to symbolic dimensions. Weber's illuminating distinction between status and class, as well as his connected perspectives in terms of social closure and style of life, is particularly relevant. It is in these respects that the German author's legacy will mainly be discussed.

For Weber, power (defined as 'the probability that an actor will be able to realise his own objectives even against opposition from others with whom he is in a social relationship') is not reducible to economic domination. In market societies, it can certainly be observed that the position of actors depends primarily on economic *class* cleavages. In many other cases, however, inequality is mainly structured by predefined privileges in accordance with conventionally or legally guaranteed *status* distinctions. Against the regression of Marxism toward economism, the advance of the Weberian approach is that it argues convincingly about two distinct modes of existence and exercise of power: one whereby power is accumulated through the impersonal logics of market competition; the other as a consequence of stratifications related to various traditional criteria of social influence (e.g. Gerth and Mills 1991, chapter VII). It is easy to show that economic wealth is not necessarily the main source of power. Other backgrounds, for example those related to ancestry, purity or knowledge, may prevail. Admittedly, Weber was not the first to have dealt with the topic, but any work on elite distinction must acknowledge his fundamental contribution.

Especially when it comes to contexts in which social relationships are based on a subjective feeling of belonging together on traditional grounds (communities, differentiated estates or orders), Weber's theoretical understanding of status proves useful – at least as a starting point.[25] His ability to enter into different systems of meaning in a 'comprehensive' way (i.e. consisting of stressing what apparently made sense for the actors concerned) also deserves consideration. History informs us of many groups which controlled a great deal of property but were unable to occupy the top rung of the social ladder. One may, for instance, think of the rich metics in ancient Greek society who did not have access to political rights and could not marry the daughters of established citizens because they were regarded as 'ill born'. For many centuries in Western Europe, wealth and power followed status, rather than the reverse. In other words, ascribed status in the social order was more primordial than positions in relation to the mode of production. Many convincing illustrations are given by Weber, for example in his description of the Brahmins within his work on Hinduism, or about the mandarinate system in traditional China. The second case (see Weber, 1951 [1915]) is interesting in so far as it shows that dominant status groups may be formed not only on the basis of race, caste, ethnicity and other kinds of hereditary prestige, but also as a result of formal, highly praised education.

This raises the issue of closure strategies. When honour is related to a fixed criterion, the status order is likely to be threatened if the system becomes even slightly open, notably if economic achievements can bestow upon commoners an equivalent estimation. Social closure may involve 'connubial' or 'commensal exclusiveness' (see Murphy, 1988) as well as 'sumptuary laws', among others. Seen from the outside, cultural conventions regarding status may seem quite arbitrary, yet it is important to take their continuity and deep-rootedness into consideration. In this regard, Weber provided a relevant discussion in terms of 'originators', 'specific bearers' and 'conservers' of particular styles of life (Roth and Wittich, 1978, pp. 932 ff.) and – theoretically coherent with the rest of his writings – institutionalisation and legitimation.

Most interesting is the fact that Weber did not view these aspects as superficial or trivial. For example, he wrote about the aristocratic 'ethos' and 'the need for ostentation, glamour and imposing splendour' in feudal contexts where luxury was 'nothing superfluous' but 'a means of social self-assertion' (Roth and Wittich, 1978, p. 1106). Besides, Weber offered occasional remarks about the sartorial styles and physical appearance of elites or their sense of dignity. Methodologically, it is worth adding that he kept a most welcome axiological neutrality. In sum, in the rich symbolic domain which treats styles of life as enhancers of social power and status, Weber is of lasting value.

Sombart

Werner Sombart (1863–1941) is also a prominent figure among those first theorists for whom elite distinction was, at least implicitly, a significant object of investigation. Like some of the other scholars considered here, his university career was not immediately a successful one, despite the quality of his writings and his renown. This was as a result of his controversial early work on socialism and capitalism, and the favourable review he had written of the third volume of *Capital* (which earned him a laudatory letter from Engels in 1885), but also it seems – strikingly enough, like Veblen – to stem from his bad reputation as a womaniser. Despite unanimous votes within several faculties and strong support from Weber, the employment of Sombart was vetoed for many years, and it was only in 1917, after years of heated discussion, that he was appointed to the most important economic chair in Prussia. On the other hand, as Sombart belonged to a wealthy upper-class family, he never encountered serious material difficulties.[26]

Intellectually, Sombart was a thinker whose ideas evolved considerably. He could be regarded as a Marxist in his youth, but with the intention to go beyond Marx and with an aversion to dogmatic communism; he later appeared to be a reformer unwilling to engage in party politics, a conservative during the Weimar Republic and, finally, with an ambivalent relationship to National Socialism. He wrote influential books such as his monumental *Der Moderne Kapitalismus* or *Why is there no Socialism in the United States?* Although several other volumes are relevant to a certain extent – e.g. his *Economy and Fashion* – of greatest importance here is unquestionably *Luxury and Capitalism* (1967 [1913]).

The kernel of his argument is that with the advent of court society in some European countries, a new class of women emerged, together with new attitudes toward sexuality. The primary cause for the development of luxury would be related to the cultural acceptance of 'sexual love' and intra-elite competition in this respect. Sombart's last proposition is that strong demands for luxury products eventually led to the growth of capitalism. Even if he does not establish the relationship between the three dimensions very persuasively, his thesis is original and to a certain extent supported by historical evidence. For the comparativist specialising in the study of elite ostentation, Sombart's line of reasoning is stimulating. Several of his distinctions – for instance between quantitative and qualitative emphasis, or between refinements leading to sensuous pleasures or respectability – are useful. Moreover, he was able to catch something essential of the role played by women. Admittedly, Veblen should be seen as the most important student of 'vicarious' display, yet his one-sided approach is not as convincing as Sombart's more balanced picture about the relation of upper-class women to the consumption of prestigious goods.[27]

Although some commentators would deplore the fact that Sombart is 'not part of the core of classical sociology' (Grundmann and Stehr, 2001), one must acknowledge that authors from several disciplines have tried to re-establish his reputation. Against the criticism of a structuralist like Braudel (1973 [1967]), who rejected his reading grid, there have been other historians or social anthropologists who have supported Sombart on various grounds, both empirical and theoretical.[28]

The sociological thinkers considered above have most certainly provided solid foundations for the study of elite distinction and it would be a mistake to assume that much of this early literature is, by now, extremely dated. However, as we have already hinted throughout this first chapter, the problem arises from awkward leanings toward reductionism. Short presentations inevitably fail to do justice to the intricacies of each analytical framework, yet it is hoped that this introduction will give readers the stimulus to explore these writings further.

2
Major Subsequent Contributions

If theoretical contributions from social scientists whose writings appeared between 1880 and 1920 can prove useful to contemporary researchers, one might expect later works to be more valuable still. However, as becomes immediately obvious for those with a comprehensive overview of the literature in question, the analysis of distinction has not followed any sort of cumulative progression. Many authors – from Goffman at the beginning of the 1950s to Bourdieu at the end of the 1970s – conferred the (somewhat uncomfortable) impression that they were starting from scratch. This chapter explores more recent sociological approaches from various schools of thought (neo-Marxist, functionalist) and key authors (such as Elias, Baudrillard and analysts of postmodernity). It also examines contributions from psycho-sociological and socio-economic angles.

(Neo-)Marxist views

Symbolic issues have seldom held centrality in Marxist thought. With their attention fixed on infrastructural relations of production and by perennially focusing upon the dynamics of class struggle, Marxist writers have tended to reduce very diverse situations to a single general equation: class determines wealth, which determines supremacy and subordination. If we return to Marx's own works, the major theme related to our topic is (apart from a handful of scattered remarks[1]) that of 'commodity fetishism'. It should be recalled that, in volume I/chapter one of *Capital* (2006 [1867]), Marx revisited the old distinction between the 'use-value' and the 'exchange-value' of commodities. Objects are created through concrete labour in order to fulfil some human needs (working being considered as central to self-worth).

26

Concurrently, however, commodities are also valued because they can be exchanged for others, through a relation of equivalence facilitated by the existence of money. In many instances, the hard labour of a worker is likely to confer great honour upon the person able to purchase an impressive commodity. The fetishism of commodities refers to the owners' belief that the mere possession of the objects acquired has the quasi-magical consequence of bestowing prestige upon them, while masking the social nature of the human relations determining the whole process.[2] In Part II, we shall discuss how external signs of superiority often contribute crucially to elite distinction. Marx's specific view prompts us to keep in mind the 'making' dimension behind the 'having' one.

Marxist authors routinely invoke the theory of 'commodity fetishism', yet symbolic aspects are clearly deemed secondary within this intellectual tradition. However, in certain variants of Marxism, one finds passages akin to the subject under consideration here. Firstly, the Frankfurt school and their descendants deserve a brief mention. Within their critique of capitalism, Adorno and Horkheimer (1979 [1944]) stigmatised the 'culture industry' and its standardised, mediocre, levelling products. This was one the first attempts to examine, from a neo-Marxist perspective, the effects of the rise of mass media and consumer society on working classes. The latter were depicted as being lured by an homogeneous mass culture which was designed to depoliticise and integrate them, while it promoted the interests of capitalism. A further corollary, elaborated in particular by Marcuse (1991 [1964], Chapter 1) two decades later, is that this system would generate 'false needs' determined by external powers promoting a 'one-dimensional' ideology working as a mechanism of social control and militating against any real change.[3] A major paradox here is that this denunciation of 'low culture' and consumerism resorts to rather elitist arguments. The above-mentioned members of the Frankfurt school felt nostalgic toward sophisticated works of art and avant-garde subversive pieces likely to elevate minds or to challenge dominant perceptions.[4] Their very abstract and top-down discourse has been criticised on many grounds by those authors who aim to show that audiences and consumers are not necessarily passive, or that 'popular culture' can be of great interest (Gans, 1999 [1974]). British Cultural Studies (the Birmingham School), notably, has turned away from high culture in favour of the popular. Essential debates, also including postmodern critics, followed. This raised several issues which we shall meet again in relation to the themes of cultivation and taste.

Thompson's descriptions of relations between the 'gentry' and the 'plebs' in eighteenth-century England equally merit being touched on in this section, as one of the very rare instances of a neo-Marxist approach which keenly stressed 'distinction' matters. An important member of the aforementioned British 'Cultural Studies' tradition, Thompson, like most Marxists – and for obvious reasons – paid attention mainly to working class populations. However, he was an unorthodox socio-historian who studied class interactions both 'from above' and 'from below'. In *Customs in Common* (1991), he pursues discussions about his favourite themes such as popular culture, hegemony, deference and resistance. Chapter II of his work, entitled 'The Patricians and the Plebs', contains comments on the 'high visibility' of the great ('formidable mansions', the 'elaboration of wig and powder', 'hauteur of bearing and expression', etc.) versus the 'low visibility of others'. He particularly insists on theatrical dimensions and on the 'conspicuous display appropriate to each rank and station' employed to exhibit authority to the villagers. Thompson's analysis proves to be fairly balanced: both impressive and paternalistic styles are taken into account, as well as the dialectic between the 'act of giving' and 'calculated extortions (under threat of riot)'. Nevertheless, he unfortunately tends to reduce this symbolic confrontation to a mere two-player game – underlined by the above-mentioned Roman dichotomous words – and disregards the presence of a 'middling sort', or intra-elite competition for display.

It is important to distance ourselves from the idea that distinction is solely domination over social inferiors. In the social sciences, resorting to signs of superiority is most often analysed in negative terms by those authors who seek to deconstruct such manifestations. Yet, as empirical research shows, symbolic competition is found within as well as between social classes. Furthermore, with regard to Marxist theory, the question inevitably raised is that of the relative autonomy of prestige in relation to material conditions.[5]

The functionalist school

Seeking to differentiate themselves from the Marxist approach, American functionalists have developed diametrically opposed views. It may be considered, however, that they, too, suffer from comparable normative defects and dogmatic one-sidedness. Whereas class conflict theorists are inclined to analyse, through the prism of fundamental inequalities, work relations and struggle, functionalist authors postulate that status competition has a beneficial effect on the social system, since the most capable persons compete to obtain the highest and most rewarded positions. In a context witnessing the triumph of achieved over ascribed status,[6] inequalities and emulation would eventually prove to be functional. When it comes to social distinction, the alternative theoretical vision provided here brings forth perspectives in terms of 'status attainment', 'ranking on a continuous prestige scale', 'achievement through commodity consumption' and 'social standing and lifestyle', within supposedly well-integrated communities sharing the same belief in the potential for upward mobility.

The fierce theoretical competition which resulted, especially during the cold war era, was often biased by ideological convictions and, therefore, did not always lead to particularly satisfactory analyses. Still, American research was usually based on serious empirical studies. Several areas of work, dealing mainly with issues of stratification but also with fashion and 'trickle-down' mechanisms, are of relevance here. As far as the last two themes are concerned, contributions by Barber and Lobel (1952) and Fallers (1961 [1954]), respectively, should be mentioned. Fashion, most notably in the fields of women's clothes and of household furniture or cars, is described as fulfilling important social functions in the United States' 'open class system', conceived as a linear continuum of strata. Far from corresponding to irrational shifts in taste, goods (and services) consumed are considered in relation to a hierarchy of patterns. Greater industrial productivity, as well as constant innovations, prompts status battles and competitive expenditure. The whole population is presented as moving 'up' in this respect, or at least to be motivated by a widespread myth of success maintained by the mass media. Within this literature, the aspect most commonly investigated is the possession of key material goods and the implications of this for cross-perceptions and self-image.

As early as 1925, Robert and Helen Lynd had collected ethnographic data on the symbolic importance of houses, back yards, cars, clubs or leisure activities within the town of Muncie (Indiana), thereby concentrating on representations of stratification in a local community. Ten years later (i.e. after the Depression), they were to analyse evolutions in this respect. These so-called 'Middletown studies' (Lynd and Lynd, 1929; 1937) mainly focused on culture – 'a culture in which one is largely judged by the things one has' (1937, p. 62) and in which 'symbols of arrival' are deemed crucial. Although several commentators esteem the Lynds' landmark explorations, especially as they include sections on the distribution of power, this tradition of enquiry is dominated by the work of W. Lloyd Warner (1898–1970). The author of many significant texts, Warner is best known for his five-volume 'Yankee City Series', based on ten years of field research in the town of Newburyport (Massachusetts). Having received mainly an anthropological education, Warner was interested in the subjective understanding of stratification and highlighted the presence of classes endowed with distinctive cultures. His community studies are the result of a lasting preoccupation with the peculiarities of the American social system. Various samples of people in Newburyport were asked to rank themselves, and others, according to their perceptions of the prestige hierarchy of their town. Particularly relevant, here, is the proportion of the work devoted to the 'characteristics' of 'upper-upper' and 'lower-upper' classes and the way in which both 'express social distance'. Concrete objects of investigation – such as clubs, houses, clothes, cars or food – were all taken into consideration.[7]

Warner's analyses have attracted a storm of criticism. First, in accordance with the above paradigmatic debates, conventional leftist critiques have taken aim at Warner's tendency to define classes less in terms of wealth or power than in terms of lifestyles. This approach has been deemed rather superficial and incidental.[8] For these commentators, his functionalist bias also led Warner to overstate the consensual character of status symbols. Second, his reputational methodology was bitterly attacked on the grounds of excessive reliance on subjective data. It was questioned whether merely recording opinions and viewpoints could truly reflect social realities. A key issue is the extent to which his informants from various strata were equally class conscious. As Lipset and Bendix rightly emphasised, in their lengthy discussion on the disadvantages of purely objectivist and subjectivist readings of class (1951, I, p. 159), Warner was apparently aware of methodological flaws, yet never rigorously addressed this issue. Third, some sociologists have harboured serious doubts about the applicability of the methods of the anthropological field worker (the pre-selection of informants, for instance) when applied to the study of modern settings. They have accused the Warner team of ignoring the contributions of the founding fathers of the sociological discipline.[9] These critiques are far from being unjustified, yet the volumes produced by this school of thought remain fascinating reading even 60 or 70 years after the original field research. The descriptions of cultural traits and the quotations of the interviewees (e.g. in Hollingshead, 1949) are of greater interest than the countless tables or the incredible enterprise of producing typologies classifying all sorts of possible interactions and situations.[10]

By contending that through his community studies he had been able to reveal 'the nature of the social class system in America', Warner posited a fallacious ubiquity for his work. As is apparent in the discussion of Veblen and Simmel in Chapter 1, self-presentation and means of appraisal in an anonymous urban context prove to be of a very different – fleeting – nature. Thus, the reading grid elaborated for the 'intimate and enduring' perceptions of inhabitants of the small town may not be appropriate when describing and analysing the 'segmental contacts' in cities where one interacts with 'strangers'.[11] In later decades, American functionalists were to work on metropolitan areas and mass society logics. Coleman attempted to show how Warner's social class theories, developed in small communities, could be applied, with some modifications, in cities.[12] They were also to produce studies on 'status attainment', 'appraisals of others' and 'prestige scale' at a national level.[13] This broader perspective stimulated research on 'reference groups' (e.g. Shibutani, 1955) and was supplemented by some descriptive essays (e.g. Packard, 1960; 1989) worthy of attention.

Elias

In contrast to many authors from the two schools previously discussed in this chapter, Norbert Elias (1897–1990) cannot be accused of having produced analyses affected by ideological preconceptions. His work was guided by a strong concern for intellectual detachment (which may have been inherited from his supervisor, Karl Mannheim). Elias's career was ruined by the National Socialists' accession to power in Germany, prompting him to flee to Switzerland, France and finally England – where he was to spend 40 years. Not until 1954, at the age of 57, did Elias obtain an academic position. He remained virtually unknown until the end of the 1960s, when his unread work, written mainly in German, was discovered, translated and published. Elias then suddenly became an intellectual celebrity and is now viewed as one of the major figures of twentieth-century sociology.[14] Creator of the 'figurational' theoretical framework – one of the attempts at transcending the agency-structure dichotomy – and a renowned author in the field of 'process sociology',[15] Elias is of special interest, here, as a precursor in the study of court society and in the cultural history of manners.

Elias's essay on *The Man of the Court* was submitted in 1933 as a 'habilitation thesis' – but never formally accepted – and published only in 1969 (1974 in French, 1983 in English) with some additional passages and rewriting. It may, however, be considered as the foundation upon which much of his later work was built. As is well known, Elias describes the process of the domestication of the warrior nobility, whereby lords formerly at the head of relatively independent political units were brought under the effective control of the crown within the context of a centralised (and fascinating) court. France was the paradigm case of subjugation to the authority of a king. An important component of Elias's analysis was an explanation of the role played by the etiquette through which 'court society represents itself, each individual being distinguished from every other, all together distinguishing themselves from non-members, so that each individual and the group as a whole confirm their existence as a value in itself' (Elias 1983 [1933], p. 103). Within such a configuration, theatrical representations both derived from, and consolidated into, hierarchies of infinitely graded rank. The courtier contributed to and gazed at the kingly pomp, thus exalting the figure of the monarch. Life at the court of Versailles, for instance, especially under the reign of Louis XIV, not only entailed the most stringent observation of daily rituals and minute rankings of precedence but also demanded a lavish existence. A significant theme is introduced here: the obligation for the courtier to live ostentatiously. The luxury and refinement of some created the exclusion of others. This is what Elias calls the 'court rationality', that is the imperative pressure for competitive display between aristocrats eager to defend their prestige.

Elias acutely focused his attention upon manners. Within court societies, the strictest control over demeanour was expected during audiences, dinners and balls. Elias's work set forth subtle reflections on poise, cultivation of elegance and eloquence, as well as on command over emotions and self-restraint. We therefore arrive at a paradoxical situation: by fully containing oneself one dominates others. We shall see that this is far from being the only possible way for elites to project an overbearing image to others. Nevertheless, Elias undoubtedly remains a key author in the discussion of 'embodied signs of superiority' (Chapter 5 below). Reference must be made here, of course, to his two-volume work, *The Civilizing Process*. In the first volume, *The History of Manners* (1978a [1939]), which traces the gradual change in table manners, aggressiveness, sexual relations and the control of bodily functions, Elias has shown how, in only a few hundred years, behaviour which we would today regard as coarse, or even squalid, progressively gave way to more refined standards. According to his famous thesis (mainly expressed in Part II of the second volume) on the micro-*psycho*genesis of self-discipline, congruent with the macro-*socio*genesis of the state (1982 [1939]), this extensive reformation of mores would eventually have led to the unexpected downward diffusion of polite manners to the lower classes through the crucial mediation of a self-restrained courtly elite. Elias's analysis of diffusion is sophisticated and quite characteristic of his theoretical model of interpretation in terms of actors and groups in constant dynamic interdependence.

The Eliasian line of argumentation intending to reveal a process of civilisation was highly debated. Elias's examination of court society and of the crucial role played by the aristocratic elite in behavioural changes has, justifiably, been questioned by some historians and on various grounds.[16] Elias has undeniably provided a brilliant introduction to the dynamics of social relations from the end of the Middle Ages to the French Revolution and he was able to identify several crucial mechanisms of differentiation during that period. He took into joint account distinction vis-à-vis lower strata and intra-elite distinction – this is far from always being the case among the other authors considered in these introductory chapters. Beyond his classic contribution on the advent and characteristics of the 'court-aristocratic figuration', we shall have the opportunity to refer to his work when we come across, for example, public and private contexts, or elites' self-observation.

Goffman

It is debatable whether Erving Goffman (1922–1988) is an interactionist or a structuralist scholar. The ethnographic micro-descriptions available throughout his works might lead one to assume that he clearly belongs to the first tradition. In Goffman's work realities appear to be ephemeral and subjective, constantly reshaped along the continuous flow of interactions. On the other hand, he also regularly offers typologies, concepts and a rather objectivist reasoning. The debate is not insignificant for us, to the extent that if one fully adopts a symbolic interactionist approach, the shape of the status hierarchy is likely to differ depending on which status-assignment system is relevant for the definition of a situation. In other words, there may be as many logics of distinction in a society as there are distinguishable patterns of interpersonal relations. However, if we consider Goffman's analysis of the ritualistic aspect of life, on techniques of information control (e.g. 1963a; 1971) and especially on 'frames' (1974), a quite different picture emerges.

Beyond these continual oscillations and the ambiguities of his theoretical positioning,[17] Goffman is an important author from the perspective of the present book in several respects. First, it is appropriate to recall that, at the beginning of his career, he published an article on 'Symbols of Class Status' (Goffman, 1951), to which we will refer. Furthermore, Goffman's reading grid proves to be most helpful for students of elite distinction because of his emphasis on the presentation of self. The dramatic approach which he developed to characterise the process by which individuals construct the world about them, and their place in it, is extremely stimulating. Goffman's models of interpretation, expressed in terms of signs employed to convey social information, 'front' and 'back' stage, or mutual aid between performers (1959) open up vast areas of research worth exploring. They may lead social scientists to study façades, front lawns or cosmetics, or the art of synecdochism (which consists of giving a general impression of status superiority through one or several attributes only). Goffman is also remarkably insightful with regard to 'face-work', the term 'face' being defined as the positive social value a person effectively claims for her/himself during interactions (1963b; 1967). The behaviour maintained by an individual asserting any kind of superiority during encounters may be more or less legitimate and institutionalised, and the image s/he tries to convey more or less convincing and confirmed by the other interactants. This leads to behavioural themes such as ease, self-assurance, commanding presence and deference. It also, crucially, leads to the subject of the prevailing definition of situations – potentially manipulated by the dominant actors – which permeates many of Goffman's writings (e.g. 1961).

There is much to admire in and borrow from Goffman. Importantly, he shows that social actors participate in myriad interactions, play many roles and evaluate themselves and others differently according to concrete circumstances. The merit of his approach is to make clear that the need to compose one's image in public is not necessarily reducible to a repetitive model but may differ – audience segregation, for instance, allows for considerable variations. It remains that symbolic representations are not elaborated within a social vacuum; they depend upon dispositions toward others, themselves very much depending upon one's position and previous experiences. Interactionist descriptions at times confer the feeling that a unique new world emerges every minute. Furthermore, Goffman has a tendency to equate everything with 'impression management'. Even for elites, life is not just 'a bowl of strategies' – to refer to Geertz's critique (1993 [1983], p. 25). It is obvious that actors can never completely control information about themselves available in a social situation. The language of the stage, as well as game analogy (Goffman, 1970 [1969]), may be relevant to a certain extent.

However, as we shall see in the next chapter, Goffman's dramaturgical theory often sounds too universalistic.

Bourdieu

One of the best-known and most influential analyses of social distinction is the Bourdieusian one. Pierre Bourdieu (1930–2002) was unquestionably a major sociologist of the second half of the twentieth century. As the initiator of a grand theory aiming to transcend classical theoretical antagonisms – between objectivism and subjectivism, structure and agency, and class and status – the French author has had a profound impact not only on his discipline, but also on several other academic fields. The success of his powerful school of thought, his ambitious attempt to overcome traditional paradigms and his intransigence vis-à-vis intellectual rivals have, inevitably, generated considerable scholarly debate.[18] Comments about Bourdieu's reading grid often prove to be Manichaean, with devotees defending it in a very dogmatic way, as against resolutely hostile thinkers rejecting it irrevocably. Neither of these extremist stances is particularly helpful and a more nuanced appraisal is instead suggested.

The work of most relevance here is, of course, the famous book on *Distinction: A Social Critique of the Judgement of Taste* (Bourdieu, 1984 [1979]). Nevertheless, it is difficult to separate this study of lifestyles and classifications within French society from the rest of his oeuvre. Indeed, this opus can be seen as an extension of previous books and as intending to expand his favourite concepts – such as habitus (see below), practice, field, positions, dispositions, etc. – following his usual perspective of constructivist structuralism.[19] Bourdieu's starting point in *Distinction* is that high cultural objects do not have any intrinsic worth (as a Kantian approach to aesthetics would have it). On the contrary, taste is socially structured and reflects the position of each 'agent' in the hierarchy. Indicators of prestige and dominant taste originating at the top become a hegemonic norm with regard to those tastes of other classes – subject to 'symbolic violence' – which can thus only be interpreted negatively. When the question of taste is extended to the field of consumption, what interests Bourdieu is less the obvious expression of material domination, that is the display of goods, than the exhibition of 'cultural capital' and a subsequent 'classification of the classifiers'. The same is true of behaviour. In other words, according to Bourdieu, distinction is based fundamentally on the power held by the upper class to impose its own categories of perception and appreciation as legitimate upon the lower classes. Here, a central thrust of Bourdieu's grand theory, 'habitus', is of relevance. This concept refers to the ensemble of largely unconscious dispositions producing action and judgements. Habitus is supposedly rooted in the social background of each 'agent'. According to this perspective, cultural judgements – culture being taken here in a narrow sense, in relation to arbitrary dominant representations – are deterministically dependent upon social positions or trajectories. In broad terms, the dominant class expresses its distinction through its sense of what is right or proper, while contemplating with disgust the tastes of subordinate classes, thus reinforcing them as subordinate. Bourdieu's argument implies, therefore, that taste is always harnessed to the struggle for recognition between and within social groups.[20]

Distinction, which has dominated the sociological discussion on these topics for many years is an important work, and one to which we shall return throughout the remainder of this text with reference to many Bourdieusian themes – such as the self-assurance of the dominant classes and hegemonic mechanisms, to name but two. Critical discussions about the originality of Bourdieu's perspective, as well as the general applicability of his model of interpretation, are postponed until the following chapter.

Baudrillard

When assessing the writings of sociological thinkers, it may be beneficial to consider the theoretical coherence of their respective frameworks. In this respect, Jean Baudrillard (1929–2007) is probably, among all the authors presented here, the scholar who displays the most noticeable development in his working life. One may roughly distinguish three periods (intersected by two major turning points) within his intellectual career. First, he was the successful structuralist analyst of the consumer society who introduced a fashionable semiotic dimension within critical sociology. This corresponds to the end of the 1960s and the beginning of the 1970s, a phase that saw the publication of his trilogy (Baudrillard, 1996a [1968]; 1996b [1970]; 1981 [1972]) on objects and signs. Second, is the (mid-period) postmodern Baudrillard, publishing rather abstract volumes and collections of aphorisms and memories. This new fragmentary vein and his tendency to touch on all sorts of subjects eventually led some commentators to regard him more as a writer producing stylish essays – a well-established French tradition – than as a rigorous social scientist.[21] During this second period, Baudrillard embraced the idea that with postmodernity, transcendental references would vanish.

The singularity of his vision chiefly consists in showing a universe of simulacra which would have taken precedence over a largely eliminated real world (e.g. Baudrillard, 1994 [1981]). Toward the end of this phase, came a second rupture, leading to a third period in his intellectual life, in which provocative journalistic writings predominated.

The most important volumes of Baudrillard's work for our purposes are those making up the above-mentioned trilogy, published between 1968 and 1972. Baudrillard began his studies with the objective of proposing a critique of consumer society from a Marxist perspective, in combination with a semiological one. In the first book, *The System of Objects* (Baudrillard, 1996a [1968]), drawn from his doctoral dissertation, his argument is based on a rediscovery of the signifying power of commodities interpreted as forming an arbitrary and self-referential system of signs with meaningful 'marginal differences' – not irrelevant from our 'distinction' point of view. In the second of these volumes, *The Consumer Society: Myths and Structures* (Baudrillard, 1996b [1970]) – his most famous opus but one he personally did not like much – and in the third, entitled *For a Critique of the Political Economy of the Sign* (1981 [1972]), Baudrillard further develops his views with reference to anthropological literature and to classic Marxist thought. To summarise his argument, within contemporary capitalist societies, most people are alienated as a result of their relation to modes of production and *also* through consumption. A new logic of ordering has replaced the traditional one; obtainable commodities are used to signify qualities about oneself, and needs are manipulated by the capitalist system for its own purposes. Although it is reductionist, and not always as original as it claims, what should be retained from the Baudrillardian approach is mainly its conception of combinations of objects within the context of a 'society of signs'.

Analysts of postmodernity

In our introductory remarks on Baudrillard, we touched on the theme of postmodernity. From Baudrillard's perspective, this refers principally to a world saturated with signs, where the distinction between reality and appearance becomes blurred. Many contemporary authors consider that we have witnessed a crucial break with modernism, one comparable to that which had occurred between modernity and tradition (see e.g. Bauman, 1992). Within the expanding literature concerned with such a multi-faceted topic, numerous dimensions are taken into account.[22] Postmodernity defies simple definition but is usually associated with the end of teleological visions and with an endurable dissatisfaction with credible master narratives, a decreasing confidence in science (after Hiroshima), the end of belief in humanism (after colonialism and the holocaust) or a playful and ironical mixing of codes in art works (once modernity reached impassable limits with the empty canvas or the empty scene). The advent of postmodernity is also, frequently, synonymous with anti-conformism and permissiveness, the decrease of community controls, free lifestyle options and a general impulse toward consumption – with a strong emphasis on immediate satisfaction. Several convergent themes emerge from this (non-exhaustive) list. Postmodernity surfaces with the decline of many norms and once-fundamental convictions, giving way to a far more fluid situation, in which relativistic and expressive concerns are central.

Such perspectives matter for the purpose of this book in so far as analysts of postmodern realities often take a special interest in symbolic aspects. According to many studies, the unprecedented profusion of styles would engender serious confusions as regards conventions embodying hierarchy. The fluidity between signs stemming from both 'high culture' and 'popular culture' – another important characteristic of postmodernity – has led to the conclusion that the traditional portrayal of social life as a continual exchange of imitation and differentiation between the elite and their social inferiors is obsolete. It is not that postmodernity tends toward an egalitarian society but rather that many codes now coexist largely independently – their appreciation having little meaning except within their respective sub-cultures. Indeed, the goal of social life would no longer be to foster one's image actively but to affirm a style and define one's own identity, knowing that there are no incontestable standards of superiority any more.

Under such circumstances, most of the above-mentioned scholars – from Veblen to Bourdieu – have been deemed obsolete. Postmodernity has included a loss of once stable meaning in classifications, and some thinkers extend this to theories of the 'end of the social'. On the other side, authors who attempt to recycle the perspectives of more traditional schools of thought seek to persuade us that class-marks would still be primordial. Although this is seemingly unlikely, there are extant empirical illustrations corroborating both logics. Casualness has clearly become a value cutting across the social hierarchy.[23] However, it would be unconvincing to argue that elites no longer develop at all a distinctive set of objects of consumption serving to express their status position, for example. It must be admitted, nevertheless, that there are now other attitudes involved, such as self-satisfaction quite unconcerned with the opinions of others. Present-day realities prove to be complex. Yet, what is striking is the affirmative tone adopted by each camp. We will return to these disputes when we consider the theme of elites increasingly playing on different registers, and at times even deliberately adopting traditional symbols of dominated strata. Suffice it to say at this point that, with a few notable exceptions, analyses lack empirical support. What matters to commentators, more often than not, seems to lie in offering deductive interpretations fitting their *a priori* ways of viewing the subject. This dialogue of the deaf must be overcome by inductive work on concrete perceptions at each social level and in various countries. As far as North American or West European elites are concerned, it is interesting to see to what extent they feel destabilised by this new lack of readability of signs of social status, or whether they remain at ease, with their symbolic superiority never being seriously threatened.

Psycho-sociological perspectives

The psycho-sociological literature deserves to be mentioned, here, if only because research in this area has sometimes concentrated on self-validation, appearance and power, or possessions as expressions of personality, among other themes indirectly relevant to us.[24] The field of psychology is traditionally defined as the science of subjective perceptions and idiosyncratic aspects of behaviour, and psycho-sociology as a branch of this discipline which deals with models of interaction. The individual-centred focus may be deemed to be problematic from the point of view of certain sociological traditions, but it is worth adding that some scholars have been concerned with making psycho-sociology more 'social' – largely considering the self as embedded within social relationships or working on shared representations (e.g. Tajfel, 1984).

Most noticeable, among the research traditions pertinent to our topic, is that of 'social comparisons'. Initiated by Leon Festinger, this was followed by an extensive line of deductive research. The approach posits that individuals aim to compare themselves with others for purposes of self-evaluation. The original statement of Festinger's (1954) theory was that they prefer to undertake this comparison with similar individuals in order to gain an accurate assessment of their respective positions and abilities. Later researchers have emphasised, however, that social comparisons can be motivated by other goals such as self-improvement and self-enhancement (Wood, 1989). In this respect, 'upward comparison' may be a source of inspiration for social comparers. Some psycho-sociologists also noted that people may prefer to compare themselves with less fortunate individuals, thereby increasing their subjective sense of well-being (Wills, 1981). These 'downward comparisons' could prove especially crucial for persons under threat, who seek reassurance through the contemplation of worse-off members of society. Social comparisons theory grew in complexity. For example, writings on 'relative deprivation' and 'inequity distress' have shown that upward comparison can be an extremely frustrating experience. It has also been underlined that downward comparisons are not necessarily good for the self in so far as they may entail a feeling of vulnerability.[25] Regardless, exploring the role of social comparison in self-esteem processes has become the major contemporary focus.

'Social identity theory' provides a complementary approach. According to this, the characteristics of a group acquire their significance in relation to the perceived differences to other groups. Thus, positive and negative comparisons might ensue, depending on whether or not evaluations between 'ingroup' and 'outgroup' are perceived as satisfactory for each social identity. The central proposition is that people strive to define themselves positively (see many contributions in Tajfel, 1978). Several strategies are envisaged in the attainment of a 'valued distinctiveness': dissociation from one's former group (individual mobility), redefinition of the elements of the comparative situation (social creativity) and attempts to reverse entirely the relative positions of the ingroup and outgroup (social competition). A useful dichotomy between 'secure' and 'insecure' social identities and comparisons is introduced. In the first case, the comparability between two or more groups is not even conceivable, because the superiority of one group is blatant (as in rigid caste societies or some colonial situations). In the second case, the status relations are much less stable because 'cognitive alternatives' are emerging. This urges the formerly dominated group to show that its inferiority is not inherent and immutable, which prompts the challenged group to reaffirm its own positive distinctiveness.

In some respects, this literature, which has developed quite independently of the above-mentioned sociological traditions – and uses a somewhat different rationale – implies, however, a certain similarity in its results. For example, some interpretations of upward-directed comparisons are reminiscent of analyses in terms of emulation. Equally, the insistence on the attainment of a sense of identity by individuals seeing themselves through the eyes of others raises the problem of possible discrepancies between the idealised view of oneself as compared with the actual self-image, which brings to mind some Goffmanian perspectives. The originality of the psycho-sociological approach lies in the stress put on the personal and emotional dimensions. To a large extent, the perceptions under examination occur before what mainly concerns us here. Specialists in 'social comparisons' deal with self-evaluations – in relation to other individuals or groups – rather than with distinction *per se*, but these are closely related processes. Furthermore, as with developments on 'valued distinctiveness', theoretical contributions sometimes go a little further and can be of some interest from an elite point of view.

Elements of socio-economics

Also of relevance to our subject are some works within the sub-field of socio-economics. In Chapter 1, we noted that Veblen and other 'institutionalist' authors seriously challenged conventional thinking in economics. By introducing sociological dimensions into classic theories of consumer demand – especially when insisting on the intrinsically relative nature of consumption – they brought up new visions which threw light on some of our themes. Veblenian approaches influenced economists such as Duesenberry (1949), who acknowledged the importance of the 'demonstration effect', whereby consumption patterns depend not only on the absolute level of spending but also on 'relative income' and on how spending compares to that of others. Almost concurrently, Leibenstein (1950) elaborated an unorthodox framework in terms of the 'Veblen effect' (where demand increases although the price is higher), the 'bandwagon effect' (where demand increases due to the attitude of other consumers) and the 'snob effect' (where demand decreases due to the fact that others are consuming a particular product). In a well-known volume, Hirsch (1977) added, importantly, that consumption becomes increasingly social as incomes rise. He argued that consumption is based on positional competition and introduced the influential concept of 'positional goods': 'those things whose value depends relatively strongly on how they compare with things owned by others' – which within a zero-sum game, is collectively self-defeating.[26]

It must be admitted that mainstream economists have been reluctant to confront the issue of the sociological bases of consumption patterns because these rather elusive dimensions do not easily fit their mathematical models of analysis centred on value and utility. On the other hand, specialists in marketing usually do recognise the importance of social factors. Many of the researchers who have entered this applied field actually have a behavioural science background. Sociology is well represented owing to the fact that inter-class relations and reference groups are deemed important for consumer motivations.[27] These works are useful because they show how consumers differ in their relation to symbolic consumption (e.g. Hirschman and Holbrook, 1981). It is often assumed that rich consumers are willing to pay more, not only because they associate high price with better quality, but also because they feel that high priced products convey their prestige to others. The premium is one of exclusivity; the consumption of select products distinguishes a privileged or sophisticated minority (see, e.g. Mason, 1981). Besides, it was suggested that consumers may attain a feeling of status and power from 'instant master-servant relationships' during shopping (Tauber, 1972), especially in countries such as Japan where salespeople are expected to indicate their submissiveness by a constantly deferential posture. Research also emphasises, however, that paying a reduced price for certain items may lead 'smart' shoppers to feel proud and to experience a distinguishing sense of accomplishment vis-à-vis others. It remains that elitist consumption may consist of hedonistically spending long days at prestige stores (which can be related to the Veblenian theme of 'conspicuous leisure') as well as in never bothering to compare prices, or even in sending one's servants on errands, thus avoiding any direct contact with other buyers.

Marketing literature is rich with detailed enquiries about consumer choice. An important recurring theme, here, is clearly that of brand image. Potential owners are bombarded with all kinds of advertisements that attempt to convince them that they will become a different person – expressing social status – if they acquire certain material goods, or that the purchased possession will render some aspects of their personal qualities more visible, thereby contributing to 'making themselves'. This raises the key issue of the relationship between collective and personal styles. A brand image is certainly the result of both objective and subjective factors; consumers associate it with the type of class using this brand. A pertinent question is whether the *homo consumens* is systematically manipulated by corporations or whether (at least within so-called 'advanced consumer cultures') it is instead the capitalist system that would have difficulties satisfying countless different tastes generated by a postmodern environment. Socio-economic approaches entail an explicit consideration of many dimensions, not only in relation to the democratisation of consumption, but also to globalisation and the consumption of Western luxury brands by the well off in the rest of the world (who wish to gain recognition at both the national and international levels). It is partly with regard to the questions provided by this sub-discipline that we shall engage with these points.

Focus must now, however, shift to the main concern of Part I: an examination of how successfully the theoretical frameworks available can explain past and present elite distinction in its manifold manifestations across the planet.

3
Grand Theories: Limits and Merits

From the panorama of analytical perspectives discussed above, dealing directly or indirectly with our subject, two contradictory impressions emerge. What strikes one is the disparate nature of the available literature – with so many different departure points – and yet the latter is frequently redundant in character. Focusing rather exclusively on their respective models of interpretation, individual theoreticians or schools of thought have largely tended to ignore each other, which has, at times, led to repeated arguments. A recurrent shortcoming is that whenever they present empirical evidence to support their position, they infer entire sociological laws on the grounds of one particular case during a given period. From a comparative point of view, this is indeed problematic. However, a mixture of criticism and admiration is often appropriate when it comes to assessing the relevance of the reading grids concerned. After discussing the symptomatic lack of willingness to engage in dialogue between authors, and then on over-generalisations or extrapolations, this chapter will emphasise how an inductive process can help to refine analysis.

Endless rediscovering

As we have seen, elite distinction has been a phenomenon of significance for many social scientists, but most have not deemed it necessary to acknowledge their indebtedness to their predecessors. Although there is a wealth of literature on this subject, one must admit that it hardly grew through building on the achievements of those who provided pioneering interpretations. Whether this negligence is a result of a lack of knowledge or a deliberate disregard for the contributions of others would be an interesting matter to pursue but is beyond the scope of this book. Generally speaking, space limitations prevent a systematic examination of the analytical relationships (legacies, compatibilities, antitheses, reformulations, extensions or inattention) between all the theoretical frameworks involved. What will be proposed here is an abbreviated discussion of some revealing aspects.

A few of the social scientists taken into consideration here did admittedly allude to ideas proposed by their forerunners.[1] However, a thorough examination of these references proves that this was usually combined with a claim to go beyond them. Many examples could illustrate this point. In his book on *The Court Society*, Elias does invoke Weber, Veblen and Sombart but states that Weber would have merely posed the problem of luxury as a means of social self-assertion and 'no more than that', (implicitly) that Sombart would have just adumbrated reflections on courts and that Veblen is 'hindered in his study of "conspicuous consumption" by an uncritical use of bourgeois values as criteria for economic behaviour in other societies'.[2] Baudrillard seems to offer support for Veblen's thesis but with the intention of providing important additions.[3] Only in a footnote, did Bourdieu distance himself from trickle-down perspectives, merely referring to the above-mentioned articles by Fallers (1961 [1954]) and by Barber and Lobel (1952) on that topic.[4]

It is still the case that what is most often notable is the lack of attention to previous literature. In this respect, some authors have been criticised for blatantly ignoring their precursors. Warner was reproached for never quoting Veblen.[5] Some of Bourdieu's commentators have taken aim at his unwillingness to situate his model of interpretation in relation to the pioneers who had paved the way in the study of social distinction. Generally speaking, Bourdieu enters into dialogue with scarcely anyone other than a few select philosophers, or the founders of sociology, and he invokes first and foremost his own *oeuvre*. Readers of *Distinction* will no doubt remember that there was no reference to Veblen (1994 [1899]) at all, not even to the latter's chapter on 'Pecuniary canons of taste' or the Veblenesque idea of 'distance from economic necessity'. When some influential contemporaries (e.g. Elster, 1983, pp. 69–70) estimated that, in many respects, the French author was merely building on some of the ideas presented by Veblen (among others), Bourdieu ultimately felt compelled to counter these criticisms – not unambiguously (Daloz, 2007a, p. 31). This raises the sensitive issue of theoreticians who, consciously or not, draw inspiration from others' seminal works and further develop them. In Chapter 1, it was mentioned that Spencer had anticipated Elias on the question of manners which, by descending the social ladder, result in ubiquitous politeness. Spencer might be a pioneer here but it cannot be denied that Elias considerably elaborated the argument.[6] To return to Bourdieu, it is not a very difficult task to show that some of his major theses – for instance on the 'natural' ease of those actors who are not wholly held in the grip of aquiring the necessities of life – are clearly present already in Veblenian interpretation. Likewise, the idea, if not the notion, of symbolic violence can be found in Elias (1982 [1939]). If one does not adhere short-sightedly to the respective conceptual apparatus of each social theoretician, in particular, and is conversant with the literature at stake, the originality of the analyses and conclusions drawn deserves careful scrutiny.

A good illustration, with regard to the lack of awareness (or recognition) of others' work, is the continual rediscovering – from Sombart to Bourdieu, through Weber, Elias and Warner – of the theme of the ability of the nouveaux riches to display external signs of wealth, while, however, revealing their social origins by the insecurity of their conduct.[7] Similarly, as we have seen in the two previous chapters, what was eventually referred to as the 'trickle-down theory of fashion' was suggested by Swift, Tarde, Veblen, Simmel and later by some American functionalists (who took no notice at all of one another), and it would have been quite legitimate in this respect to mention Spencer as well. A topic such as the undue appropriation of symbols is also telling of the way authors reconceive identical ideas – and here, Veblen, Weber, Simmel, Goffman and Bourdieu could be mentioned – without any quotation or footnote referring to their predecessors' or contemporaries' contributions. It goes without saying that the question of the reliability of signs carrying social information is a crucial one, and it is not surprising to see it addressed by many authors who impose their own vocabulary. But the problem is that of a marked reluctance to mention the insights made available to them by other theoreticians, thereby conferring the (incorrect) impression that every thesis contained in their books is their own. It would not be difficult to furnish other illustrations of theoretical amnesia relating to our subject. This might not mislead all readers, but devotees imprisoned by the dogmatic jargon of their own school of thought often appear blind to this problem of rediscovery.

On dubious generalisations and extrapolations

In the sociological literature dealing with elite distinction there is a manifest tendency toward generalisation. Innumerable quotations of passages betraying the intention to offer theories transcending both time and space could be presented here. Certainly, analysts need to offer conceptualisations applicable to a wide range of distinct contexts, but the danger involved is that of excessive universalism. Some of the scholars considered in the two previous chapters elaborated models based on a key principle underlying their grand theory, whereas others were prone to derive generalised laws from their research on specific case studies. In any event, the intention was to erect a single, homogenising, framework of analysis aimed at encompassing all sorts of situations – Weber's ideal-typical constructions and Elias's configurations constituting a relative exception. Yet, it is worth pointing out that the models available are more or less well-suited to the interpretation of concrete observations in a particular society.

The goal of early sociologists was mainly theoretical. What they seem to have been overly concerned with was figuring systems aspiring to the highest scientific ideals. Consequently, the basic processes or principles they built their work upon permeate all their writings. For instance, Spencer's views on class distinction, and more generally speaking on 'ceremonial institutions' (1893), are clearly affected by his evolutionist as well as organicist positions. Spencer enjoyed constructing orderly models and his fundamentally deterministic philosophy is governed by the idea of universal, inevitable laws derived from physics. Even though the unprecedented scale and scope of his synthesising project is impressive, Spencer was more concerned with teleology and theories than with realities. Equally, Tarde's obsessive concern with the 'Law of Imitation' (1962 [1890]) led him to a reductionist line of reasoning on the recurring aping of one's superiors. As is elaborated later, people do not always consider elites standing at the apex of the system as exemplary. Similarly, Sombart's central thesis on the advent of court society, 'sexual love' and the promotion of the demand for great luxury, is plausible and stimulating. The problem is that he confines his attention almost exclusively to this dimension. The task for the comparative analyst is to highlight the limits of such generalising enterprises. It is thus important to complement Sombart's one-sided picture and show that challenging luxury serves many other purposes. An extreme case is the Marxist research tradition, which tends to reduce anything symbolic to infrastructural relations of production and anything social to class. Without even having to refer (in a Weberian way) to ancient privileged groups whose status was not systematically derived from economic standing, it is not difficult to demonstrate the limits of economistic theories – including in market-dominated societies.[8]

As we saw in Chapter 1, Simmel did not deploy grand systematic explanations. Yet, in his influential theory of fashion and distinction (Simmel 1957 [1904]), he did not merely propose a model of interpretation about the situation in Berlin in the early twentieth century. Had Simmel been content with developing his subtle reading in terms of personal and collective styles about this particular context, there would be little controversy. The problem is that his famous article sometimes shows wider ambitions (referring to Renaissance Florence and Venice, dandies, etc.), not to mention the use of expressions such as 'The human being is a dualistic creature' and 'the essence of fashion', which have a rather universalistic ring. In any case, it is unlikely that the model of distinction as understood by Simmel can easily be applied across contexts. For instance, one does not inevitably discern a tendency of the superordinate classes to relinquish old status symbols. Even if we examine the period in which Simmel was writing, providing counter-examples is relatively easy.[9]

Veblen's perspectives can also be seriously questioned from a comparative standpoint. One can only concur with Elias who, as mentioned above, justifiably criticised the former for failing to understand the behavioural logics and the mentalities of environments different from the American bourgeois society with which he was familiar. A radical writing in the *Monthly Review* expressed this with style. According to him, 'Veblen's reflections about history and pre-history are infected with his view on the contemporary United States. He saw the past through a lens encrusted with the American present and, as a consequence this past was permeated with emulatory consumption and invidious distinction'.[10] Indeed, especially when attempting to reflect on aristocratic contexts, Veblen is no longer convincing. When he asserts, for instance, that since the status of hereditary nobles was definitively fixed at birth, and they tended to live in their own cocoon, they would not have been forced to show their rank, he makes a most unfortunate omission by neglecting intra-elite competition within court societies. Veblen's Americano-centrism is a complex one, since one has to consider his Norwegian roots. He was also apparently very much influenced by the work of the anthropologist Franz Boas on the famous *Potlatch* system. According to several commentators, the Veblenian scheme on conspicuousness is no more than an analytical transposition to the industrial era of the North-West American Indians' extravagant display and ostentatious destruction of properties.[11]

Functionalist theories are equally ethnocentric. However, it must be recognised that authors from this school of thought were mainly interested in the North American context and that, as far as questions of status symbols, prestige scale and standing are concerned, they rarely attempted to apply their model further afield.[12] The problem lies instead in the assumption that 'the social class system of America' can be characterised on the sole basis of community studies. Warner went as far as saying that 'To study Jonesville is to study America' and that cities such as Dallas, Seattle or Indianapolis and small American towns are 'essentially alike', in the introduction of his study of this rural town (Warner and collaborators, 1949, pp. xiv–xv). In other words, here we have a very questionable tendency to extrapolate, but only with regard to this large country.

The founders of sociology were primarily concerned with change in nineteenth- and twentieth-century Western society. However, a few like Weber or Elias sought to essay a theory of historical dynamics and, for this reason, determined to analyse the societal aspects of 'pre-modern' or extra-European communities. Elias can be classified among the authors for whom the social sciences ought to aim for large-scale theoretical synthesis. Yet, his approach in terms of configurations makes him a rather unusual kind of comparative sociologist. If he is clearly an anti-relativist, because of his insistence on the respective logics behind various types of configurations (Elias, 1978b [1970]), he cannot be accused of extrapolating or of aspiring to explain everything with a single grand theory. Unfortunately, this does not prevent him from drawing a debatable parallel between the *Potlatch* system and prestigious consumption within courtly society (1983 [1933], p. 67).[13] Furthermore, he remained an evolutionist (like Weber) and his strong emphasis on a process of civilisation drastically limits the range of possible cases, even if it avoids one-dimensional universalism.

This brings us to highlight another category of criticism which can be addressed to some of the authors concerning us here, that is the tendency to abstain from referring to some elements that might provide arguments for a revision of their theory. As will be developed in Part II, the study of elite distinction leads one to work on prestigious goods (clothes, vehicles, residences and luxurious eating), refined manners, gesture, the display of entourage, physical appearance, etc. In this respect, it is instructive to note that social theorists often tend to favour some of these facets at the expense of others. Elias acutely focuses his attention upon manners, which is consistent with his intention to reveal patterns of gradual diffusion.[14] Yet he says relatively little about extravagant adornment, indulgence in lavish banquets or, strikingly enough, the lack of sexual restraint which used to be so obvious in seventeenth- and eighteenth-century aristocratic life (see, e.g. Stone, 1977). One may wonder whether Elias (consciously or not) minimised those aspects that would seem to contradict his thesis about the rise of distinction through self-control? With this hypothesis in mind, one could attempt to give an overview of the objects of investigation ostensibly favoured, and of those (purposely?) neglected, by all of the social theoreticians considered above.

Weber is still viewed as one of the pioneers in the field of comparative history. However, much of his work (for instance on Confucianism and mandarins) is now deemed outdated or too imprecise by specialists. Weber was sceptical about grand theories which purported to be valid at any time and place, which is why he developed his ideal-typical methodology. Such an approach may potentially lead to scientifically rigorous perspectives, although assembling various historical cases by reference to the same abstract type at times entails simplifications or mere allusions. It has been a common complaint that the term 'charisma' is too imprecise, and covers phenomena too disparate to be of serious analytic service. Equally, Weber's 'traditional authority' ubiquitous ideal-type has justifiably been questioned by anthropologists (notably Goody, e.g. 1996). Moreover, while Weber certainly had an encyclopaedic knowledge of both Western and Asian civilisations, his theoretical acquaintance with more 'primitive' contexts was rather more limited (unlike a Spencer or a Durkheim), which is problematic for an author who sought to embrace all power situations. He convincingly argued about the specificity and heterogeneity of the 'West'. He also favoured a useful 'comprehensive' approach which consists in stressing what makes sense for the actors concerned. It is still the case that his evolutionist views on modernisation and rationalisation sound universalistic.

As for Goffman, apart from a few relativistic remarks (see principally 1963b), his perspectives on staging prove to be far too influenced by the limited number of settings studied. Indeed, when reading his works, one is constantly torn between admiration (generated by the remarkable subtlety of so many of his ethnographic observations) and dismay (when confronted with astonishing ethnocentric generalisations).[15] He does not seem to be conscious that relations to 'roles' or, to take another example, the way embarrassment is experienced vary hugely in different cultural contexts. As we have seen, Goffman is far from being unimportant to researchers studying elite distinction, but the major weakness of his work is its obliviousness to historico-cultural context. A similar feeling occurs from reading the Baudrillard trilogy mentioned above on objects and signs. One cannot but be disconcerted by so many over-generalised structuralist accounts in his first book (1996a [1968]) or by the doubtful anthropological parallels between modern consumer society and the *Potlatch* – assuredly a recurrent point of reference in the literature – or the *Kula* in the third (1981 [1972]).[16] The main objection is that a considerable number of theoretical speculations are made on the basis of very little evidence, which leads thinkers to mistakenly postulate invariant logics. Such queries could easily be multiplied. When we turn to psycho-sociology, it appears that the extensive line of deductive research derived from Festinger's theory of 'social comparisons' – largely based on laboratory studies – is inherently related to Western settings, where people are likely to think of themselves in terms of separate individuals possessing a uniqueness which is developed as an end in itself. There are obviously societies in which this type of perception, and consequently many of the assumptions of the sub-discipline, would not be prevalent.[17] The same is true, to a large extent, of the price/quality and prestige sensibility schema in marketing literature, or of sweeping proclamations by some (admittedly not all) analysts of postmodernity.

Last but not least, Pierre Bourdieu can certainly be put within the category of extrapolators – his singularity residing in the fact that he manifested generalising ambitions at a time when it was far less common to formulate a grand theory applicable to all societies. Each social theoretician must have a starting point somewhere and, in this respect, an awareness of the experiences in the field that have most influenced their scholarly work is always instructive. Quite often, there is clearly a tendency to rely on material from the monographs which have given these sociologists prominence. Undeniably, Bourdieu's theoretical framework is based on considerable empirical research on the peasant society of the Kabyle in the 1950s, and later on French society. However, to speak bluntly, it would appear that his comparative horizon was confined to these two cases, which he has attempted to establish as typical illustrations of pre-capitalist and capitalist society, respectively.[18] In largely evading the question of wider cultural and cross-national differences – apart from the two cases constituting his points of reference – he left himself open to criticism by scholars pursuing research on this topic. The question of whether or not Bourdieu's theory of distinction was applicable to the United States prompted most critical engagement. Following some seminal contributions around the issue of social boundaries and cultural norms from a comparative perspective (Lamont and Lareau, 1988; Lamont, 1992), this debate has mainly evolved into discussions centred on the question of taste displays.[19] But one could also mention European (e.g. Longhurst, Bagnall and Savage, 2001) or Australian studies (Turner and Edmunds, 2002) and, of course, a plethora of works on postmodern logics in late capitalist societies. As will be suggested below, we cannot unproblematically assume that such an analytical framework can be applied to Scandinavian, sub-Saharan or South-East Asian countries, for instance. Likewise, his attempt to defend the applicability of *La Distinction* to Japanese society (Bourdieu, 1994), by bringing up a handful of local references, cannot convince anyone even only a little acquainted with Japanese culture.[20] This, of course, did not prevent him finding sociologists willing to import his reading grid and to make themselves the apostles of his approach all over the world.

Perhaps some of these critical remarks have seemed ill-conceived to the ardent admirer of a particular author. Yet, as will be clear in the rest of the present work, empirical research reveals that all of the theories reviewed thus far do have some validity for the comparative study of elite distinction.

The analytical models confronted with comparative research

In their writings on our topic, many commentators have attempted to prove the superiority of one standpoint over the others. For instance, Mennell (1985, pp. 112 ff.; 1989, pp. 83 ff.) tries to persuade us that Elias's reflections on elite prestige consumption are more convincing than those of Veblen, Sombart or Weber, because his argumentation is more developed and is based on less elusive empirical grounds. Holt (1998) endeavours to show the ways in which the Bourdieusian theory of tastes exceeds the functionalist approach (particularly that of Warner) in terms of status symbols. On his side, McIntyre (1992) offers support to Baudrillard's views, which would go beyond those of Marx and Veblen. We could provide many other illustrations of converts who are of the opinion that their favourite thinker always surpasses other analysts, or of detractors unrelentingly voicing objections against one author.[21]

The approach advocated in this book starts from the very different premise that the theories elaborated by the above-mentioned scholars are all stimulating, *if we do not see them as reading grids that could systematically be applied across cases and contexts, but rather as tools useful for interrogating particularities.* Needless to say, the intention of this relatively eclectic perspective does not consist in juxtaposing largely incompatible theories. It entails instead an awareness of the limited validity of exclusivist conceptual frameworks. As should be clear from the discussion above, the major pitfall of most theories is to ignore the lack of similarity characterising symbolic relations between elites and other strata. To consider that distinction and emulation, imitation and differentiation, are merely the outcome of universal logics or will always be, *mutadis mutandis*, the same old story, is to fail to enter the world of their plural significance. Comparative studies on social distinction should question the explanatory value of analytical models by contrasting singularities.

What such an approach involves is thinking inductively rather than deductively. This means beginning with an examination of empirically observed realities and, only at a second stage, having recourse to the most appropriate instruments. The chief merit of in-depth field studies on elite distinction lies precisely in avoiding the temptation to generalise *a priori* on the basis of grand theories held to be universally valid. Although the sociological apparatuses discussed above are all worthy of note, it is relatively simple to supply empirical findings which do not readily fit in with their respective predictions. The existence of such discrepancies necessitates not a further elaboration of alternative theories with global explanatory ambitions, but limited ones succeeding in making sense of non-negligible variations across time or space – and of the logics underpinning them. In other words, the scientific reasoning suggested here is not one that attains the highest level of abstract generalisation but one that takes into account various logics of meaning. Placing the issue of meaning centre stage leads us to rethink the merits and demerits of the classical approaches to social distinction and challenges the supposed universality of some mechanisms. The result is certainly not 'sterile empiricism' or 'subjectivism',[22] but a non-dogmatic perspective seeking to illuminate the diversity of scenarios.

Although the following parts of this book will largely be devoted to discussions of singularities versus commonalities, let us offer a first illustration at this stage. Among those dimensions which are important to an understanding of divergent manifestations of elite distinction, a particularly eloquent one concerns the issue of ostentation/ understatement. The following passage of Veblen's *Theory of the Leisure Class* (1994 [1899], p. 24) is often quoted. 'In order to gain and to hold the esteem of men it is not sufficient to merely possess wealth or power. The wealth or power must be put in evidence, for esteem is awarded only on evidence.' This kind of statement is comprehensible, considering the dominant 'upstart culture' of his time, in a Northern American context which might be taken as the epitome of superiority assertion through external signs.[23] Yet, it prompts the question of the extent to which material symbols need to be exhibited for any self-completion to work. Arguably, if they are not verifiable, self-reported levels of superiority are hardly credible. Gronow (1997, p. 35) writes that 'A mere bank account or share portfolio is not a very good investment in this respect.' However, as Elias justifiably pointed out, in industrialised societies one is able to preserve great prestige without providing public proof through costly display. Social pressure would no longer have the unavoidable character it once had (especially under the court configuration). Bourdieu, for his part, reiterated the idea that when their superiority is well institutionalised, upper groups would tend to resort to rather discreet determinants of status, whereas the nouveaux riches would boast, thereby revealing their underlying lack of confidence.[24] The originality of his approach lies in the attempt to move away from the usual reflections about conspicuous display, while concentrating attention upon more elusive dimensions such as judgement and cultivated dispositions. This is certainly a fertile research direction, although it runs the risk of neglecting concrete dimensions which might also remain at the heart of social distinction practices.

One variable is significant when studying ostentation versus 'subduedness', namely, the assurance for the social actor wishing to express his/her worth that his/her interlocutors are already aware of his/her status. This is obviously related to another key variable, the more or less anonymous communicative context. In smaller communities, people share a great stock of background knowledge about one another and superiority may not need to be demonstrated.[25] In contrast, in urban settings, and particularly in large cities (as was pointed out in Chapter 2), external appearance does not just confirm an already known status but pertains to a constant reassertion of self. Therefore, considerable impression management is often necessary (see, e.g. Lofland, 1973). However, it proves difficult to generalise about status affirmation/confirmation and (in)conspicuousness. As an instance of this, it is notable that dominant groups or individuals might enjoy an institutionalised superiority but still be overtly ostentatious; conversely, elites may acquire high-value goods without displaying them. This is a topic to which we shall return.

It is also important to reason and analyse culturally. For example, specialists point out that an assertive display of face is frequently indispensable. In Lebanon 'if you don't *fannas* (show off) you are dead', writes Gilsenan (1976, p. 198), and this may involve lying. Almaney and Ahwan (1982) similarly discuss the practice of *mubalaqha* (exaggeration), which could be said to be imperative in the Arab world.[26] In contrast, in Scandinavia, the effects of the *Jante lagen* (referring to the informal rule that discourages feelings of superiority) can be seen among most members of the social elite.[27] They are even more powerful when it comes to political representatives, who cultivate an image of 'conspicuous modesty' (Daloz, 2007b) which is hardly found anywhere else.

More complex still, but equally important, is the need to bring to light various cultural patterns of elite/non-elite relationships. Particularly in societies which are structured according to vertical axes (be they clientelistic or linked to ethnic or religious identities), 'symbolic struggles' prove to be experienced in rather specific ways. In what may be called holistic contexts, many of the above-mentioned analytical perspectives about social distinction do not appear very useful. For instance, the tendency to reduce consumption to a materialist acquisition of goods by individuals makes it difficult to understand community-centred activities, such as banquets designed to display communal wealth and status. In his article on 'The Material Culture of Success' in Cameroon, Rowlands (1994) describes how conspicuous consumption is rarely just 'a personal and private act of gratification'. Rather, it is mainly concerned with 'public ceremonies', where both authority and generosity are supposed to be emphasised. In a similar vein, works on leader/community relationships in Nigeria (Daloz, 2002a) reveal that followers expect their respective 'Big Man' to display external signs of wealth. Supporters gain 'social credit' from his luxurious objects, as they reflect favourably upon the group as a whole. Thus, clients expect their patrons to uphold their rank and any failure to do so would come as a grave disappointment since it would denote the community's (or faction's) lack of substance. In this setting, social distinction does not only pertain to a self-glorifying quest by elites but also meets generalised expectations. Competitive display certainly functions as an exhibition of prosperity and power. However, it also reassures the supporters of a Big Man about his capacity to supply and satisfy a network of dependants in a particularistic manner – which is the key aspect to acquiring social legitimacy in such a context (Daloz, 2003). Otherwise put, there is paradoxically – at least from a 'Western' point of view – a kind of proxy 'enjoyment' by the clients of a Big Man's prestige goods. This begs an important distinction made by Campbell (1995) in his critical comments on Veblen: '[...] between those situations in which observers are impressed by one's ostentatious expenditure, although they do not benefit from it, and those in which the good opinion of others is linked to the fact that one's wealth has been spent on them' (p. 42).

Asia also provides instances implicitly contradicting assumptions made in some of the above-mentioned theoretical frameworks. In Singapore, Malaysia, Thailand or contemporary urban China, the members of the new middle class appear to be constrained by 'traditional morality' emphasising the necessity of communal reciprocity. Although it may be viewed with envy, wealth is definitely admired. However, conspicuous 'private' consumption by the nouveaux riches might be resented and obligations to 'one's people' remain very strong. This has theoretical implications because we are not just dealing with a class-differentiation standpoint here, as many orthodox models would have it, but with contradictory images of success, conspicuousness and cultural legitimation.[28] In holistic cultures, as opposed to individualist ones, preservation of one's collective image seems to be the major goal and a 'positive face' is fundamentally related to a community's or extended family's status, which is itself dependant upon each (dominant or dominated) member's attitudes.

These preliminary considerations lead us to affirm that some aspects of social distinction making perfect sense to the actors concerned within a certain context are meaningless in others. It would be tempting, but misleading, to interpret such differences from a purely evolutionist/teleological point of view or to reduce this complexity to a number of structural variables, such as a process of individuation (at once socio-economic, political and cultural), which claim to explain different perceptions and practices. Admittedly, some situations are rather ambiguous – and this is undeniably the case of many East-Asian or African societies 'in transition'. Yet, what is particularly fascinating, from a comparative point of view, is to show how elites may themselves be constrained by the cultural environment they share at a societal level. Far from being mere ideological smokescreens, some deeply engrained patterns of relationships are part of common cultural heritages and prove to be meaningful all the way up the social ladder. What this necessitates is an explicit consideration of cultural dimensions. If, obviously enough, purely societal logics require full attention, they do not necessarily exhaust the analysis of distinction.[29]

In summary, although the theoretical traditions presented above have generated insights, most of them have been prone to fitting realities into preconceived moulds. Indeed, many of the theses advanced seem somewhat strained. This may be related to the fact that the major contributors have 'instrumentalised' the subject – which was rarely their principal one – and that they were preoccupied with offering reading grids consonant with their own respective system of sociology. Once again, this does not mean that these frameworks are not penetrating, but that they have often led scholars to types of research that are biased: neglecting the intra-elite dimension of distinction (Marxists, Simmel), reducing presentation of self to the strategic (Veblen, Goffman) or unconscious pursuit of status (Bourdieu), treating prestigious goods as nothing more than signs (Baudrillard) and so on.

Comparative research on the symbolic dimensions of social distinction is likely to reveal important variations. This should become a major focus of investigation. It is imperative to emphasise both similarities and dissimilarities and, as far as is possible, to offer interpretations of them.

Part II
Key Manifestations

The socio-historical literature on upper-class behaviour or material possessions and anthropological fieldwork on dominant groups worldwide are rich with close observations. Monographic studies allow us to see a multiplicity of local definitions of distinction that are mediated by a complex array of factors and roots.

Drawing on some of these contributions and on personal research, the object of Part II is to highlight the major means through which elites can signal their prominent position in social life. Each chapter, therefore, explores different facets thus divided for purposes of exposition; however, as will be emphasised, there are connections between them. Chapters 4 and 5, respectively, deal with external and embodied signs of superiority. Then, in Chapter 6, 'vicarious display' will be examined, showing how eminent actors have recourse to their entourage to increase their own distinction.

A caveat is in order at this point. It will obviously not be possible to account for the tremendous variety of forms that elite distinction may take, nor to do justice to the many titles among the widely dispersed, and often densely allusive, literature. Part II offers an overview of some key manifestations and is written with the intention of bringing concrete aspects directly to the forefront of the discussion.

4
External Signs of Superiority

Among all of the attributes of social eminence, the possession of prestigious commodities is perhaps the most obvious. Elites enjoy value goods which not only make their everyday life more comfortable and pleasurable but also serve as symbolic expressions designed to authenticate their standing. Dominant groups often tend to define themselves – and to judge others – in terms of material symbols. Elegant clothes, vast houses, luxury cars or even delicacies (e.g. caviar) function as badges of social rank, denoting the superior status of elites against the groups below or vis-à-vis outsiders. We will consider adornment, residences, vehicles and culinary aspects in the following pages, but it is first appropriate to reflect on several issues of a theoretical nature.

Some premises about prestigious goods

By definition, the game of social distinction entails a sense of self-worth and a claim to superiority, and especially when it comes to asserting oneself over others, external signs prove to be crucial resources. In this respect, it is important to bear in mind that, throughout history and until quite recently (Galbraith, 1958), the vast majority of populations have been 'poor'. Distinction, and *a fortiori* ostentatious exhibitions which proceed from a sharp contrast with regard to the common lot, must therefore be perceived against this background.[1]

We may think of this question in terms of luxuries versus *'real human needs'*. However, as we saw, this usually leads to rather philosophical debates about the nature of luxury goods. From a less normative standpoint, anthropologists working on 'primitive' communities have established a distinction between 'subsistence goods' and 'prestige goods'.[2] The second category includes materials intended for adornment, money and wealth or ritual use. Amassing, exchanging and distributing prestige goods are significant activities because they are the means by which leaders or chiefs define their own status and that of others. They also provide a medium for demonstrating the standing of one's own community vis-à-vis elites representing neighbouring polities. On their side, sociologists dealing with 'modern' societies similarly contrast goods which are purchased to serve basic needs to those designed to display pecuniary strength and signal a superior social rank.[3]

Such differentiations are heuristically valuable but are far from being unproblematic from a comparative perspective. Historians have demonstrated that the luxury goods of one generation may become the 'standard items' of the next and the 'necessities' of the third.[4] As they move from being rare to being commonplace, many commodities thus lose their high-status denotation – as has happened with cars during the last 100 years, even though the most prestigious models remain out of reach for the greater part of the population. Equally, the strict nature of the subsistence/prestige goods dichotomy has been criticised by several ethnologists as a result of their field research.

Regarding the sociological thinkers presented in the previous chapters, it must be emphasised that some, by essentially paying attention to prestigious goods as status symbols or 'pure signs', have unfortunately underestimated the functional dimension of these signs. This is particularly noticeable in the approaches of both Veblen and Baudrillard. Yet, prestigious goods should also be studied from the perspective of their practical value.[5] For instance, although private jets must certainly be analysed in terms of status enhancement, one cannot deny that they fulfil concrete functions of rapidity and 'comfortableness'. Likewise, the Bourdieusian thesis according to which, by choosing goods that privilege aesthetic form over immediate material satisfactions, the dominant class would indicate that they have sufficient resources to be unconcerned with prosaic needs is sometimes borne out, but cannot be endorsed systematically. An alternative vision of 'utilitarian' dimensions might prompt scholars to study the usefulness of the artefacts with which elites surround themselves, irrespective of intentions of distinction. This is certainly not to suggest a purely reverse emphasis, which would be equally dogmatic, but to understand that, most often, prestigious goods prove to be composites: they provide substantive and symbolic satisfactions. Both deserve to be taken into consideration seriously.[6]

What should be kept in mind from the previous paragraphs is that it is advisable to avoid simple dichotomies or monolithic views which tend to obscure the actual intricacies that can be detected empirically. This does not mean that all attempts to establish categorisations are improper. On the contrary, several important distinctions about prestigious goods are particularly relevant from a comparative viewpoint: for instance, between the most durable (like precious stones passed down from generation to generation) and the ephemeral ones (such as luxury food), between movable and immovable ones or between those which seem to exert a universal fascination and others valued only in some places. We shall have occasion to return to these aspects. Furthermore, other issues which merit specific discussion – especially distinction through antiquity or novelty and through profusion or sophistication – will be addressed later.

An additional theme which should be mentioned at this stage is that of the visibility of signs associated with high status. If we talk of *external* signs of superiority, an outward exhibition is inferred. This, however, is not a simple matter. As noted earlier, distinction may require studied understatement, whereas too much concern with displaying one's rank through personal possessions would eventually undermine one's reputation. Conversely, in some settings, openly flaunting one's assets is expected, while inconspicuousness is likely to be interpreted in terms of diffidence or lack of wherewithal.[7] Another way to reveal the complexity of this question of visibility consists in differentiating between 'position goods' – which strongly depend on how they compare with things owned by others – and 'non-positional' ones (Frank, 1985), to use socioeconomics categories. Elites may acquire high-value goods without displaying them, perhaps because they are 'money-rich but time-poor' upper-class people, or because not all 'status consumption' is supposed to be put conspicuously on display, or even enjoyed publicly.[8] Moreover, it is essential to understand that the general tension between concealment and exposure works rather differently from culture to culture. In some contexts an imagined presence behind closed doors and high walls may carry considerable status whereas, in some others, hypervisibility is indispensable, which might, for instance, bring people to cut down all the trees around their newly built mansion. Comparative studies on outward signs of eminence require nuanced conceptions and an open mind with regard to models of interpretation applicable to case studies.[9]

Large-scale empirical research might well lead one to stress dissimilarities as to which prestigious goods are given priority when projecting an image of superiority to others.[10] Nevertheless, it seems that luxury food, distinction through the size of dwelling, means of transport and sartorial dimensions (i.e. refinements related to the fundamental needs of sustenance, shelter, mobility and clothing) remain highly desirable in most societies. It is relevant, therefore, to focus attention on these four domains, although they are by no means exhaustive.

Adornment

Throughout history, lavish displays of finery and wealth in the form of jewellery have been a key component in proclaiming social worth. Clothes, as well as serving as a means of protection (against the cold, the burning sun or even malevolent forces), provide visual information that conveys many different messages by reinforcing identities, arousing sexual interest, eliciting deference, etc. Since specialists from various academic disciplines have shown the enormous range of human behaviour when it comes to the symbolic universe of dress, generalisations are seldom convincing. For instance, if in most civilisations the contrast between being dressed and undressed has long been essential, ethnologists have demonstrated that relative nakedness is not necessarily a sign of inferior status.[11] Distinction may involve being veiled from head to foot or displaying one's undergarments.[12] Comparativists have come to realise that there are countless logics of elegance, each with its specific significance. For example, clothes more or less follow, conceal or distort the lines of the body, but the most striking illustration is probably the use of colour, given the many contradictory conventions.[13]

It is important to highlight the fact that smart attire is one of the least onerous distinctive signs one can obtain. If owning a house is still unaffordable for most working-class people at the present time, wearing a suit or an elegant dress and momentarily putting on an outward 'good show' has been an achievable ambition for many. An improved appearance may give one a relative self-confidence. The autonomy of the sign allows the artificial affectation of a superior condition – the reason why one finds so many reflections about 'imposture' or 'pretension' in the literature on dress. In the United Kingdom, during the interwar period, many clerks or salesgirls suffered from malnutrition even while their wardrobes were full of lovely dresses (Horwood, 2005). In France, some Congolese immigrants use most of their salary to buy impressive designer-label clothing and parade on the Parisian avenues but rent a miserable suburban dwelling. It seems likely that they will not delude people for long, except perhaps when they return to their own country.[14] As Marx noted earlier, luxury goods may function as a signal of credit-worthiness[15] and this seems to be particularly true of impressive apparel (Bell, 1976). More generally speaking, it is interesting to study how distinction in one sector – being well-dressed, driving a fancy car, etc. – can serve as a foundation for conquering others. Here, a functionalist approach is probably appropriate but, as will be shown, it is also pertinent to consider cultural aspects.

Clothes magnify their wearers 'quite literally in some cases', as Peter Burke (1987a, p. 145) reminds us, in so far as they are often designed to make them look bigger or broader than they really are. It is usually accepted that tallness and a strong build command respect. Consequently, many artifices have been concerned with creating an impressive appearance. Witness, among many other examples of aggrandising garments, the high-shouldered sleeve padding of some Renaissance monarchs and courtiers, or the recourse to platform shoes (for a long time, a status symbol). Headgear also constitutes a relevant topic in this respect. From a structuralist point of view, it may be contended that it reinforces the feeling of transcendent verticality,[16] although it is important to take into consideration a multiplicity of symbolisms (e.g. Clark, 1982).

Shape, amount and superiority of materials, aesthetic dimensions and, in certain contexts, 'fashionability' contribute to the distinctiveness of attire. If perfectly cut dresses and creative tailoring are at times deemed primordial, the appeal of expensive, bright and most comfortable fabrics proves to be widespread when it comes to conceal the 'commonness of nakedness' and to beautify bodily appearance. One could elaborate on shimmering silk, brocade velvet, lace, furs and feathers or (from a more quantitative perspective) on multiple layers of clothing, long trains, embroidery, ribbons and buttons. We clearly do not have space here to examine these elements in detail.[17] However, one interesting phenomenon and one noteworthy thesis deserve to be mentioned. Historically, when clothing became associated with status pretensions, sumptuary laws were often enacted. In Europe, for instance, particularly from the end of the Middle Ages, such legislation forbade aspiring groups from wearing fabrics which aristocrats thought to reserve for themselves. Even within the nobility, lords were frequently required to wear a prescribed range of ornaments according to their respective rank.[18] We shall return to this socio-political theme of reserved styles and materials, from a comparative standpoint, when we deal with the historicity of elite distinction (Chapter 7). The thesis – developed mainly by Veblen (1994 [1899]) in relation to his approach in terms of 'conspicuous leisure' – importantly argues that sumptuous and delicate attire not only draws attention to the 'conspicuous consumption' of the wearers but also to a dissociation from physical work.

Continuing this line of argument, a few words must be said on the question of neatness. Although historical comparisons show a great deal of variation as regards conceptions of personal cleanliness, there is no doubt that, in many societies, scrupulously dirt-free clothes have been an imperative means of validating status, in sharp contrast with the bulk of the population. During the Victorian era, one could speak of the 'clean upper classes' versus 'the great unwashed'. Conjointly, as a result of new standards of behaviour and technical progress, spotless shirts, neatly pressed suits and impeccably polished shoes are not the prerogative of the elite anymore. Until fairly recently, however, such a final touch pointed to the fact that one had servants, or at least access to careful laundering services on a regular basis. The immaculateness of clothes, particularly that of vulnerable pieces like sleeves or collars, was a chief indicator of distinction. Wearing irreproachable light-coloured attire can also indirectly prove the adroitness of the wearers (for instance their capacity to eat sophisticatedly) and the fact that they pay visits to undirtied places only. Moreover, if enjoying a lavish wardrobe permits elites variety of dress and, when appropriate, the ability to follow the changes dictated by fashion (two important subjects to be treated later), it also contributes to avoiding excessive wear and tear, knowing that individuals' social standing is often judged through the newness of their clothes.

Dressing well used to be an obligation for all people 'of position'. A few exceptions notwithstanding, it is acknowledged that at least until the Renaissance period, women of the elite had less luxurious clothes than men. This trend has reversed progressively since the Renaissance in Western Europe, leading to what psychologist J.C. Flügel (1930) called the 'Great Masculine Renunciation'. Flügel contends that from the end of the eighteenth century, men have ignored dazzling and varied forms of masculine adornment, in order to adopt a less elaborate style denoting seriousness. Another well-known specialist of sartorial matters, J. Laver (1969), went as far as saying that women's clothes are governed by a 'seduction principle', aiming at making them 'more sexually attractive', whereas men's clothes are governed by a 'hierarchical principle'. It is also possible to follow Veblen, according to whom men of the upper groups have transferred their 'conspicuous waste' to their spouses or daughters, thereby showing their own superiority vicariously through their entourage (see Chapter 6, hereafter). Although such views are over-generalised, they nonetheless offer suggestive roads. In many societies, gorgeous wives or mistresses are openly flaunted by men and it is not unjustified to provide interpretations in terms of 'ornamental reification of women', as feminist authors are prone to do. Yet, this is just one scenario among many, as we shall see.

Beyond the enhancements of dress, jewellery is paramount when it comes to displaying one's superior social status in public. It sets apart the wearer because of its brilliance, of its value, writes Simmel, and it operates a sort of 'circle radiation' in which 'every close-by person, every seeing eye, is caught'. This perfectly fulfils a desire to distinguish oneself, 'to be the object of an attention that others do not receive'.[19] It should be added that jewels are used as means of increasing beauty and desirability. In this respect, such external signs must be considered in close relation with the bodily ones: a glittering necklace draws attention to the daring décolletage, and vice versa. What is more, precious metals or stones are held in exceptionally high regard because of their timelessness. They are valued as lasting possessions in old elite families and as prominent signals of achievement for rising groups. Although there are obviously accounts of contexts where men displayed chains, brooches or bracelets – not to mention the present wearing of watches, cufflinks or wedding rings – jewellery has more usually been worn by women. Therefore, what has been outlined in the previous paragraph clearly applies to jewellery, but one could also mention many other accessories.[20]

Most of the observations and analyses presented above remain valid to a large extent. However, several consequential dynamics have led to shifts and to the actual complexities of the contemporary situation. First, the industrial revolution has brought ready-to-wear copies of smart clothing to the lower classes, who tried to ape the upper ones. The materials used were cheaper and the designs often simpler, but a process of imitation was at work – and here Tarde's model of interpretation certainly is useful. This gradual change frequently resulted in the emergence of a 'Simmelean tension' between adoption and differentiation in the pursuit of fashion. Yet, both historical and sociological research shows that this has not been the only observable attitude. Some high-status people have continued to favour a rather habitual style and remained immune to the gaudy displays of some of their subordinates. Others have allowed themselves to wear more relaxed, non-distinctive clothing. It is well known that by the end of the eighteenth century, informal country outfits had become quite acceptable in England, and did so later in some other countries. Besides, a relative simplicity of dress can have political overtones. What is most remarkable in the evolution of clothing is that we are not just dealing with 'trickle-down' differentiation logics but also with reverse (upward) patterns of diffusion. For example, the ordinary man's full-length trousers eventually displaced the aristocratic knee-breeches, and denim jeans have become a ubiquitous item of apparel. Elites themselves have often shifted to more casual styles and manners of wearing clothes.

However, here again, nuanced analyses are required. Garments might less easily serve as accurate symbolic representations of social status than in the past. The democratisation of clothing is a reality, and so is the cacophonic proliferation of codes emphasised in the literature concerned with postmodernity. Top designers are nonetheless still producing luxury clothes distinguished by exquisite workmanship and quality materials. Likewise, ties are possibly increasingly perceived in terms of constraint, but some are splendid creations and the ability to tighten and to wear them with sartorial flair undeniably remains a source of distinction (Finkelstein, 1991, Chapter 4). On the other hand, breaking free from certain conventions may also be an elitist way of asserting oneself over others.

Residence

Beyond their fundamental function as a shelter, dwelling places have often been the essential indicators of social standing. There are, however, great variations. First, one must recall that in numerous 'traditional communities', habitations were used to express collective (e.g. clan) identities and group unity. It is only after a long period of evolution that residences became status symbols.[21] Even now, the stylish façades of vast private houses can still be a minor source of collective pride, in so far as they are liable to attract admiring glances from strangers. Second, environmental and climatic factors and the availability or relative lack of space, as well as numerous specific cultural norms, have shaped local perceptions. In certain contexts, surrounding land is considered to be more important than the buildings themselves or a desert tent can prove more ostentatious than a permanent edifice. Admittedly, some structural dimensions – like the threshold – are transcultural. Yet, research shows significant differences when examining concrete realities and meanings: 'inner' and 'outer' areas can be clearly marked by physical boundaries (doors, fences, gates, sliding paper partitions or curtains) but also by purely symbolic and conventional – though no less commanding – borders.[22]

The history of housing, both with respect to architectural form and furnished contents, is well documented. Some of the authors discussed in the earlier chapters have investigated this subject from the point of view of social differentiation. Elias, among others, devoted the beginning of his work on *The Court Society* (1983 [1933]) to an analysis of the physical structure and appearance of aristocratic and bourgeois dwellings in France under the *Ancien Régime*.[23] He emphasises how dimensions and ornamentation varied with rank and proposes a subtle interpretation of internal layout in connection with status. On his side, Warner graded the houses of 'Yankee City' and 'Jonesville' in terms of size, condition and location.[24] Dimensions and situation, as well as interior decoration, are evidently at the heart of elitist strategies. The study of residences equally leads to a consideration of elements such as distinctive architecture, furniture – and more generally all sorts of prestigious goods for which the house serves as a showcase – but also grounds. It is to these elements that we shall now turn.

The size of buildings is frequently proportionate to social status (or to the official power exercised). However, as Marx (1932 [1849], p. 32) noticed, this is rather a question of relative, as opposed to absolute, hugeness. A larger palace arising in the neighbourhood is very likely to make the previous ones look small, even if these are, objectively, vast. Conversely, houses of modest size may be regarded as sufficiently satisfactory as dwellings if the surrounding ones are smaller. What is critical for elites is to demonstrate their dominance vis-à-vis subordinates and to exhibit at least as much supremacy as their peers. An interesting historical development in this respect is the one which saw nobles used to an undisputed pre-eminence within their locality, thanks to their castle, being subjected to a sudden residential competition when gathered by the king, or the queen, under a process of 'courtisation'. A big house is not only a matter of external impressiveness, it also signifies inner space and gives room for the display of prominent features: a wide staircase, a huge chandelier or a very long table, for example, which themselves contribute to the imposing character of the place.[25] Last, but not least, space permits the decent and hospitable accommodation of guests, which may prove to be crucial within a context of intra-elite competition.[26] Having numerous, spacious rooms, however, raises the issue of care and cleanliness and calls for the presence of servants – who may themselves play an important part in distinction strategies.

Another aspect of special interest when one studies dwelling from a distinction perspective is that of location. Superiority in this respect is chiefly expressed through two, differing, logics which are revealing about the nature of social relationships. The first is aloofness. From Roman emperors who had their residences built on the Palatine hill – that is above the crowded city – to medieval lords in their high towers dominating and guarding over their lands, to British colonial officers purposely settling down at some distance from the communities they had to administer, standing symbolically apart has been a key to demonstrating one's supremacy. The second logic combines visibility and closeness. In contexts where primarily vertical relations are the norm, leadership mainly involves exchanges cementing clients to patrons in mutual self-interest. In sub-Saharan Africa, local 'Big Men' do indeed try to distinguish themselves by constructing the most impressive edifice, but generally in the very place where they have their roots, that is, among their community and followers, even if this is a miserable village or an overcrowded suburb. Undoubtedly, in such cases what is at stake is a collective sense of distinction from rival groups and a suggestion of ascendancy depending on proximity.[27]

In cities and towns where horizontal cleavages prevail, area segregation has not always been the rule. For centuries, in a city such as Paris, social differentiation was related to levels rather than neighbourhood. Poor people were relegated to garrets or basements, whereas the richest enjoyed the first and second floors; consequently, there was potential for continual interaction between persons from different orders or classes. Further developments (linked to the industrial revolution and migration) led to more homogeneous spatial arrangements with exclusive residential sectors at one end (usually most remote from local industrial plants and pollution), overcrowded tenement buildings at the other and more or less finely graded neighbourhoods in between. In many places, a local address can immediately be interpreted in terms of social milieu. Functionalist authors have emphasised that when upper-class people pay for a house in the United States, it is not just about providing a shelter for their family but about living in the 'right' neighborhood, which will bring the approval of their friends or colleagues and reflect their social status.[28] The current phenomenon of 'gated communities' – those protected 'golden ghettos' which can be found in some unsafe North American and in Third World megacities – certainly indicates that these trends are not declining (see, e.g. Hill Maher, 2004). Nevertheless, works from geographers or specialists of urban studies reveal the variability of social distinction strategies related to location.[29] In many places, well-to-do families have deserted city centres and moved to new suburbs where they may enjoy a greener environment. In this case, people from the poorer segments of the population have more or less 'reconquered' the heart of cities where wealthier ones only come to work or shop. However, it is also common to have working-class inhabitants and immigrants confined to the downgraded peripheries and elites preferring a renovated condominium along the main avenues of the cities. In the 1980s, it was fashionable for 'Yuppies' to opt for luxurious dockland flats alongside socially deprived residents (distinction being expressed, here, through the conjunction of space and centrality) and, since then, a process of 'gentrification' of formerly low-income areas has often been witnessed. Technical progress has also contributed to radical shifts. New means of transport have thus favoured the development of residential areas ringing the cities and incited elites to live on the top of steep hills which offer unrestricted panoramas, whereas these places were previously considered hard to reach and therefore left to low-ranking people. Similarly, the advent of lifts has somewhat modified the respective prestige of floors, with living on the first or second one now being less prestigious than residing in the top ones with a view.

The examination of residences also brings one to study interiors. From a comparative angle, a very good question is of whether the latter are deemed more or less important than the external aspects of a house. A Goffmanian approach in terms of 'front' and 'back regions' can be used appositely. However, one should beware of universalistic generalisations. In some cultures, beautiful façades play a paramount role in magnifying the status of the owner of a house, in others it may instead be the ceilings, the wall hangings, the floor-covering or the patio that have become the major source of pride and distinction. As with other social categories, elites may spend more money on rooms devoted to public functions than on adjacent 'private' ones – and one inevitably thinks, here, of the literature on living-rooms[30] – but this calls into question the notion of a strict separation between the two spaces. Such a dualistic conception may or may not make sense, and views may also fluctuate markedly over time.[31] Proxemics (that is the study of the human use of physical space) equally informs us about strongly relativist premises as far as the size and fullness/emptiness of rooms is concerned. In some contexts, elites appreciate immense and rather bare spaces, possibly making some foreigners feel ill at ease (Hall, 1966). Reciprocally, social distinction may come from the display of redundant decorations in fairly small spaces, such as those purposely overfilled ante-rooms planned to impress waiting visitors.

The importance attached to furniture varies from one society to another. In some civilisations (e.g. China and Japan), it may be considered even more valuable than the house itself, whereas in others (the Near East) large pieces are notably almost absent. The above-mentioned question as to whether prestigious goods are valued mainly as outward symbols of status or as utilities is particularly significant when one studies furnishings. Some items are decorative while others are indisputably functional. Some are used daily and others, in the principal reception room, often remain protected with covers when no distinguished guests are expected. Some are also meant for the exhibition of precious objects, such as buffets flaunting silver, ceramic plates and fine glassware or display cabinets full of antiques. A large number of sofas and assorted armchairs may be a sign of an active social life. Among the items put on view, it is appropriate to differentiate between those which are related to the history of the owners of the place, their successful entourage or their prestigious ancestors (flattering portraits, trophies, framed degree certificates) and possessions with exceptional value, the accumulation of which is appreciated as a suitable indicator of social position. It is the logics of self-presentation which are of most interest here for scholars, with respect to what they tell us about social perceptions.[32] This may lead to standard accounts of lifestyle or taste. What are frequently overlooked are the cultural dimensions, such as distinction entailing the art of regularly changing the layout of the things in one room or, on the contrary, the imperative of conferring an impression of continuity in the narrative presented to the viewer.

Equally, gardens and parks may have significance for status purposes. As Warner (1959, p. 46) wrote, 'Landscaping transforms the surroundings of the house into a superior aesthetic form, functioning for the exterior setting much as the beauty of furnishings and decor for the interior.' For many successive generations of landowners, prestige was strongly associated with land in so far as the latter was a major source of revenue. A shift to more visual dimensions must certainly be understood in terms of evolving mentalities within some societies, but it is also appropriate to consider it from a social distinction standpoint. Devoting part of one's property to non-economic and purely aesthetic purposes is an indirect way of showing one's wealth and taste, and this can easily be interpreted along Bourdieusian lines. A truly comparative treatment of this topic would require us to enter into the varied relationship between culture and 'nature' (or 'landscapes') – those unsatisfactorily Eurocentric notions – and to take into account, for instance, the very rich Arab, Indian, Chinese and Japanese traditions. Nevertheless, a close examination of 'Western' patterns is already quite revealing. The Italian Renaissance garden tried to rediscover (what was imagined to be) Roman precedents, but proved, in fact, rather original. As with the case of 'Arcadian gardens' and their numerous temples, what this involved was not just rare fruit trees, terraces and stairs, but evocations of antiquity through the presence of statuary and allusions to literature. Distinction before others depended on a good knowledge of classical studies. French formal gardens also conformed to such highly conventionalised configurations. However, they introduced an even more artificial domestication of nature. The neat and carefully planned geometric lines, designed to be viewed from the residence, emphasised the full control of the elite over an ordered environment. Clipped trees and shrubs, perspective created by seemingly endless rows, fountains going off when distinguished guests passed by and flowerbeds changed overnight all contributed to this elitist impression of domination.[33] With the English landscape park tradition, we have yet another way of generating a sense of distinction. There, the intention is to identify empirically the originality of a place and to build on it by heightening the illusion of naturalness. All deformities are concealed, variety and contrasts aim at creating a feeling of perfection with smooth surfaces and ornamental trees producing subtle effects of light and shade. In other words, superiority is related to the selection of the most beautiful aspects of nature.[34] A belt of vegetation can often be found around the perimeter of the parks, in order to screen them from surrounding lands, as if the property was a world of its own. At the present time, however, very large estates – which require gardeners working constantly to maintain their impressive appearance – have become a rare privilege. Places of retreat and exclusive access to an attractive countryside with no neighbour in view, now belong to what Baudrillard (1996b [1970, pp. 72–73]) calls 'new rarities', along with such elements as pure air or even silence, which were previously taken for granted, or considered unimportant.

Vehicles

From ancient rulers who had to demonstrate their existence all over their territory, to aristocrats moving from their castle to their residence in the capital city for the 'season' or to the 'jet set' participating in high life activities across continents – among many other examples – the ability to travel rapidly, comfortably and in style has been a priority. This is why elites frequently attach great value to vehicles, which prove to be a primary object of competitive display. One could look to antiquity and evoke beautifully decorated chariots that were significantly buried, in some places, with their deceased owner. Horse-litters, gorgeous coaches, sedan chairs and all types of elegant carriages would deserve separate consideration in relation to technical improvements.[35] For what concerns us here, it should be underlined that these means of transport allowed important people more comfortable and less fatiguing journeys, but were also a crucial means of attracting attention. Indeed, many specialists of the seventeenth and eighteenth centuries in Western Europe concur that there was no more visible form of prestige than ornate coaches and equipage. With their elaborately carved bodies including a large amount of gilding, painted panels or insignia on the sides, a rear platform for footmen and sometimes accompanying postillons riding beautiful horses, it seems clear that such vehicles could contribute to elite distinction.[36]

The advent of the car prompted mixed reactions: it was rejected as hopelessly vulgar by some British aristocrats (Cannadine, 1994, pp. 62 ff.) but enthusiastically adopted in France where it quickly became associated with elite circles and events.[37] Cars were at first fancy toys for the rich and they could still be regarded as outstanding symbols of success in the 1920s. However, because of the development of production, a second-hand market and the subsequent fall of prices, within 30 years cars denoted middle-class status and have since become a common machine in industrialised societies. Such a rapid diffusion confers a relative specificity to the analysis of cars from our perspective. In a well-informed study, Gartman (2004) argues that a social distinction reading grid would mainly be valid for the 'first age' of the automobile, but much less so for the next two, characterised, respectively, by mass production schemes – making sure that no model looks 'cheap' – and pluralistic postmodern logics entailing an unprecedented diversification. Laudable as its non-dogmatic concern to analyse various stages with reference to differing models of interpretation undoubtedly is, this evolutionist approach is nonetheless debatable. The buggy's owner might not necessarily envy the driver boasting in an expensive limousine, but this does not mean that prestige vehicles – whether sports or executive cars, or massive 4x4 SUVs – do not play any part in status competition nowadays.

This is all the more obvious when one takes into account the situation of 'developing countries' where the possession of a car remains a luxury for many. It might be considered that these societies would just be 'late' and will eventually go through similar dynamics. Yet, once again, it is important to enter the realm of meanings and cultural comparisons. In some places, the centrality of the car is such that persons are mainly identified by their associated vehicle, which can be

washed several times per day.[38] In Nigeria, where the desire for ownership of a Mercedes Benz verged on the obsessional in the 1980s, the
adjective 'V-boot' (meant to refer to the then rear line of this make)
was interestingly used to designate any ostentatious style. One could
say, for instance, that a lady had a 'V-boot' hairstyle. In other words, if
cars are instrumental goods concretely allowing demarcation of oneself
from the masses doomed to walk or to use packed public transport, it is
imperative to examine local representations and how vehicles symbolically contribute to image shaping.

Cars are usually presented as individualised means of mobility that
have become synonymous with autonomy and a promise of greater
freedom. In many countries, they have made possible some new leisure activities[39] and have facilitated the suburbanisation of the population. It is worth adding that cars are rich in ambiguity, as several social
scientists have emphasised.[40] On the one hand, they can be seen as
eminently private goods, allowing one to have a personal space even in
the middle of a metropolis. On the other hand, since drivers are largely
dependent on surrounding vehicles, road facilities and highway codes,
they also belong, unquestionably, to the public sphere. As far as demonstration of social standing is concerned, they probably represent one
of the most easily observable external signs of superiority, even if one
cannot always discern the passengers inside them.

Driving often generates a feeling of empowerment.[41] This may well
result in challenging behaviour toward others. In the past, running men
were tasked with shouting at other people to get out of the way of their
master's palanquin or carriage.[42] In certain extreme cases, the vehicle
can be used as a menacing device aiming at intimidating pedestrians or
other drivers. Settlers, in some colonies, loved to sound their hoot and
to deliberately frighten the natives. Currently, in Moscow, VIPs who
regard themselves as above common people drive their powerful auto-
mobiles at breakneck speed without taking anyone else into consideration. From a neo-Marxist point of view, there is subtle analogy between
the respective 'performance' of cars and social hierarchies on the road
(Lefebvre 1971 [1968], pp. 101–102), while aggressive overtaking is interpreted in terms of 'symbolic violence' by a Bourdieusian author such as
Boltanski (1975). Horsepower and class-consciousness may be related.
Furthermore, the ability to handle a sports car deftly may also have an
elitist dimension. However, pressing the accelerator is not the prerogative of just those who occupy the top of the social ladder. Quite to the
contrary, some dominated individuals look for a kind of compensation,
or even revenge, on roads. As with ostentatious dress, it is quite possible

to have a strategy consisting in devoting the bulk of one's money to acquiring an imposing vehicle.[43] It remains, nevertheless, a fact that cars offer many ways for elites to distinguish themselves.

When a car is described as being prestige, it is usually related to exceptional design, shiny metal, high-speed potential, very complete instrumentation and stylish accessories. It is also easy for authors interested in luxury goods as 'pure signs' to highlight the superfluous character of several characteristics (see Baudrillard, 1996a [1968, pp. 83–85] on tail-finned cars). When scrutinising what is favoured, one realises that the codes are quite sophisticated, not to say contradictory. Sports cars can be astonishingly spartan, but the powerful engine is the deciding factor. Reciprocally, prevailing considerations for luxurious models are aesthetics, manoeuvrability, a spacious passenger compartment and no compromise in comfort, but they do not necessarily require an outstanding engine. Moreover, as we shall see later, cars' distinction may be based on antiquity as well as novelty. Comparative observations also reveal some attitudes which are symptomatic of cultural divides. To give just one illustration, we may mention contrasted views vis-à-vis the expensive 'under-the-hood' options which are often advertised on the outside of vehicles. Unlike their Nigerian counterparts who are infatuated with these aspects (Daloz, 1990), it can be observed that in Switzerland a majority of Mercedes Benz owners do not want indications about the type, characteristics and the engine capacity of their car (such as E 320 or 'Kompressor') to appear on the boot, because such conspicuous indications are deemed both redundant and 'vulgar'.[44]

This area of the discussion involves a return to the idea already expressed that distinction is not only a question of domination over social inferiors but also, and often primarily, a concern with differentiation between elites themselves – as the world of yachts, helicopters and private jets demonstrates.[45] Dream vehicles such as Lamborghinis or Aston Martins (produced at a rate of a few hundred units per year) offer a way of standing out from one's relatively less wealthy neighbours with their BMWs or Cadillacs. Considerations related with carmakers traditions, objective and subjective factors in brand choice and national stereotypes are frequently involved.[46] Elegantly upholstered interiors, the use of precious wood, gorgeous hub caps or stunning insignia certainly play a prominent role. But research on this theme equally brings one to study less obvious dimensions. One of them is personalised registration plates. In many countries it is quite possible (officially, or thanks to bribes or connections) to have meaningful combinations that add character to the vehicle. In Nigeria, the numbers 1, 11, 111 and 1111 are particularly sought after as if this repetition is a good indicator of primacy. Messages can be more or less subtly distinctive and all sorts of plays with numbers and letters are conceivable.[47] Certain plates also confer concrete privileges, such as the right to use exclusive express lines, or to park freely anywhere. This links to an interesting parallel subject: that of the private appropriation by some powerful members of the elite of attributes which are usually reserved for special public purposes. In this respect, tinted windows can serve as a good illustration. In Lithuania, because of their association with the mafia, these were finally prohibited for everyone except top officials and some specific departments within the police or customs administrations. However, it appears that some prominent citizens are abusing the system.[48] Yet again, we are confronted with the necessity to understand what is immediately perceived as a sign of social distinction locally, from both a top-down and a bottom-up perspective.

Culinary aspects

Considering that food is vital for survival, it is certainly difficult to treat it as a 'prestige good' exactly like others, as above. Nevertheless what people eat and how they eat might play a major role with regard to social distinction – increasingly so when elites indulge in lavish feasts while the bulk of the population barely has enough sustenance for subsistence. It is therefore crucial to know whether or not we are dealing with societies with sufficient food supplies for the whole population. This said, it is also important to note that what can be regarded as a fundamental biological requirement is deeply affected by cultures. Indeed, the realm of culinary matters is eminently variable, and thus so is the world of table manners with their fascinatingly contradictory codes.[49] Some specialists claim that hunger is shaped as early as the foetal stage, or that appetite is not a universal phenomenon, but a feeling strongly related to an increased regularity of food supplies and a civilising process of self-control.[50]

What proves to be most interesting in the case of culinary aspects is the way that distinction usually takes place within a social atmosphere of commensality. A few exceptions notwithstanding (such as some sovereigns of the past ostentatiously being served alone in the presence of onlookers, or even avoiding eating in public), what is involved is the sharing of a meal with others. This does not necessarily reflect equal status but at least a relative closeness and, frequently, an affirmation of solidarity or membership. The two symbolisms (a sense of communion and the staging of differences) might appear at first as not being easily compatible, but they are. As a matter of fact, their simultaneity may pertain to an edifying spectacle, quite essential from a socio-political perspective.[51] A wide variety of ritualised interactions aimed at indicating precedence or submission between hosts and guests are liable to be deployed – for instance, who is served first, who is allowed to eat first who is toasted, etc. – depending upon the local rules of etiquette, the number of companions at the table and upon the layout of the premises. From feasts to much more limited gatherings, most occasions providing an outlet for social prestige might be designed to emphasise positions. In this respect, specialists from various disciplines teach us about the rather contrasted realities of such demonstrations throughout history and in different geographical locations.[52]

Strikingly, when one studies how elites use luxury food and grand eating for display, one regularly encounters the many facets presented above, or those following: residence (which should allow guests to be entertained decently), adornment (dressing up), impressive vehicles (indispensable to arriving at receptions in grand style), manners (marking social inclusion), cultivation and linguistic competence (conversational aptitudes, expertise about wine and food) and entourage (select guests, glamorous company and competent servants). To go into even a little detail about the countless logics of distinction related to ingredients, tableware, accessories, decoration, conventions or practices valued as social symbols would oblige one to devote quite a number of pages to the topic.

A primary aspect is scenography (that is the way a space is constructed), with high tables – if there are tables – and seating plans indicating the social hierarchy. However, to restrict ourselves to the external signs dealt with in this chapter, two key dimensions are of chief concern. Obviously enough, the first has to do with what is actually served and eaten. Being able to offer food of the highest quality has often been a major source of distinction, although comparative research leads us to realise that in some parts of the world (e.g. China, India, France or Italy) one attaches far more importance to sophisticated dishes than in some others. In Paris, during the eighteenth century, aristocrats and financiers vied with each other to be considered as having 'the most refined table of the capital city' and as being able to please the palate of demanding epicures. Holding dinners of unprecedented elaboration at that time undoubtedly played a central role in intra-elite competition, but this would hold true for many other places or historical periods. Saving the best pieces or serving a greater quantity of food to the most prestigious guests or hosts has also often been a crucial way of underlining rank differences. In addition to their gustatory qualities, the luxury of dishes may additionally express itself visually. Aesthetic appearance is a significant part of the culinary arts and, along with hyperbolic names for dishes, proves to be a crucial determinant of status in certain contexts.[53]

The second dimension is that of the place settings: sets of dishes and plates, cutlery, glasses, table linen and other accessories supposed to contain or to surround the food. As regards presentation, one usually makes a distinction between the *service à la française* (which consists in laying a large amount of crockery on the table, in an elegant, orderly way) and the *service à la russe* (a series of already-filled plates being brought to the diners on a regular basis), among many other possible solutions. Both methods give opportunities for ostentatious display: the first because of the profusion of dishes and food set at once, and the second because it requires an array of servants.[54] In either case, expensive and beautiful items in gold, silver, porcelain or crystal, frequently stamped with armorial bearings or initials, contribute to the grand appearance of the table. As for accessories, an Eliasian perspective in terms of the process of civilisation and emulation is definitely pertinent. It should also be highlighted that it is precisely during the advent of the production of cutlery on an industrial scale – the nineteenth century – that elites adopted new items such as fish, cheese and desert knives, or special instruments used for eating crabs, oysters, melon or snails. Here, a 'trickle-down' analysis is applicable, as is often the case for this period in Western Europe. Indeed, what mattered was not just the possession of such devices, but also how to use them properly. Even at the present time, some infrequently used utensils may appear as fearsome traps for unaccustomed diners.

When studying the expression of social distance through the act of eating, one is presented with vastly different situations. Elites may receive close friends or strangers, stand a crowd of supporters a treat, be accepted in various circles, dine out in an exclusive restaurant, etc. In other words, the company may be heterosocial or not, and the gathering more or less homely or official. Eating out in restaurants is of particular interest for sociologists, especially because of the ambiguous private/public nature of such a social event (see Finkelstein, 1989 and, principally, Warde and Martens, 2000). The advent of the modern restaurant is commonly related to an age of 'democratisation of luxury' (after the 1789 Revolution in France) witnessing cooks, who had formerly served aristocratic households, transforming themselves into restaurateurs welcoming rich bourgeois patrons eager to enjoy *grande cuisine* and to display their new elite status. Of course, there are restaurants and restaurants. Distinction is usually related to exclusiveness and reputation because of sophisticated gourmet food, high-class service, and decorum – that is the precise opposite of the cheap standardised products and uniform appearance of fast-food establishments. Social visibility (being seen in fashionable places and potentially catching a glimpse of famous personalities), conspicuous expenditure and competition (lengthy forward reservations and hierarchy of tables) are important elements. In any event, what is involved is not merely filling one's stomach but communicating the right messages to others.[55] At a lesser level, the ability to feel at ease in various types of ethnic restaurants (mastering the codes and manners of eating, as well as the exotic names of the specialities) might equally suggest a sense of distinction, indicating openness and cosmopolitanism, as well as perhaps, indirectly, the fact that one has travelled widely. However, postmodern interpretations in terms of 'omnivouresness' – to be taken literally here – are also eligible.[56]

With these types of signals we are moving away from dimensions of 'having' to focus our attention on aspects of 'being'. This is the subject of the following chapter.

5
Embodied Signs of Superiority

Upright bearing, 'sophisticated' accent, or even just an imposing air of determination instantly function as signs of distinction in some contexts, irrespective of whether or not they are confirmed by external attributes. To a certain degree, such embodied markers might equally be considered as outward manifestations. However, in contrast with prestigious goods – which can be acquired at once by each and everyone with sufficient resources, including upstarts – what is involved here are more subtle, but also more deeply anchored means of demonstrating social worth. These signs convey the impression that elites are *intrinsically* superior to ordinary people. This apparently natural superiority reveals itself principally in posture and gesture, behavioural standards, good grooming and cultural background. The ensuing chapter, therefore, deals with the following topics: assertiveness, distinguished manners, beautified bodily appearance and the display of cultivated accomplishments.

Self-confidence and assertiveness

When observing elites, an ostensible feeling of ease is frequently noticed, as if they are more self-assured than members of subordinate groups. Contrasting with the prevalent tenseness of the majority of people (perceptible in anxious looks, for instance, or hand-wringing when under stress), what is implied is a relaxed attitude and a certain control over one's emotions. These combine to give an impression of confidence in relation to the world. Some elements of posture (commendable gait, lifted-up head, shoulders held back, steady gaze, etc.) additionally appear to act as an advertisement of self-esteem and status. In this regard, ethological research has produced interesting analyses on how dominance is signalled through expressive movements and can prove useful to some extent.[1] However, reference to this tradition of study is not uncontroversial. The question is: despite our common heritage how much can we reasonably expect to learn from any parallels between human and animal body language?

Contributions by ethologists must be supplemented by a full consideration of the cultural variability of human deportment. Scholars from several disciplines have pointed out that even the most common postural habits and corporeal manifestations, such as ways of standing or sitting, crying or smiling, are in fact the product of cultural contexts.[2] Whether deliberate or inadvertent, gesture is seldom a purely natural and universal language, but largely takes its meaning from conventionalised repertoires. The elite specialist comes across magniloquent gestures as well as dignified postures, and symbolic demonstrations of bodily control as well as deliberately sprawling positions. Walking with long strides might be a typical way to assert oneself, but (as Veblen emphasised it) a slow pace may also indirectly refer to conspicuous leisure.[3] It is important to decode the significance of a particular bearing in the contextually relevant setting.

Many sociologists tend to regard the ways individuals move, carry and position themselves in social situations – the 'hexis' – as a good indicator of class membership. For Bourdieu (e.g. 1977), who has paid especial attention to embodied dimensions,[4] the ease and grace of the upper classes contrast strongly with the deficient assuredness which characterises the middle ones. Because of their respective habitus, members of the dominant stratum are deemed rather indifferent to the others' gaze, whereas members of the middle one – as a result of their telling desire to be noticed – lack this (distinctive) naturalness and self-confidence. Being an incorporated manifestation of deep-seated 'dispositions' governing conduct, the hexis cultivated by the dominant classes cannot be effortlessly mastered. Deportment lessons from a very young age (conferring, for instance, the habit of holding one's back straight), attending top schools and regular contact with other members of the upper social ranks, eventually create poise as a second nature. Reciprocally, according to Bourdieu, those who endeavour to acquire such propensities at a late stage are likely to be doomed to achieving only contrived postures.[5]

There is certainly evidence to support such a reading. Undoubtedly, both primary and secondary socialisation are conducive to the construction of a 'public body' and composure. Nevertheless, we must not lose sight of the fact that social life is full of differing interactions. In particular, when confronted with other men and women occupying the higher echelons of society, members of the elite might themselves prove to be more – or less – at ease. Even in circumstances when they have to mingle with social inferiors – on the occasion of a working-class wedding, for example, or in the army – it is not at all certain whether they will stand out or appear bashful. The same is true for travellers exposed to exotic customs. A relevant contribution, here, is the analytical work by Goffman (1967) mentioned above, on the 'display of face'. In most encounters, each participant must adjust his face. Social actors who assume a high degree of dominance are most likely expected to live up to a certain level of self-worth. Yet, this does not mean that presentation of self must be systematically based on an over-confident attitude.

On the other hand, it is, of course, a fact that social relationships are full of ritualised signs which can immediately be interpreted in terms of claims for prestige and indications of submissiveness. Deferential postures (from prostrating, kneeling, bowing and curtseying to stooping) as well as domineering ones are documented by ethnology and history.[6] In contemporary 'Western' societies, where the more pronounced gestures of reverence (implicating lowering of the body) have been reduced in scope, what might merely be involved is whether or not one knocks, responds to greetings, holds doors, continues standing, etc. What still remains is the visual manifestation of the balance of power between social actors. Distinction may conceivably consist in always expecting humility, respectful behaviour or flattery from others. However, once again, a comparative outlook leads one to realise that a wide range of attitudes, as well as body language patterns, can be adopted and prove efficient: swaggering along or remaining solemnly reserved at all times, staring at people around or conspicuously looking right through others, etc.[7]

As previously hinted, there are many connections between the various facets of social distinction. In this regard, it is instructive to take into consideration the interesting links between posture and clothing. Dress, especially those voluminous, heavy or rigid articles so much favoured by many elites for centuries, can dramatically affect bearing and gesture. By restricting or liberating movements, they, so to speak, 'create' a certain body. Veblen (1994 [1899]) notoriously condemned the artificial character of the corset: not only tightening the waist – thus emphasising the breasts and buttocks – but also forcing the wearer to sit, stand and walk in a particular manner (this perfectly fitted his analysis in terms of 'leisure class' and 'vicarious display').

During an earlier period, ruffs also had direct consequences on overall appearance.[8] Both items contributed to a disciplined physical outlook exhibiting pre-eminence and pride, in stark contrast with average people 'walking small'.[9] In the nineteenth century, male shirt fronts, or high-standing collars holding back the neck, played an analogous role.[10] Retrospectively, we tend to view such items in terms of discomfort and impracticability, not to mention potential health risks. However, it is important to understand that, paradoxically, they could produce self-assurance and even a satisfying sense of well-being, in so far as they conformed to the prevailing codes of distinction.[11] This said, the high theatricality of impressive clothing, liable to allow for elegant gestures, frequently called for a real learning process: Marie-Antoinette, for instance, had a *'Professeur de grâces'*, who taught her how to deal decorously with long trains. In the preceding chapter, it was stated that occasionally dressing up may give modest people a relative self-confidence. Nonetheless, how individuals wear clothes usually reveals much about their respective status. This is also the case with regard to their posture (and their potential awkwardness) when they sit on more or less comfortable pieces of furniture. Some chairs or sofas indeed require great physical control and can, therefore, be used to demonstrate – and assess – ease (see Hellman, 1999).

Distinguished manners

The term 'manners' is employed to refer to the prevailing norms of conduct within a given society. It is not without ambiguity in so far as it relates to how one should behave correctly toward others as well as to the possession of a certain sophistication. What is involved is both a degree of thoughtfulness vis-à-vis the people one meets, and of personal polish enabling this. One can adopt a restrictive or a broad definition of manners (encompassing, for instance, some bodily aspects touched on above and the language dimensions to be discussed below). What matters, from a sociological point of view, is to analyse them in connection with social stratum. More precisely, from the perspective of the present book, it is appropriate to look at how excellence of manners may become employed to convey status between elites themselves, as well as toward social inferiors, or foreigners (which requires 'intercultural sensitivity'). Standards of expected behaviour, and related logics of (dis)approval, vary significantly from one society to another and across historical periods, yet social scientists are not condemned merely to compiling catalogues of culturally specific norms. The following are some of the ways in which the relation between manners and distinction can be understood.

Historically (at least in Europe), there has undeniably been some interconnection between the rise of 'mannered societies' and the development of urban settings (in which social actors were increasingly led to deal with unknown others), the advent of courts and that of a 'civilising process' – as the adjectives 'polite' or 'urbane', 'courteous' and 'civil' respectively suggest. From these considerations, it should be apparent that the key theoretical contributor is Norbert Elias. However, specialists in antiquity or in the Middle Ages, as well as anthropologists, have good grounds to deny the fact that cultivated comportment would essentially be a modern (that is post-medieval) and Western affair. Elites from many civilisations have undeniably developed what can be regarded as a growing refinement of manners over centuries, which naturally begs an open mind, fully taking into account the socio-cultural relativity of conceptions. In ancient or non-literate cultures, acceptable behaviour could derive from informal, but no less compelling, principles bounded by orally transmitted traditions. One should therefore beware of reductionist views.[12]

When seen from a comparative perspective, elitist manners prove irreducible to one single logic. They may, for instance, involve sheer arrogance and great shows of extravagance. If nobles in Europe did indeed elaborate sophisticated forms of courtesy among themselves, aristocratic behaviour could allow considerable licence. Nowadays, there are still plentiful examples of capricious people at the top of the social hierarchy who are purposely insolent. In such cases, distinction is expressed through a demonstration of freedom from restrictive norms. One may also decide to adhere to mannered conventions when they serve well, but to circumvent them unscrupulously when they hinder the attainment of certain goals. Frequently, the appropriate behaviour will be dictated by circumstances and by the nature of interactions.[13] This calls attention to two dimensions which are indirectly relevant to our theme. The first concerns a smart capacity to judge social situations and to match behaviour to the occasion – which, according to Bourdieu, is a fundamental component of the upper-class habitus. The second involves the exemplarity of elites and their possible claim to moral superiority, liable to be seen as a chief determinant of status in some contexts.[14]

The development of a normative literature on suitable conduct has clearly been most important for the long reformation of manners and mores in the 'West'. In this regard, it is essential to differentiate between humanistic treatises aiming at universal application – e.g. Erasmus's famous [1530] work *'On the Civility of Children's Conduct'* – and books intended for elite circles – such as Castiglione's *The Courtier* (1974 [1528]) – explaining how elaborate manners can advantageously contribute to status. Throughout the subsequent centuries, it is possible to follow the parallel developments of these two veins, respectively advocating an egalitarian civility or recommending distinctive codes. As far as the second (evidently of greater interest for the purposes of this volume) is concerned, what is sought is a supreme capacity to give a perfectly mastered representation of oneself, supposed to reflect inner qualities. Within court societies, the highest status was expected to be substantiated by excellence of manners: the sovereigns being allegedly the most knowledgeable, and accomplished, gentlemen and ladies. Although in actual fact a question of high birth and 'good' breeding, manners were understood in terms of natural superiority. A major contradiction, here, is that self-restraint leads to distinction and domination over others. This may be analysed along Eliasian lines (1983 [1933]) as a process of 'domestication' (of the self and of the entire group) and as the elaboration of a sophisticated system of mutual recognition between people 'of quality'.[15]

It is also pertinent to point out that etiquette is often plainly a matter of self-protection. Due to their complexity, knowledge of the rules of intra-elite interactions is an important exclusionary resource used by the established members of fashionable society to recognise and reject outsiders. Certainly, legitimate ways of behaving are explicitly codified in books (about table manners, etc.) which can be acquired by aspirant social climbers. However, there is concurrent use of what McCracken (1990, p. 34) calls the 'invisible ink strategy': this consists of the employment of all sorts of hidden snares to test the status of newcomers. In other words, if refined politeness may be comprehended in a commonsensical way as facilitating contacts between strangers, it may also operate as a closure stratagem. The student of elitist behaviour interested in this realm of 'good manners' actually encounters different models. Distinction might involve public rebukes against uncouth individuals or never judging others (at least outwardly), with noticing 'wrong things' being considered as impolite.[16] It may also involve treating people deemed inferior condescendingly. A classic episode, reported by several authors, is that of George Washington bowing before a black woman. Questioned by a companion about this deferential attitude, he responded, 'Would you have me outdone by a negro in politeness?'. The implication of this is less a manifestation of respect toward a 'down under' than vis-à-vis the distinguishing codes of one's own milieu. Similarly, the author of the present work once greeted a renowned Parisian professor using a mere *'Bonjour'*. The immediate reaction was a *'Bonjour Monsieur'* ('Good morning, Sir'): the intention through this marked politeness being, in all probability, a criticism of his younger colleague's overly familiar tone, therefore heightening his own distinction. It remains that elite politeness frequently finds expression in treating others tactfully.

As we saw in Chapter 2, it is debatable whether the 'civilising process' originated mainly in courts or other societal points of reference, before descending down the social ladder. In either event, such a process of diffusion greatly affected the logics of distinction. According to some authors, the advent of a formal equality between citizens has paradoxically accentuated the crucial character of manners for social differentiation. Whereas new rights can instantly be granted and acquired, the self-mastery of polished manners is viewed as a question of prolonged exposure – definitely taking several generations – and therefore as the most enduring means to express ascendancy. With the 'slackening of mores' subsequently affecting societies, certain attitudes considered as outdated by a majority of people (such as kissing a woman's hand) would remain, more than ever, a major sign of social recognition within some circles.[17]

On the contrary, for other analysts, high-status groups have no alternative, within a context of the emulation and dissemination of upper-class manners, than to express defiance of conventional standards. While members of the petite bourgeoisie reveal their social level by an all too rigorous adherence to formal correctness, individuals at the top demonstrate their superiority through casual and spontaneous attitudes,[18] which may even verge on impudent behaviour aimed at distinguishing themselves from those obsessed with decency.[19] Such an interpretation is without doubt stimulating. It can be claimed, with empirical backing, that aspirant middle classes particularly have considered manners as a social passport to higher ranks, in clear opposition to 'coarse' peasants or working-class people. On their side, members of the upper classes might not need to conform to 'good' manners so much, as they take their worth for granted. However, this is far from the case systematically. The contemporary situation is certainly more nuanced, complicated and dynamic – all the more so when one takes into equal account the question of the importation/ exportation of norms and attitudes of resistance or syncretism (see Chapter 8). Within increasingly permissive 'Euro-American' societies,

we have perhaps entered yet another stage where loose manners supposed to demonstrate 'authenticity' or unaffectedness are admired.[20]
The ways of expressing oneself through manners at the present time
are rather diverse. Consequently their sociological analysis needs to be
multi-faceted.

Physical appearance

Obviously enough, physical attractiveness is not something directly
dependent upon social position, but rather on the whims of fate – as the
popular expression '(not) being blessed by nature' conveys. However,
sociologists are justified in stressing that societal determinants, such
as living and working conditions, diet and access to care services and
cosmetics, are likely to have strong effects on physical appearance.[21]
Lower-class men and women for whom existence is a continual harsh
struggle, as well as social climbers who have made strenuous efforts
to improve their situation, inexorably bear the stigma of such striv-
ing on their faces and bodies.[22] Similarly, elites who benefit from a less
demanding way of life are likely to enjoy a longer-lasting finer appearance. One recurring theme is that of smooth, as opposed to calloused,
hands. Spencer, Veblen, Weber, Goffman and several functionalist
authors have devoted analogous lines to the topic. Most frequently
commentated upon is either the mandarins' extraordinary long nails
as an advertisement of abstinence from manual work, or the delicate
well-cared-for hands as a major means of signalling and identifying
social status.

In many stereotyped representations (manifestly related to the distribution of rank in society), elites are associated with outstanding
beauty, whereas ugliness commonly chimes with low birth, social inferiority or wickedness.[23] Commentators since Herodotus at least have
depicted some major sovereigns as the most handsome human beings
on earth – which could readily be exploited as a sign of divine sancti-
fication and shining superiority. Likewise, fairy tales are symptomatic-
ally full of charming princes and matchless princesses. Needless to say,
beauty criteria vary enormously across contexts – from the deliberate
deformation of physical features to radical aversion for any artifice –
and comparative research can easily challenge the generalising ambitions of some structuralist models.[24] In the (admittedly special) case of
the 'West', the degree to which canons have evolved is amazing, as a
glance at the evolution of nude representations in painting since the
Renaissance is enough to show.[25] From a socio-historical point of view,

however, it is important to move from ideal artistic references and to enter the realm of everyday-life perceptions.

Particularly fascinating for our perspective, in this respect, are instances of 'full reversals'. Let us take stoutness as a first illustration. In many different contexts and until quite recently, it was, more often than not, a mark of distinction. Fleshy bodies denoted the potential to consistently eat beyond one's fill – hence to one's prosperity, social rank and, most likely, idleness. One could also take pride in corpulent children, spouses (or fattened concubines) vicariously emphasising an elite standing. Nowadays, obesity would contrarily tend to be read in terms of unhealthy eating patterns, poor self-control and, therefore, as an indicator of low social status. Another striking example is that of paleness. For centuries, in Europe, a pale complexion was considered as one of the most important physical attributes a woman could possess. This was evidently linked to the conspicuous faculty of being saved from laborious activities outdoors. Hat veils, parasols – often status symbols in themselves[26] – and whitening creams could also usefully preserve or accentuate paleness. Since the 1920s, a bronzed skin (note the precious alloy connotation) is considered attractive because it suggests that the individual has the means to spend holidays in enjoyable resorts. Clearly, such revolutionary shifts result from a combination of factors: the development of medical knowledge, entirely new mentalities as regards slenderness or open-air activities, etc. From an elite distinction angle, the second illustration is perhaps not as spectacular, in view of the fact that what is sought after is still the expression of conspicuous leisure. Yet, it is far from being negligible for the comparativist, especially when one realises that a protuberant stomach continues to be a sign of success in certain parts of the world[27] (the same is true for paleness).

As physical beauty is a significant component of social accomplishment, elites often feel impelled to cultivate their personal appearance. It is of the utmost importance for those with pretensions to status to remain constantly vigilant about the excellence of their image. In many dynasties therefore, heirs to the throne usually enjoyed beauty care attention from the cradle (Kantorowicz, 1957). Nevertheless, the body is a 'given', and latitude for intervention in this respect is relatively limited. One may establish a basic distinction between everyday logics of enhancement and extensive operations aiming at correction or rejuvenation.

Until the twentieth century, devoting time and attention to make-up, hairdressing and other beauty techniques, in order to be presentable for social engagements, was essentially an elite activity. The Veblenian reading grid is most appropriate here, in so far as taking care of one's bodily appearance involves having leisure at one's disposal, as well as assistance from skilled people – servants in the past and beauticians nowadays.[28] Toward the end of seventeenth century in France, perfecting one's appearance had become so absorbing an obsession that some ladies spent hours at the dressing table. Since such a considerable amount of time could not entirely be frittered in absence from the social scene, it became fashionable to invite and entertain a following of admirers in one's *cabinet de toilette*. Consequently, more money had to be invested in the decoration of these – henceforth 'semi-public' – rooms. What we see at work, here again, are remarkable linkages between various dimensions of elite distinction.

Considerable differences can be found about this important side of everyday life, and the same applies, of course, to standards of hygiene. However, worthy of note for our central topic is the fact that in many societies, precious substances or materials have been used for both cosmetics and toilet requisites. Archaeological excavations show that the most valuable objects discovered in elites' tombs are frequently related to body care (e.g. carved ivory hair combs in ancient Egypt or China). Equally, ointments, lotions, powders or 'waters of youth' were preferably concocted from noble ingredients, such as gold dust or pearls. This not only means that in the course of history, wealthy men and women were willing to spend large amounts of money on cosmetic preparations and tools, it also points to noteworthy symbolic connections between rare elements and the body, in which preoccupations with distinction are obviously present.

The theme of beautified appearance has many interesting ramifications, from the use of fragrance to create physical desirability to the elitist world of spas and the metamorphoses of rooms dedicated to bathing and washing, etc. We cannot consider these aspects in any detail here (see, e.g. Gunn, 1973), but one item merits a brief discussion the mirror. It is now taken for granted that one may easily view oneself. Although pieces of polished metal have existed and been used for this purpose since antiquity, the mirror, however, was for a long time an item available only to a privileged minority. For centuries, elites had to content themselves with pocket ones, or at best with wall mirrors rarely exceeding 20 inches in height. The adjustable cheval glass and, later, wardrobes fitted with mirrored doors, allowing to examine oneself full-length, served significantly as status symbols. This is not merely anecdotal: what is at stake is the ability to see oneself no longer solely through the eyes of others.

Accounts of reconstructive surgery can be traced as far back as early antiquity (in India), although the development of expertise in this field finds its roots mainly in the treatment of World War I invalids, and subsequently in the Hollywood system aiming at 'generating' flawless stars. Throughout history, such aesthetic operations were rather the prerogative of elites (e.g. aristocrats disfigured by syphilis). This remains the case at the present time, particularly when they travel to expensive beauty surgeons in faraway destinations. However, a new industry has emerged and liposuction, hair transplants, face-lifts and breast enlargements or reductions are now accessible to wider sections of the population (Black and Sharma, 2001; Taschen, 2008).

Generally speaking, there is no question that the diffusion of cosmetics and perfumes during the twentieth century has considerably reduced the elitist dimension of grooming. Beauty salons are thriving all over the world. Yet, their more or less sophisticated character does reflect hierarchy of income (as is true of the consumption of beauty products) and social distinction in this sector is still easily noticeable. The 'sociology of the body' sub-discipline encourages us to view complex dynamics whereby bodies are perhaps increasingly exposed and 'liberated' but remain, nevertheless, constrained by compliance with new imperatives and canons such as bulging muscles which are not solely the sign of relentless physical efforts implying a dominated social position, but of health and fitness indicating leisure.

Cultivation and linguistic competence

Admission into upper ranks may depend largely upon the display of cultivated accomplishments and the total mastery of sophisticated language. 'Cultural Capital', to use a Bourdieusian expression, is one of the chief ways of being socially constructed as 'distinguished'. This obviously refers to the fact that one has benefited from a 'good' education, most probably in an elitist institution whose goals are not just to inculcate knowledge but also to instil constant self-confidence and what can be called an 'aura of differentness'. Intellectual skills may be expressed through elegant verbal communication – preferably full of erudition – and the capacity to talk in a broad, abstract manner, without systematically returning to one's own experiences.

However, such demonstrations do not necessarily command social admiration: they may prove utterly out of place in some high spheres in which sentences burdened with learned references, or too much subtlety, are liable to be considered as odd and counter-productive.[29] One general comment is in order here. An often overlooked key aspect in the literature on social distinction is the question of meaningfulness. It is too readily assumed that most markers are immediately comprehensible by all and sundry. Admittedly, elites' manifestations of superiority may be impressive without being intelligible or even fully accessible and visible.[30] Yet, when someone exhausts himself using witty speech with an interlocutor who misses every allusion, can we just propose an interpretation in terms of 'symbolic violence' as with the Bourdieusian school of thought? The argument here is that, in order to make sense, distinction strategies require at the very least a slightly competent audience.

On the other hand, it remains true that linguistic proficiency is indeed an important clue to placing people in the social hierarchy, as Veblen, Elias or Bourdieu, among others, have emphasised. Many key signals can be differentiated: the possession of a rich vocabulary, selection of the right expressions, perfectly correct spelling, impeccable grammar and also 'correct' pronunciation. Particularly interesting is the fact that distinction simultaneously requires the ability to speak (or write) in strict accordance with the rules of one's language *and* to make use of it in an inventive way. This raises the ambiguous question of style, to be elaborated later (Chapter 9). Elites may also achieve distinction through the deliberate use of foreign language snippets, or of Latin expressions, for example.[31]

Addressing an audience is a major act of self-presentation, as is the capacity to sustain conversations through both form and content. Among those elements which appear significant when composing an image under such circumstances, eloquence is undoubtedly central. It involves the art of attracting attention and persuading – *ergo*, rhetorical expertise. The ability to avoid nervous mistakes and to remain clearheaded under the emotional stress of verbal confrontations may equally be considered crucial.[32] This brings us back to the themes of self-command and confident behaviour discussed above. It can be argued that three dimensions predominantly function as an advertisement of status in this respect. The first is, perhaps paradoxically, the propensity to speak slowly. A rapid delivery may certainly be interpreted as a sign of mental agility, but it usually entails imprecision and the need to correct oneself, whereas steady speech, emphasising a precise choice of words without any hesitation, indicates self-mastery and confidence. The second consists in not excessively raising one's voice, thereby showing that one is used to easily obtaining satisfaction, as opposed to the person whose vociferating attitude betrays the fact that s/he is regularly challenged by others. The third dimension concerns a sharp understanding of when one should remain silent, listen (attentively or not) to other speakers or intervene appropriately.

Yet, how far may we generalise? Ethno-linguists underline a remarkable variety of codes. Appropriate interruptions may contribute to distinction in some contexts but irremediably undermine status in others. In many societies, who speaks first is often a strong indicator of higher position but, in some places, distinction is conversely expressed through withdrawing into almost total silence. Also, attitudes may prove very different along the flow of interactions. Even from a purely physiological point of view, evidence shows that voice is prone to changing according to the social level of the interlocutor with whom one is dealing, because throat muscles are more or less relaxed. Above all, one should not forget that language and cultivated behaviour are highly conventional and tied to a specific culture. Where stratification is rigid, the vocabularies of the various strata do not diffuse readily and a 'respect language' may also be resorted to: involving honorific and sentence-final particles.[33] Additionally, pronunciation may betray not only regional origins, but also social identity. In this regard, an upper-class accent associated with best higher education may prove to be an essential way of asserting oneself over others. However, in many parts of the world, this kind of distinctive feature would be meaningless, or deemed secondary.[34] A final point about contemporary trends must be raised. As with manners, it appears that the old formality of 'proper' language and grammar is on the wane. One would almost think that transgression – e.g. enlivening one's speech with a few vulgar, at times deliberately shocking, expressions – is a new way of distinguishing oneself for some upper-class people, with a view to expressing a sense of spontaneity.[35] This is only one inclination among many; it does not replace previous ones, but adds to them, thereby contributing to the present confusion and the difficulty of providing sociological generalisations.

6
Vicarious Display

In this chapter we will explore how elites use their entourages to call attention to their distinction. The performance of others around them is relevant to the self-definition of upper groups in different ways. They may increase the prestige of the latter because they relieve them of certain tasks, because they put their talent at their disposal or by virtue of their own status or impressiveness. It is principally to Veblen that we owe consideration of the subject of 'vicarious' display. The author of *The Theory of the Leisure Class* showed how dependants – particularly wives, children and servants – can actively contribute to fostering an elitist image. However, further penetrating analyses (by Sombart on courtesans, for instance, or by American functionalists on exclusive clubs) are also relevant, and others will be suggested here. The following pages discuss in turn how relatives, close proximity to socially renowned individuals, glamorous female company, skilled staff and outstanding artists might serve to confirm status.

Relatives

In everyday social life, it is common to meet people for whom another's success proves to be a source of self-esteem. What is sought is an indirect recognition through the accomplishments of, more or less closely, related persons. Whether they themselves have little or nothing to do with these achievements, and whatever the nature of the bond they share, they claim to benefit from such an association. As we shall see, elites often look for validation by surrounding themselves with other prestigious social actors. At a more primordial level, however, vicariously asserting prominence concerns one's own kin. In nearly all societies, parents acquire a sense of pride from their children's attainments, and vice versa. On the other hand, sociologists show that kith and kin may also constitute a source of vulnerability.[1] The poor performance or 'bad behaviour' of one family member is liable to have negative effects on the image representation of the whole group. In other words, references to relatives are potentially double-edged.

From a comparative perspective, a pluralist reading of the implications of this is required. First, it is appropriate to recall that, in many parts of the world, the notion of family must be extended well beyond immediate members. In Chapter 3, we drew attention to the fact that the classic analytical frameworks elaborated for (post)modern Euro-American contexts may not be successfully applied to other settings. Such is clearly the case in 'holistic' environments where it is customary to witness members of large communities trying to project themselves socially upward by basking in the reflected glory of so-called 'brothers' or 'sisters' with whom they have hardly been in touch. Reciprocally, persons perceived as 'black sheep' may stain the reputation of a number of people allegedly sharing a group identity. Second, if, in both 'traditional' and 'modern' contexts, to bear an illustrious name is often considered as symbolic capital entailing an a priori distinction, 'well-born' people are essentially duty-bound to contribute towards the prestige of their family and to protect the reputation of their ancestors. However, to draw on Riesman's (1950, p. 40) felicitous formulation, the question remains over the degree to which status-claiming groups standing at the apex of the social system train their children merely 'to succeed them' or to 'succeed' (i.e. to demonstrate their individual ability and win personal prestige).[2]

Elites generally make the most of matrimonial opportunities to strengthen their social standing, putting pressure on their children, if needs be, to marry at or above their level. Nevertheless, unions may severely disrupt important symbolic continuities. At the beginning of Edith Wharton's novel, *The House of Mirth*, (1997 [1905], p. 9), mentioned is made of the anxiety about the daughter-in-law having all the family jewels 'reset' or the drawing room 'done over'. More commonly, the visible items inherited, or subsequently purchased, by the husband or the wife are liable to affect not only the image of their spouse but also that of more or less distant relatives, which may prove consequential for high-status families regarded as 'total units'. Of course, marriage is an institution of society which has extraordinarily diverse implications in different cultures (endogamy or exogamy; matrilocal, patrilocal or bilocal residence; monogamy or polygamy; dowry or bride price, etc). However, what is at stake everywhere, from our perspective, is the prospect of increasing or undermining standing in the eyes of each side.

To a large extent, we may apply the same type of reasoning to young children. The dream of many parents from the uppermost rungs is to see their own distinction reflected in the image projected by their sons or daughters. This obviously involves the inculcation of 'good' manners but also, for instance, sartorial strategies. In the past, some little boys have been compelled to wear elitist confections of fashion, such as ruffs, and girls crinolines.[3] As mentioned above, Veblen (1994 [1899]) argued that the active businessmen of his time delegated the task of conspicuous consumption – central for 'invidious distinction' and social esteem – mainly to their wives and children. In the contemporary world, specialists in marketing equally illustrate how some well-off parents enjoy purchasing luxury brands for their children in order to signal their privileged financial status through them. Indeed, this pressure is often exerted by the offspring themselves (see e.g. Darian, 1998). However, in this case, we may also arrive at a reverse situation in which some of the children's choices prove embarrassing for their parents. The profusion of lifestyles and the non-conformist attitudes emphasised in the literature concerned with postmodernity may lead to some inconsistencies in terms of kindred image.[4]

Finally, it is appropriate to mention that very elegant pets (such as beautiful Borzoi dogs wearing clothes and accessories ostentatiously matching those of the owner exercising them) probably furnish yet another example of distinction relying on the outward representation of closely related living creatures.

Flaunting elitist connections

Elites usually have a rather active social life. They may be expected to participate in several types of prestigious gatherings throughout the year, but also to organise 'home performances' (dinners and parties). In the sociological literature, as well as in standard elite studies, what is principally analysed are the processes of networking and the constitution of a 'social capital' (in the Bourdieusian sense of the expression).[5] Indeed, upper groups often prove more conscious than lower ones with regard to the strategic importance of making and cultivating useful contacts. In the present book, however, we are less occupied with this conventional approach than with exploring how flaunting connections contributes to elite distinction.

'[...] The social identity of those an individual is with can be used as a source of information concerning his own social identity', writes Goffman (1963a, p. 47), 'the assumption being that he is what the others are'. This may well lead elites to shun people who are not as accomplished as they (think they) are. Their status, or their greater resources, normally allows them to shine in prominent circles, in which it is important to be seen. Which receptions people attend, and whom they entertain, may be perceived as a clue. Yet, a caveat needs to be mentioned. If in 'individualist' cultures, non-kinship relationships are largely a matter of personal choice, in other (more holistic) settings, who one's acquaintances are is less easy to control.[6] As Weber emphasised, the logics of honour may clearly restrict social intercourse, but in patrimonial contexts, they also involve vertical interactions between actors of various statuses, e.g. a lord and his clients (Roth and Wittich, 1978, p. 932 and p. 1068). For sub-Saharan elites – among other possible examples – prestige is more clearly connected to the capacity to attract and move with an impressive number of (subordinate) supporters than manifestly to withdraw oneself from social inferiors.

In societies where horizontal cleavages prevail, it should be considered whether distinction is related to the fact that elites operate within a strictly homogeneous network of acquaintances or are sensitive to all kinds of superiority. For members of exclusive social groups, being seen with outsiders, whatever the talent the latter may deploy, is liable to damage their reputation. Hence the decisive ritual of presentation.[7] Conversely, as a result of socio-political changes or of the increasing visibility of certain sectors (e.g. arts, sports or the media), it may be of concrete as well as symbolic interest for established elites to socialise with individuals who have succeeded in rising to heterogeneous top positions. A good illustration is that of the French society during the nineteenth century. Whereas the *Ancien Régime* was a pyramid of estates, there was an evolution away from the enclosed aristocratic life towards a more open type of social intercourse, within a far broader circle of elites comprising people who made a name for themselves under various regimes and in diverse capacities. There developed what evocatively became to be referred to in the capital city as *'le Tout-Paris'*: encompassing not only aristocratic families, but also the upper bourgeoisie, some famous artists, etc. This did not mean that the traditional cleavages were no longer relevant, or that membership was open to anybody claiming some success (including, for instance, *demi-mondaines*), but that distinction could be related to interconnections with people having gained recognition through miscellaneous activities (Martin-Fugier, 1990). Yet it is still the case that elites from each sector may prove more or less worthy of consideration in the eyes of their counterparts from other sectors.[8] This theme must be related to classical sociological interrogations about the cohesiveness of versus the disunity of upper groups (see, e.g. Dogan, 2003), many of which have given rise to rather dogmatic assumptions, in terms of 'power elite', 'ruling class' or pluralism. However, from our viewpoint, the issue is not just stratification, but its symbolic consequences. In this respect as well, it is difficult to generalise, with elite configurations obviously differing both from country to country and historically.

A comparativist analyst interested in the social modalities of flaunting connections is led to witness many types of concrete arrangements. In some places, for instance, it is customary to display one's Christmas cards, which are proudly shown to visitors as a demonstration of one's large number of acquaintances.[9] Similarly, in Nigeria, most business companies, governmental institutions, churches and associations, but also eminent individuals, enjoy having their own calendars printed and distributed to selected persons. It is therefore not uncommon to see rooms literally covered with calendars, thus signalling to the standing and size of one's social network (Daloz, 1989). More usually perhaps, especially at the top level, what is mainly involved are gatherings scaled by exclusiveness. Space limitations preclude the discussion here of a large number of such manifestations. In the paragraphs that follow, we shall turn our attention to two significant configurations, the prestigious salon and the upper-class club.

Originally a French aristocratic institution, the salon has long served as a central locus for elite (including bourgeois) sociability in many cities. This term, or its equivalent, refers to a (private) reception room and by extension to the distinguished persons regularly or occasionally frequenting it. The salon is of interest for our purposes in several respects. First, designed to promote social position at the top of the ladder, it must be an attractive place which might require many of the conspicuous elements discussed in this section of the book: it should be not only a comfortable and pleasant residence, but should also provide gourmet food and first-class service, contain impressive works of art, and so on. Second, it is synonymous with eloquent conversations and refined manners under the supervision of the host holding it, most often a lady.[10] Third, intermixing entertainment and distinction, salons endeavour to set tone, to impose themselves as tastemakers and to prove influential in many ways. Fourth – and this more directly meets our present concern with the exhibition of elitist connections – there is a well-understood competition between salons as regards their ability to attract the most remarkable celebrities. The renown of a salon is related largely to its capacity to bring together persons endowed with an assortment of virtues. At stake are the issues of selective access and of the symbolic interdependence between the various actors involved. For the newcomer to a famous salon, the first visit is generally a fearsome test. Certainly, the host aims to make all her guests shine, but it is crucial for the latter to be equal to the situation, that is to be suitably appealing to others and therefore to contribute to the good reputation of the place and of the whole group.[11] Salons are indisputably on the wane, nevertheless, they are still a useful gateway to the upper levels of society in some places.

Elite clubs represent more modern and also more formal structures (with codified rules, processes for co-optation, an official list of members and annual dues). Although they can be seen as voluntary groupings potentially 'open to everybody', such institutions are used as a source of distinction in so far as they explicitly separate those who can afford to belong and have the right connections or credentials from the 'excluded' others. There are, of course, all sorts of clubs (specialised or not; local, national or international, etc.).[12] Just like the salons, they are assigned varying degrees of social prestige, depending upon the characteristics of their members. From a comparative perspective, it is obvious that the relevance of joining clubs varies from one society to another. In the United States, as American functionalists have amply shown, they constitute a major way of expressing the positioning of individuals or families within the social hierarchy.[13] But this is far from being the case everywhere. In France, for example, it appears that membership is less important a priority for the shaping of a distinguished image. In countries where informal socio-political and economic links prevail, such organisations usually exist (as a sequel to ex-white clubs in post-colonial settings), but personalised, clientelistic relationships or adherence to certain secret societies are often deemed far more crucial. Whether or not we are dealing with 'front stage' cultures, to use a Goffmanian expression, or with societies with a predilection for institutionalised arrangements are probably key explanatory variables. Furthermore, elite clubs are substantially affected by the historical national repertoire of each country (a British club is quite different indeed from a Japanese one). A number of typologies have been developed for analytical purposes. However, what we need are systematic comparative studies.

Glamorous female company

Because of the prominence of sexual desire in human life, the display of fine-looking (mainly female) companions frequently plays a primordial symbolic role in strategies of distinction. Of greatest importance here is the fact that gorgeous spouses, or mistresses, not only suggest sensual pleasures but often carry added enhancements (dress, jewels, etc.) that contribute to the vicarious assertion of the wealth of their husband or lover. It is common for male members of the elite to be seen using their status or economic resources in order to attract either many women or the single most lusted-after female. This calls attention to the key theme of the relation between social power and sexuality[14] and that of the all too often ancillary position of women in this 'game'. As has already been noted in Chapter 4, distinction sometimes involves ostentatious exhibitions aiming at stressing a visible contrast. In this respect, elites may not only express a (distinctive) lack of concern over sexual access, but also affirm their supremacy through a predatory sexuality. For dominant men, the open flaunting of success with woman is all the more imposing in that many others develop a sense of frustration because of low responsiveness, or even suffer from the pains of abstinence. However, attractiveness is of course not entirely dependent upon social position and it is necessary to transcend simplistic interpretations.

We are touching on a subject where, despite enormous socio-cultural differences, theoreticians have been prone to find abstract regularities and to generalise. Veblen will serve as our main illustration here. He famously wrote that the first conspicuous form of property was the ownership of women and saw some continuity between the 'barbarian' practice of seizing them from defeated enemies and that of marriage depicted as a new form of subjugation in 'civilised times'. Whether they are captives of a raid or modern housewives, what enduringly remains is the women's status as decorous living symbols: in Veblenian terms, 'trophies' designed to show off men's success. As far back as historians can see, we have evidence of females (of rank or not) being captured and proudly brought home as proof of men's 'exploits'. In the age of Genghis Khan, for instance, Mongols with no wife were regarded as nobodies and women tossed about by events could pass from one 'master' to another throughout their lives. There is no doubt that female abduction has been a recurrent practice over centuries. The problem is that Veblen was hindered by his abstract theorisation and did not see much difference between remote times and his own period. Similarly, Marxists, like Engels (1940 [1884]), reducing women's status to the question of private property, or rigid structuralist anthropologists like Lévi-Strauss (1969 [1949]), who thought it possible to provide generalisations as regards the rules on the exchange of women between communities, did not eschew the universalist pretension of grand systemic explanation.[15] The same is true of Bourdieu, in that he essentially considered women in their capacity of 'repositories of capital' for someone else or as 'socially inclined to treat themselves as aesthetic objects' (2001 [1998], p. 99).

Some scholars provide analytical frameworks which are already a little bit more sensitive to important variations. For example, drawing on the evolutionist scheme of Lenski (1966), Collins (1975, pp. 234 ff.) makes distinctions between four stages. In what are termed 'low-technology tribal societies' sexual stratification is supposed to exist only in a mild form. Especially in hunting and gathering communities, it is acknowledged that women cannot be used as property in a bargaining system. The second stage is that of 'fortified households in stratified society', in which male sexual dominance is maximised. The concentration of force and resources in each unit leads to the instrumentalisation of women, who are exchanged between households in order to gain power through political manoeuvres. The third stage is that of the 'private household in a market economy'. There, the use of force is monopolised by a centralised state, which fosters expansion of commerce and industry. A free marriage market emerges in which young women progressively begin to acquire a status of their own and the 'ideology of romantic love' is brought forth.[16] Finally, a further shift occurs with the attainment of a high level of affluence. Despite a rise in employment opportunities, women remain far from being economically equal with men, and even the most attractive ones may feel forced to exchange their seductiveness for the material security offered by a physically less appealing male. Nevertheless, the 'sexual market' is much more open and a dating system prevails, not necessarily leading to marriage. Within his typology in terms of 'tradition-directed', 'inner-directed' and 'other-directed' societies, Riesman (1950) had already shown how some major dynamics have led to a stage of freer, but also much more anxious, competition in the realm of sex.

Such background evolutions are interesting to some extent but are far from being entirely satisfactory because their wide categories mask great disparities in conceptions.[17] Regarding the vicarious display of women within concrete social environments, it is important to understand what is valued or despised, accepted or forbidden. We can mention a few alternatives that hint at the real diversity of cultural logics. An obvious one is whether the flaunting of (un)lawful companions is expected, tolerated or unthinkable. Another one is whether distinction is related to overt ascendancy or self-restraint towards ladies.[18] It can also be underlined that bragging about one's virile capacities is significant to a greater or lesser extent from one culture to the other,[19] and that in some places some women may appear all the more desirable since they have previously been associated with other prominent members of the elite, whereas the opposite would hold true elsewhere. Likewise, the capacity to seduce rivals' female companions is a major way of enhancing one's profile in some contexts but will irremediably undermine it in others. It would not be difficult to carry on with such an enumeration of contradictory codes, but the point can already be made; it is necessary to take into consideration the relative heterogeneousness of representations and to develop a complex view of this topic, knowing that some situations are ambivalent.[20] A good question, already tackled in Chapters 3 and 5, is to what extent elites distinguish themselves by strictly adhering to the principles predominant in their own society – with possible reversals from one period to the other – or by, more or less conspicuously, taking liberties with them.[21]

The expression 'to go out with somebody', which can be found in several languages as a euphemistic way to designate a relationship, is symptomatic of the importance often attached to being seen with a partner. However, in many cultures, distinction is, on the other hand, related to the confinement of women. Wives or concubines may be reputed for their high distinction and live in the most luxurious environment, with many servants, but remain closely guarded. As we observed in Chapter 4, social distinction may involve concealment as well as visibility. In this respect, gynaeceum or harem imaginary could carry as much status as conspicuous display in other contexts.[22] To a somewhat lesser degree, semi-seclusion, supplemented by conventions such as the veil or the chaperone, may also be understood in terms of social superiority.

In individualistic societies where the choice of the partner is open, the big issue is what is designated in common language as 'love', a most ambiguous notion which may have rather different meanings from one cultural repertoire to the other. The logics prevailing behind the fact that one feels drawn toward somebody else can be divided, *inter alia*, into biological, psychological and sociological standpoints. What appears to be primordial is attraction related to, and entailing, physiological reactions, which scientists are endeavouring to uncover. From a psychological point of view – and this is of some relevance for our analysis – we have the narcissistic feeling of having been chosen or accepted by somebody else, seeing oneself in a favour- able light through her/his eyes and catching the attention of others as a couple.[23] On their side, sociologists are well aware that 'love' is to a large extent a socially constituted behaviour (e.g. Goode, 1959), whereby concrete possibilities of encounters/interactions and social expectations do matter. This involves a certain degree of mutual admiration: to 'love' somebody also means that one finds worth in the selected partner (for some reason or other) in a more or less (un) calculating way. From the symbolic perspective which interests us here, what is at stake are the consequences in terms of image when the couple goes forth into society. Once again, it proves difficult to generalise: in some contexts a discreet, silent and overtly submissive wife is a source of distinction, whereas in others an entertaining, witty and self-assured one, will be appreciated; equally, to openly flaunt good-looking, but socially inferior, mistresses might under- mine one's standing, or might not.[24]

These aspects of social competition are complex because they not only imply rivalry between men (endeavouring to be seen with matchless female companions whose assets cheapen the other ladies' smartness) but also, quite often, among women. It sounds artificial systematically to see the latter as mere pawns, reduced at best to the decorative role of 'objects' of ostentation whose value essentially accrues to the worth of their male partner. In this respect, Sombart's (1967 [1913]) already mentioned approach linking together 'sexual love' and luxury is illu- minating. He analysed this as an intra-elite game in which desirable femininity becomes a central emblem of distinction. Lecherous kings, or powerful courtiers, used their status to make erotic conquests and, on their side, women patently knew how to use their favours to secure a dominant position. In such a configuration, a ruler showers money and presents on his 'triumphant' mistress who seizes each occasion for the display of herself: the two of them being at the centre of admiring looks. Historians confirm that sovereigns addicted to lasciviousness and luxury could be quite dependent on their female companions. Indeed, it was frequently the favourites who encouraged extravagant expend- iture. Admittedly, for every 'courtesan' who was profitably able to use sex as a means to status, there were many not so successful in extracting grants from their protectors. Moreover, all of them were liable to the disappearance, or even just the fall from grace, of their respective male companion.

Let us now consider another period when sexuality outside the confines of marriage and vicarious display were widespread institutions: that of the French Second Empire (1852–70). It seems that it was by then essential for every man of fashion to keep a mistress. Undoubtedly, this most often involved an unequal relationship with socially dominated women (ballet girls, *grisettes*). However, it cannot be denied that at the top of the ladder one found the 'queens of the *demi-monde*' who embarked on a 'career of love', so to speak, by exploiting the insatiable needs of their rich devotees.[25] The high visibility of these women certainly contributed to extolling the glory and the wealth of their lovers, but it was also an investment of sorts with a view to attracting the attention of other potential admirers. If we turn our attention to the lawful wives of the elite during the second half of the nineteenth century, it appears that Veblen's one-sided picture in terms of 'conspicuous consumption' allotted to them principally to strengthen the status of their husband does not always hold true. In her book on *Shopping for Pleasure* in London, Erika Rappaport (2000, chapter two) shows, on the contrary, that spouses could indeed jeopardise their husband's status when overspending in department stores, those new 'halls of temptation' which offered credit facilities. With regard to the United States, when one reads Edith Wharton (who knew the milieu analysed by Veblen quite well), we see wives and daughters craving for some measure of individual prominence at the expense of their husband or father.[26] For their part, functionalists such as Barber and Lobel (1952) showed that upper-class American women of their time did take initiatives and that one could not reduce everything to mere logics of 'vicarious consumption'.[27] Focusing on Berlin at the beginning of the twentieth century, Simmel (1957 [1904]) acknowledged that women were in a 'weak social position'. However, he described fashion as a kind of compensation for them – unlike Veblen – thus offering an interpretation not purely in terms of reification.

The intention here is not to provide a counter-argument but, as elsewhere, to give nuanced views and to point to the limits of some excessive generalisations. Particularly when considering more or less ancient periods, or non-Western settings, it is important to overcome the universalistic nature of some discussions about gender relations which run the risks of anachronism and ethnocentrism. To study the current boom of 'modern' concubines in China certainly requires one to exceed *prêt-à-penser* ideas regarding the 'ornamental sex'. The same applies to West Africa.[28] As men's social superiority has been a predominant feature in most contexts (and homosexuality the exception rather than the rule), we have been inclined to discuss the issue of vicarious exhibition from a heterosexual male point of view. However, instances of exceptionally powerful women playing a reverse, though similar, game with men have not been non-existent (Catherine II of Russia being probably one of the most notorious cases). Further to notable changes, the notion of glamorous company as a mode of vicarious display should be less and less restricted to females these days.

Servants

The manifest function of servants is of course to relieve those who can afford them of certain tasks, particularly the more menial, tiresome or tedious ones. What is essential for elites in general is to devote themselves to activities which are deemed important for their social image, or very pleasant, and openly to leave the rest to others.[29] As Sombart (1967 [1913]) reminds us, the 'seigniorial mode of living' could even involve ignoring mundane money matters and entrusting senior staff to liaise with creditors.[30] A key symbolic aspect is to be served. Domestics certainly are expected to carry out concrete services, but they are also kept as indicators of their masters' social status, that of a person who gives orders. In this respect, historians specialising in the study of servants in the nineteenth century have stressed the fact that employers behaved more brutally to their staff if their own previous station in life had been closer to the latter.[31] From a social distinction point of view, a first dividing line is between those who keep servants (be it a single maid-of-all-work – once an indispensable status symbol for the petite bourgeoisie in many countries) and those who do not. In the higher-status groups that concern us, householders may employ a very large staff, with a multiplicity of duties possibly calling for a clear division of labour. At this level, elite competition depends also upon outdoing rivals in the smartness and competence of one's servants.

Since antiquity, skilled slaves or servants have often played a significant role in assisting elites with their 'staging' of social superiority. It appears that some tasks could not be easily completed without some assistance.[32] The practical and symbolic value of servants is all the more obvious when they provide outstanding expertise converted into factors of distinction for the persons employing them. In a mutually reinforcing way, elites take advantage of the talent of their staff, and impressive accomplishments indicate that they have the means to be surrounded by able people.[33] In the particular case of upstarts, to engage a very distinguished butler may be a means of compensating for a serious lack of manners. This must be related to an important topic discussed by sociologists, that of specialised intermediaries (not only servants but also, in more contemporary situations, interior decorators, landscape designers, etc.) whose responsibility is to make up for a worrying lack of confidence regarding 'good' taste and 'appropriate' style on the part of those who employ them. When considered within a comparative perspective, this theme appears complex because attitudes are widely divergent. Elite distinction may consist in systematically leaning on servants. This may go as far as deliberately insisting on one's own incompetence in order to draw attention to the fact that one has employees dealing with particular matters.[34] At the other extreme, we find elites eager to demonstrate their personal skills in specific domains, which might involve a recurrent refusal to delegate a great many tasks, or at least a constant and overzealous supervision.

A second dimension which should be mentioned, regarding servants as contributing to status-enhancement or maintenance, concerns the issue of how they were clothed. We are touching here on a more latent function, analysed by Veblen (1994 [1899]) from a 'vicarious display' point of view. Originally, servants – and a fortiori slaves – were dressed rather poorly. It later became fashionable to flaunt liveried servants who bore the insignia of their lord.[35] According to Veblen, domestics must be considered as members of prominent men's entourage being conspicuously in charge of asserting prestige or wealth, just like wives and children – all the more so in the eyes of active businessmen themselves compelled to maintain a certain understatement in clothing. A remarkable phenomenon noticed by the author of *The Theory of the Leisure Class* is that if servants are supposed to be clothed quite elaborately, their impressive attire is often out of date, thus avoiding any possible confusion with their masters. In the nineteenth century, male attendants would typically wear the costumes that nobles displayed years earlier (with powdered wigs, knickerbockers and silk stockings).[36] Several historians (e.g. Burke, 1987a, p. 140) have drawn attention to the fact that the servants wearing gorgeous clothes were mainly the ones meant to accompany their masters or mistresses. A particularly interesting case in this respect is that of the footmen: initially these were purposely tall and handsome servants parading on the platform of coaches, who 'gradually migrated to serving at table' (Strong, 2002, pp. 235–37) and were eventually requested to follow ladies going shopping and to carry parcels.

It is probably safe to say that servants function as mere foils in the game of distinction. Yet, this immediately points to the question of to what extent they feel involved in this game and may also themselves develop a sense of distinction. Admittedly, relationships between elites and domestics can be read in terms of power and obedience, at times exploitation and resistance (expressed through acts such as petty larceny) and impossible admiration. As Hegel declared, after Montaigne, 'No hero is hero for his servant'. However, service in close proximity does not just lead to desacralisation. As a result of the largesse this proximity is liable to yield, and above all because they do know that they are strategic actors when it comes to create an aura of prestige, some servants may paradoxically gain dignity via the transcendent image of their master or mistress, through which they identify themselves.[37] In other words, they too may enjoy a kind of vicarious satisfaction, e.g revelling in the idea that their employers possess more prestigious goods than others (see, e.g. Maza, 1983). Upper servants proud of mastering codes related to distinction may prove particularly uncompromising about them, not only showing arrogance toward all those they perceive as less refined than themselves, but going as far as to form an opinion of their employers and their guests according to such criteria. Strikingly enough, domestics sometimes seem to be more obsessed by the issue of ranks than the upper classes employing them. In this respect, the description of social distinction stratagems between the house steward, the housekeeper, the butler, the under-butlers, the lady's maid, the lord's valet, the cook, nannies, footmen and several types of more junior staff within big establishments in Victorian times is amazing. Countless theatrical conventions – at table, when addressing each other – aimed at constantly stressing precedence or submission 'downstairs' appear to be more firmly established than 'upstairs' (see, e.g. Horn, 1975).

To return to elite distinction *per se*, a complex of interrelated changes in 'Western' countries has led to the gradual disappearance of resident servants from all except the wealthiest households.[38] In the modern upper-middle class, the non-working housewife has for some time taken the place of domestic workers as an indication of social respectability, but this is not even true anymore. At best, one might employ a part-time cleaning lady or an au-pair. Full-time servants have become a prerogative unattainable for many – and, therefore, more than ever a key status symbol. However, when looking at this from a comparative

perspective, a very different picture emerges. In 'less advanced' countries, but also in some with a high immigration, being served is still
taken for granted in the eyes of well-to-do families, and this frequently
involves a mix of abuse and paternalism.

Art patronage

'The high life aspires to the beautiful life', writes Adorno (1974 [1951])
and this fact often prompts elites to gather magnificent objects that
serve as expressions of their social rank. Beyond their intrinsic beauty,
impressive collections indirectly point to their owners' superior
resources and power, that is those used to acquire rare and precious
items from afar (through conquest and looting, tributes, exchanges or
purchase).[39] Historically, it appears that the prevailing logic has been
omnidirectional accumulation of every coveted valuable liable to dazzle viewers. In certain contexts, however, the capacity to patronise tal-
ented artists has progressively emerged as a more prestigious attribute
of social superiority – taste operating as a new sign of distinction – and
this has led the art gallery to supplant the cabinet of curiosities in many
European castles. Different points of relevance deserve consideration
here, such as the flattering representation of elites in works of art, the
question of the visibility of the collections and the evolution of the status of the artist. The following paragraphs will address these, and a few
others, in summary.

The association between elites and artisans or artists – metalworkers,
jewellers, sculptors, painters, musicians or writers – able to produce a
wealth of exquisite craft or 'art' has been a recurring feature in many
societies.[40] What is involved is evidently the magnification of the glory
of the patrons in exchange for protection and remuneration. Craftsmen
are, for instance, requested to beautify residences in order to fortify the
self-esteem of the owners who aim to attract the admiring glances of
their peers. The crucial contribution of artists to their employers' desire
to convey the correct message about their social image is obvious in
portraits, those major acts of self-presentation. Most telling is the fact
that elites are usually depicted to their best advantage: originally in
conventionally dignified postures, subsequently with more concern
to give an accurate reflection of their individual characters, but more
often than not wearing impressive clothes and with physical defects
smoothed out. Significantly enough, a portrait painter's reputation
could depend in great part on his ability to capture the details of lavish costumes. Additionally, we frequently find in the background of

aristocratic portraits several elements symbolically contributing to confirm their status: an impressive residence (or a fine curtain, or a column metonymically alluding to it), members of their family (plus, at times, a servant) dressed up; possibly some allusions to an elitist style of life, etc. Equally revealing is the fact that, in Europe, members of the upper groups often liked to collect portraits, busts or medals representing important figures of the past and of their own time: the juxtaposition with their own household portraits could be used in this way to allude to their belonging to the higher spheres, or a least to their aspiration toward elevated status.

Our aim with such random illustrations is merely to point to a few among the possible ways in which elites have utilised art and artists to call attention to their own social worth. It goes without saying that a fuller inventory would require the examination of all sorts of artistic expressions (such as the symbolic value of some landscape or still-life paintings in certain cultural environments), especially when considering non-Western civilisations. Beyond aesthetic realisations, the issue of expertise is also at stake. Not only does it matter for elites to acquire and have original works produced by famous artists, but it is gratifying to be able to speak of them competently.[41] A standard question, not uncontroversial, is to what extent art collecting is an end in itself or, essentially, a means of self-representation? Relatedly, are we talking of private delight, exclusive enjoyment (at best shared with a few other connoisseurs) or deliberate display? The best way to study this is to consider who actually has access to works, what is exhibited and what is kept hidden. In many palaces, portraits were often purposely hung in public rooms, whereas other paintings (meant for pleasure) could remain out of sight and still others had a semi-private status.[42] The instrumentalisation of art in a perspective of intra-elite competition is manifest in many contexts. For courts vying with each other, large collections were undoubtedly a source of distinction. This entailed not just systematically showing them to every important visitor but also having the main paintings engraved and assembled into volumes proudly offered to other courts through ambassadors. The latest form of pretension in this domain is perhaps the presentation to museums of artworks conspicuously featuring the name of the donor. Another sub-theme worthy of attention is the often ostentatious nature of spaces dedicated to the display of artistic treasures.

From a vicarious angle, the key aspect to be clarified is of course the nature of the link between elites and artists. There is frequently involved a degree of reciprocity whereby the two parties know that they are liable to benefit from each other. For instance, from Pindar's panegyrics extolling his famous contemporaries' (real or exaggerated) merits, to official court historians officially in charge of describing the grandeur of palaces and the pageantry of festivities in the most flattering terms, many poets have contributed to celebrating elites and, on their side, have gained fame from this exercise. Great figures or very wealthy people need acclaim and glorification through realisations exalting them in the eyes of their contemporaries, and they look for artists who can produce art providing a permanent mirror of their claims to superiority. In other words, we are dealing with a logic of (unequal) exchange between patrons and artists. The lack of balance in such transactions is related to the respective stature of each side. In the Middle Ages, artisans working for courts or for the Church were often treated, at best, as upper servants. For centuries, artists have been keen, revealingly, to dedicate their works to their protectors in an ostensibly submissive and obsequious mode. Many of them were actually ordered to place their talents exclusively at the service of one patron, but the latter could also (strategically) lend them to other elites. Nevertheless, even sponsors who believe that they are fully in charge may prove to be much influenced by the artists they employ. Conversely, artists commonly had to constrain their creativity in order to please their protector (see, e.g. Haskell, 1980). In Europe, since the Renaissance at least (and more visibly since the eighteenth century), the progressive transformation of the status of the artist has been remarkable. Those very much in demand have been in a position to discuss terms with highly placed amateurs. What has emerged is a new situation whereby elites may have to compete to attract the most reputed artists. Equally, some salons may take pride in the fact that they contributed to launching unknown artists – the vanity of the hostess who has 'discovered' their qualities being bound to their success – but eventually have to battle to retain the honour of their company. When certain creations become particularly crucial for the image of upper groups, and when very successful artists manage to gain a relative independence within the framework of an open market, these individuals may indeed aspire to an elite status themselves (Heinich, 2005). The same is true for a few exceptionally gifted artisans.[43]

In thus placing the emphasis on the logics of patronage in former centuries, the intention here has been to highlight some key mechanisms and social dynamics from a *longue durée* perspective. It should be stressed, however, that the collecting of works of art remains a significant activity for elites worldwide. As a matter of fact, looking for items which are especially scarce – indeed often unique – and ostentatiously costly, proves to be one of the ways found by the very rich to mark their prominence by extending the consumption ladder.[44] When contemporary artists are concerned, this may still involve patronage, although art galleries increasingly function as intermediaries.

Part III
Variability

Comparative analysis obviously entails searching for both recurrences and differences. However, one of the central strands that runs throughout this book is a relative scepticism vis-à-vis the reductionist character of certain generalisations put forward in the grand theories available. Consequently, and in reaction to this, what is proposed here is mainly an exposition of some heterogeneous forms and underlying logics of distinction. The overall objective is of course not hyper-empiricism, which would make comparisons problematical. The aim is merely to underline contrasts when they are observable.

Hence, in Part III we shall provide illustrations serving as a defence of our position on variability. First of all, Chapter 7 is devoted to the historicity of elite distinction. Chapter 8 will then discuss attitudes towards tradition and novelty. Finally, Chapter 9 will address from a comparative point of view some of the thornier issues in the field of social distinction, such as those of style and dominant codes.

7
The Historicity of Elite Distinction: Selected Themes

A researcher concerned with the comparative analysis of distinction is of course particularly interested in the studies available about those places and periods in which the ostentation of the elite was outstandingly spectacular.[1] At stake, in all probability, were self-affirmation and glorification (quite often in relation to political power), but important dissimilarities should not be under-estimated. Our aspiration here is obviously not a systematic comparison between such cases. The more modest ambition of this chapter is to focus attention on five revealing themes, namely: the significant variability of attitudes toward distinction in 'primitive' communities, the prevailing logics behind sumptuary laws, the effects of political revolutions, the issue of constraints when upholding social superiority and the impact of a new world of mass consumption.

Early stages: accounts from anthropological works

In opposition to the illusory conviction that elite distinction would universally be the same story between high-status groups and those below, contributions from the field of anthropology are crucial. The chief merit of this discipline is the acknowledgement of diverse cultural representations across the globe, which thus helps us to avoid excessively ethnocentric generalisations.[2] Many descriptions within anthropological literature are rich in information about why and how 'traditionalistic' communities challenge or support status distinctions. Differences are often presented along an evolutionist line of reasoning, emphasising several stages. The first is that of hunter-gatherers operating in small units. It has been recognised that this category, although useful from an analytical point of view, incorporates rather different types. However, it appears that, in most of them, sharing practices and egalitarian ethics prevail. Many ethnographic monographs clearly indicate that prestige may exist in such 'foraging' communities but strictly in connection with activities that benefit the whole group. For instance, high regard is likely to be accorded to good hunters, but this does not lead to formalised differences in rank. Actually, levelling mechanisms are frequently resorted to in order to prevent any thought of institutionalised superiority (see, e.g. Wiessner, 1996). Nevertheless, the wearing of some trophies may mark out some members of the set to a limited extent.

A second stage is that of communities with no hereditary status but in which 'Big Men' leading factions emerge. Neither exploitation nor differentiated socio-political positions exist as yet, but individuals demonstrating their mastery of skills, thus commanding respect, are able to construct a following and to earn rank. They amass and redistribute valuables with a calculated generosity so as to create a network of obligation.[3] The circulation of such valuables – which are both the signs and means of superiority – is considered a key to power within the context of 'prestige goods systems'.[4] As is shown in the abundant literature on the gift, generosity which is not reciprocated occasions unequal relationships. On the other hand, within the context of endless competition to attract followers, dominant actors may fall prey to blackmail by those supporting them, especially when they do not regularly distribute accumulated goods.[5]

The next stage of this evolution – necessarily presented in a simplified way here – is that of the first stratified societies, able to generate surpluses and store riches that rulers convert into power. The most prestigious goods are then usually monopolised by elites. These items serve to distinguish their bearers from the bulk of the population and may be passed from one generation to the next. Dominant roles tend to be associated with the ownership, sometimes with the ostentatious consumption, of goods difficult to obtain which fulfil a purpose of hierarchy construction. What matters is not only to establish one's authority over 'one's subjects' but also within the framework of regional elite interaction (which may involve alliance building, gifts and counter-gifts, conquests and tributes). In the second case, prestige goods operate as powerful statements of status helping to raise the standing of the group as a whole.

Reflections upon these themes have been dominated to some extent by specialists of economic anthropology favouring a Marxist standpoint (in terms of causal precedence of relations of production, surplus turned into social advantage, proto-class, etc.).[6] Such perspectives certainly underline disparities. However, many other anthropologists have, with good reason, warned against the universal pretensions of economistic theories, and commented on the necessity of supplementing their evolutionist approaches with an examination of the relativity of the embedded conceptions implied.[7] For what concerns us here, this begs a full consideration of wide cross-cultural variation in prestige logics and related meanings transmitted through socialisation. In this regard, evidence provided by ethnologists enables us to view a degree of the complexity and richness of representations related to 'prestige goods'. In many 'traditional' communities, marine shells, for instance, have functioned as status markers, decorations or money, and they were often displayed, gifted or circulated between people not only because they were prized for their shapes, colours or sheen, but also because they were imbued with several symbolic meanings (from fertility to peaceful exchanges).[8] It is of course quite acceptable to go no further than a structuralist-Marxist analysis focusing on control of the raw materials, possible value added by the labour that transforms them into shaped ornaments and eventually exhibition/distribution, seeking to maintain hierarchical systems. Yet it is also instructive to examine such prestige goods in relation with local cosmogonies, involving contextually relevant classifications, and to cast some light on their social significance from a comparative point of view.[9]

It is tempting to offer many more illustrations (in reference to so-called 'primitive' contexts as well as some 'early civilisations') but there is no space to pursue them here. The kernel of the argument, however, is that anthropological descriptions allow us to realise that the world is composed of largely dissimilar universes of meaning. Against those inclined to make rapid ahistorical statements, or retrospective judgements, based on the assumptions of one favourite explanatory scheme, historians calling suitable attention to major divergences perform the same, indispensable, function.[10]

Sumptuary laws compared

In Chapter 4, we hinted at the importance of sumptuary laws. Aimed at bringing under control manifestations of social superiority, and notably to regulate the desire for lavish appearance, sumptuary exclusivity constitutes a key theme with regard to our central topic. These laws can be found in vastly different environments (from antiquity to the twentieth century, among many types of political regimes or religious contexts). Occasionally providing for 'positive injunctions' (e.g. to dress up in accordance with one's rank), they more typically take the form of negative prohibitions: forbidding some social categories from acquiring and displaying certain items. Three principal purposes may be roughly distinguished. The first is related to moralising preoccupations with promoting a virtuous frugality for various ideological (or more concrete) reasons.[11] A second motive, of economic nature, lies with the scope of protectionist views pointing toward the import of luxurious products from competitor states.[12] Above all, however, sumptuary laws can be analysed as a defensive reaction by established elites concerned with preserving an exclusive access to what 'materialises' their higher position.

In this respect, it appears that such legislation has been enacted particularly when 'fixed status hierarchies were challenged from below' (A. Hunt, 1996, p. 147). A classic example is found in the symbolic rivalry between the nobility and the rising merchant class in Western Europe, during those centuries which witnessed the long transition from social stratification through predefined privileges to new logics based on socio-economic achievements. Whereas since time immemorial prestige goods had been used to confirm pre-existing hereditary statuses, with the advent of capitalism and the strong upward thrust by new socio-economic forces, they became status markers regardless of the owner's original background. The aspiration of the bourgeoisie to a more dignified presentation of themselves led many to purchase conspicuous signs of social position (see, e.g. Huppert, 1977). What sumptuary laws endeavoured to counter was not only such a desire to adopt emblems deemed 'above their station' but, more fundamentally, the subversion of the old system of stratification. Societies composed of different estates or orders often proved obsessively concerned with the issue of visibility and discrimination. This applied to all ranks, from the highest to the lowest, and could entail exaltation as well as infamy. For aristocratic elites constantly expecting deference from subordinates, immediate recognition through conventional signs was crucial in so far as it was perceived as a guarantor of proper status identification. Yet, with the advent of newly wealthy groups wishing to be confused with the upper circles and able to emulate their external appearance, the whole symbolic system was disrupted, and this explains the attempts at official regulation.

As might be anticipated from this brief summary, several of the conceptual tools introduced earlier can be of some use here. We are obviously dealing with the theme of imitation (Tarde, 1962 [1890]), the

Weberian one of 'closure strategies' (Murphy, 1988) and that of increasing competition within urban contexts (e.g. Sombart, 1967 [1913], pp. 100 ff.) or court society (Elias, 1983 [1933]). As a matter of fact, numerous influential social theorists have helpfully tackled this significant question of sumptuary laws from their own analytical standpoint. However, beyond one-sided interpretations prone to elide the unevenness of the processes at work, a comparative perspective is liable to widen our reference points and to add further theoretical complexity. In the space available here, our concern is merely to single out a few interesting contrasts.

For instance, sumptuary laws may exhibit not only inter-class but also, first and foremost, intra-elite dimensions. In medieval England, or in China for centuries, the primary preoccupation was clearly with distinct boundaries among the top ranks. At the other extreme of the spectrum, one finds cases where no explicit reference to social category was made (e.g. the *Lex Sumptuari* in Rome toward the end of the Republic). Regarding legislation precluding any status fluidity (frequently evidenced by historians working on the early modern period in Western Europe, or on late-feudal situations), these laws could be aimed at the rising bourgeoisie (as in France and Japan) or at the old aristocratic families (as in some Italian or German cities). Equally, they could concern large territories (within a context of state development and centralisation in some parts of Europe), or just a town, and could prove more or less effective. Divergences may of course be related to the local realities of power, that is which group is dominant and which one is perceived as a threat to the social order. Nonetheless taking into account divergent occurrences, and the widest possible range of inferred information, might lead to relevant analytical considerations.

Moreover, case studies on sumptuary laws (e.g. Hugues, 1983, 1986) crucially inform us about the primary attributes of success, and how these work in different cultures. Preventing other groups from adopting markers reserved for a privileged elite frequently involves rather arbitrary relations between signs and their social referents. The most obvious example is that of those colours deemed more prestigious being monopolised by certain categories.[13] Of potential concern, however, are many 'key manifestations' of elite superiority presented above: wearing silk, gold or silver embroideries, conspicuous items of jewellery, long shoes or trains; the number of horses drawing a carriage; the guests one is allowed to entertain, what can be served to them and on which type of plate; the façades of residences; the appearance of servants; display at the occasion of weddings and burial ceremonies; and even the depth of décolletage. It is particularly interesting to compare what is held to be significant across time or space. There are countless illustrations that may serve to testify to the diversity of representations. A good example is that of architecture. According to specialists, there have seldom been sumptuary laws related to this sector in Europe. In Asia, by contrast – whether in Japan, China or the south-east – it was often deemed central. What could be involved, *inter alia*, were the size of the residence, the colour of the walls, the decoration, the number of courtyards, the size of doors, the luxury of door-knockers and the location. Spencer (1893, p. 197) equally stressed limitations in the height of buildings (as in ancient Mexico) and the fact that, for some Dahomean kings, a good way to honour someone consisted in allowing him to build a multi-storey house.

With the advent of open consumer societies (to be discussed below) sumptuary laws have, of course, lost a great part of their raison d'être. However, they have not entirely disappeared and linger under some authoritarian systems.[14] Besides, even in the absence of formal rules dictating conduct, it may remain customary for some subordinate people to abstain from flaunting items (such as cufflinks in some Japanese corporations) which are understood as a prerogative for their superiors.

Revolutionary reactions

A recurrent theme in this chapter is the impact of the political system on the modalities of elite distinction. With sumptuary laws, we clearly see the significant bearing that the political order may have on the social order (which raises the question of the – eminently variable – degree of differentiation between the two spheres).[15] When it comes to revolutionary episodes endeavouring to undertake complete breaks, the intrusion of the political realm is even more patent. The key issue here is to what extent the circulation of elites is accompanied by symbolic upheavals. Comparative analysis helps to reveal a multiplicity of scenarios. In some cases, the conditions for elite distinction truly undergo a radical shift. Yet, in many others, those who have taken over (political/social) power and claim supremacy merely work the good old system to their own advantage. Some situations also prove ambiguous. The history of twentieth-century politics is not without examples of revolutionary regimes which called officially for the eradication of former class differentiations, but eventually appeared full of apparatchiks enjoying substantial privileges. Equally, some ruling elites admittedly led a parsimonious life (e.g. members of the Taliban), although this did not prevent them from constantly asserting pre-eminence over any other group. Unlike those elites whose power is derived from hereditary status, or from the control of capital, the incumbents of command positions in post-revolutionary situations evince a form of superiority that is neither rooted in 'tradition' nor strictly economic.[16] They obviously do not rule because they owned wealth, but it should be considered to what extent they claim a kind of social distinction because they rule.

A far as extremist reactions against the abuses of a former socio-political system are concerned, one of the most impressive chapters in world history remains the 1789–94 French Revolution. What is particularly interesting in this case is the fact that symbolic dimensions did not follow as a secondary aspect mirroring deeper socio-economic battles, but stood at the very heart of the debates and processes of change. The social ordering of the *Ancien Régime* was characteristic of a stratification by status progressively giving way to a new one by class within a context of commercial development.[17] Whereas conventional markers of nobility as well as a privileged access to spectacular consumption used to trace the social hierarchy unequivocally, the rise of merchants or financiers led to a confusion of rank that potentially threatened the hegemony of traditional elites. *Grands seigneurs* and other courtiers endeavoured to defend the time-honoured symbolic boundaries intended to seal their supremacy against those who were frequently presented as usurpers. On the other side, radical political discourses against wastefulness increased considerably.[18] Courtly pomp, according to some Enlightenment writers, should be understood in terms of parasitic oppression taking the country to ruin, instead of provoking awe or respect. Marie-Antoinette's extravagant wardrobe, and the fact that she refused to reduce her expenses in a context of large rises in taxation, thus became the major symbol of the excesses that were denounced (see, e.g. Ribeiro, 2002).

Consequently, the French Revolution aimed not only to erase hereditary privileges and to confiscate nobles' properties, but also to obliterate all social distinctions that were not justified by utilitarian principles. The only permissible honour was that which signalled function, not title (Wrigley, 2002). Wigs were replaced by Phrygian caps, while patriotic women often gave their more precious jewels 'to the Nation' and adopted three-coloured attire in order to manifest their support for the regime. With the end of the monarchy, the Declaration of 1793 emphasising egalitarianism and the 'Reign of Terror' which followed, any elegance or style was viewed as a form of unacceptable social selfishness.

The use of simple, even ragged, clothing evolved into revolutionary display. The intention was to eradicate the ancient symbolic system denoting inherent status superiority. This attitude became more pronounced with the advent of the *sans-culottes*. The latter tended ostensibly to abandon the flattering and seductive role formerly ascribed to clothes (notably the close-fitting breeches which were favoured by male aristocrats because they emphasised shapely legs). If the revolutionary tribunals scrutinised dress and physical appearance with obsession, almost every sector could be encompassed. It was for instance advisable to avoid refined language, and over-familiarity with other citizens was strongly encouraged. Moreover, cleanliness often appeared suspicious to authorities, whereas sweat (suggesting manual work) was praised. As Lynn Hunt (1990 [1987]) demonstrates, even the most intimate objects (such as beds, chamber pots or shaving mugs) could be stamped with 'public signs of revolutionary ardour' and, according to her, private life then had 'to endure the most systematic assault ever seen in Western history' (p. 13).

The twentieth century, with its extremes of totalitarian politics, was to offer other illustrations of an ever-expanding public domain endeavouring to impose its presence upon practically all sectors of life. In his book dealing with prestige processes and dynamics of subversion, Goode (1978, pp. 215 and 302 ff.) underlines how quickly the deference traditionally shown toward elites may vanish (e.g. peasants or workers no longer doffing their caps to former social superiors). On the other hand, it is important to note that regulatory interventions from above in the name of an egalitarian ideology seldom last. In the French case, a few months of intransigent austerity were followed by the 'Thermidorian reaction' and the Napoleonic era, which indulged in paroxysms of ostentation. Even for revolutionary elites able to wield power for several decades (as in the USSR or China), it has proven difficult to perpetuate ascetic principles. Baudrillard (1996b [1970, pp. 51–52]) remarked that if the points of reference are quite different in such systems, the quest for 'something more' (e.g. a small *dacha*) often remains symbolically essential. A key dimension here is the attitude of the elites themselves. To return to the French case, many members of the Jacobin club were famous for the slovenliness of their dress. Yet, paradoxically, major figures such as Robespierre or Saint-Just always took great care of their appearance. In communist systems, personality cults and the rise of '*nomenklaturas*' led to a blurring of what was (un)desirable.[19] The discrepancy between the image projected by the dignitaries of a regime and its official ideology may be consequential. This, however, is a very complex matter, mainly for reasons connected with the issue of power legitimation. Firstly, the abolition of traditional forms of deference combined with the imposition of a new 'political culture' may have detrimental feedback effects, eventually bringing elites to revive some old practices selectively for the sake of their own authority.[20] Furthermore, regardless of the nature of the regime and its ideology, the necessity for the dominant actors to demonstrate prominence in varying ways is inescapable.[21]

Processes of (in)formalisation

With these few reflections on historicity, our preoccupation is not to propose accounts for general dynamics of change. Actually, when one has realised that the cultural contextualisation of elite distinction matters, it proves useful to reason not only in a macro-evolutionist way (when appropriate) but also in terms of *in*volutions.[22] Nevertheless, in the remainder of this chapter, we would like to draw attention to some developments worthy of consideration. The first concerns the frequently constraining nature of elite distinction and the trend toward more 'relaxed' attitudes.

Since antiquity, it has been acknowledged that those who occupy the upper ranks of society are obliged to be 'on show' most of the time and that social eminence is often synonymous with rigid formality. This is usually interpreted as a prerequisite designed to establish or confirm their superiority vis-à-vis the groups below and, with regards to rulers, as a necessity for giving a dignified representation of the polity in the eyes of the local population or those of other political entities. As suggested above, political and social status is not always clearly differentiated and the same kind of dramatic effects intended to constitute hierarchical relations may be deployed. Indeed, numerous social scientists have been eager to offer readings emphasising universalistic logics of manipulation calculated to dazzle the commoners. It is perhaps possible to discern some trans-cultural symbolic stratagems which ubiquitously prove effective for elite distinction but, as has been shown in significant works, attention to local perceptions is also required.[23] In any case, from an elite viewpoint, it is important to emphasise that the cultivation of a superior appearance regularly entails substantial constraints and unceasing self-observation. Here, both Veblen's and Elias's analytical frameworks are particularly useful.

Many of the attributes discussed above which determine elite distinction can be considered from this angle. If some aspects of appearance (manners, posture and linguistic competence) are related to lengthy training but acquired once and for all, many others (such as grooming) need constant repetition. In his excellent book on bourgeois clothing during the nineteenth century, Perrot (1996 [1981]) underlines that a lady might have to change attire several times per day in order to abide by the 'imperatives of propriety' with all their subtle codes. Likewise, the cravat of the man of fashion had to be artfully re-tied every morning through a painstaking series of operations. In some (aristocratic as well as haut-bourgeois) contexts, the supremacy and ranking of elites are profoundly 'representational'. The latter endeavour to exhibit their status or class position to all others by creating a surrounding 'aura'. This proves very demanding because it commonly involves impractical elitist 'hindrances' (e.g. corsets or stiff collars) used as instruments of distinction, and also because those persons who occupy the heights of the social hierarchy are submitted to the merciless gaze of fellow elites endlessly evaluating them. A pertinent question is whether such constraints are considered tedious or taken for granted.

As early as the end of the seventeenth century, it can be noted that some aristocrats began to react against the constraining norms introduced to persuade others of their superiority. Louis XIV himself eventually used to escape, on occasion, from the grandeur of Versailles to the castle of Marly where the number of guests and domestics were purposely limited, and the rituals significantly reduced. This quest for informality was to become even more obvious during the eighteenth century. A revealing phenomenon, for instance, is that of members of the highest nobility who preferred travelling abroad incognito in order to evade 'annoying ceremonials'.[24] The strict observance of formalities of etiquette was progressively supplanted by a mounting interest in private pleasures and convenience. In other words, some members of the elite were no longer systematically obsessed with the requirement of cutting a figure on the public stage. Two related aspects can be discerned here: a desire for more intimacy and a growing concern for comfort.[25] This does not imply that decorum was less important, but only that it did not have to be expressed solely through elegant performances entailing a permanent duty of self-control, and instead through expressions of delectation. It may be argued that sequential changes in this constant direction were to follow in the long run, with further revolutions into casualness (in the 1920s and the 1960s) and freer individualistic attitudes.

From a comparative perspective, however, it is more appropriate to look at this subject in terms of a long-standing tension between the need to make some concessions for the sake of distinction and hedonistic pursuits. Contemporary 'Western' elites probably tend to regard many ancient rituals and signals of worthiness as anachronistic and unbearable, but some features have persisted, and new uncomfortable practices have also appeared.[26] Moreover, we have to admit that, in some societies, elites still take most pride of certain constraining behaviour standards durably marking their superiority to the groups below, whereas others have been cultivating relaxed attitudes for generations.[27] In the discussion of elitist manners, we emphasised the fact that these are irreducible to one single logic and may involve sheer arrogance as well as an ostentatious restraint. Following Elias, one may contend that self-command has increasingly become a measure of respectability. Nonetheless, even in the 'West', these dynamics have not always been manifested to the same degree in different epochs, and the highly organised rules which previously governed conducts in past centuries have undoubtedly given way to pluralistic manifestations. Besides, many codes are obviously culture specific. Does reclining at dinner connote a damaging lack of self-discipline or an elitist attitude? Weber (1951 [1915]) contrasted the flamboyant agitation of the Islamic warrior and the steadily dispassionate attitude of the mandarin. We must remain mindful of fundamental cultural differences when we make comparisons between such processes of (in)formalisation, including in the present world.

The outcome of the mass consumer society

Another process worthy of consideration is the development of consumerism. Given the importance of the links between social position and acquisition practices in many societies, patterns of consumption are evidently of great interest for investigations of elite distinction. As with several other notions employed in this volume, the word consumption is not devoid of ambiguity. Two senses, at least, can be differentiated: that of purchase and that of 'using up'. As was already emphasised when we dealt with Veblenian and socioeconomic perspectives, it is necessary to move away from abstract thinking in terms of market exchange and to introduce concrete sociological dimensions. In this respect, many historians, anthropologists and other social scientists have produced rich studies on the meanings of consumption in various settings. There are still serious disagreements about the birth of consumer society, which some scholars trace in the eighteenth century (and as far back as the Renaissance) in Western Europe – that is before the Industrial Revolution – or, rather, in the late nineteenth century.[28] It is perhaps more judicious to reason in terms of a succession of 'outbreaks': early competitive acquisition of commodities by privileged groups and their challengers, the acceleration of the eighteenth century involving new (middle-class) consumers, the further explosion of mass consumption in the context of societies having attained a higher level of affluence and, eventually, contemporary forms of shopping in a 'postmodern environment'. What matters for us, notwithstanding the differences between historical interpretations, is the shift from an essentially intra-elite competition to a situation whereby a wider public has access to a continuously increasing number of commodities.

As regards the first stage, pioneering reflections by both Sombart and Elias (respectively on courtship and intensification on the demand for luxuries, and on 'court rationality') can still be seen as fundamental. They showed how crucial it became for aristocrats to engage in a riot of consumption with a view to bearing out their status. These reflections have undoubtedly been extended by more systematic historical explorations including concerns with various aspects of consumption (e.g. commercialisation, advertisements, techniques of sale, credit, women's consumption, etc.). However, even in the literature incorporating wider perspectives, the issues of competitive display, consumption hierarchy, material culture and status remain central. For example, McKendrick, Brewer and Plumb (1982) rely heavily on a Veblenian line of argument and employ notions such as 'conspicuous consumption', 'emulation' or 'Veblen effects' to interpret the consumer boom in eighteenth-century England. The relevance of the Veblenian reading grid to societies of that time is debatable.[29] It appears that other explanations deserve to be considered in conjunction here. An interesting contribution in this respect is that of Campbell (1987) who argues that in order to understand fully the advent of modern forms of consumption we must take into account what he calls the 'Romantic ethic'. This refers to new forms of subjectivity and emotion communicated particularly through novels. It is contended that consumerism offers a means of expressing one's individual essence. This approach is not necessarily incompatible with a distinction perspective. Nonetheless, such cultural focus is helpful because it suggests an additional dimension to ubiquitous (in this case Veblenian) explanations. It stands as a reminder to social scientists that their work should enter the world of mentalities and consider their possible evolutions. As has been noted on several occasions, the degree of individualism/collectivism (to use expressions favoured by psycho-sociologists) exhibited in various societies is a key variable when it comes to the study of elite distinction, and this certainly applies to consumer cultures.

The transition to a mass market in the late nineteenth and early twentieth centuries is related to momentous economic and social changes which are well-known: the development of mechanised production techniques, changes in methods of distribution, urbanisation, 'spread of purchasing power to ever "lower" sectors of the population, the deregulation of all traditional constraints over consumption (free choice), [...] the centrality of democracy and equality as modern values' (Slater, 2005 [1996], p. 71). The broader availability of goods to larger and larger sections of the population does not mean that social distinctions lessened, but there is no doubt that it had significant consequences for the ways in which elite superiority was experienced. In the first place, many products which had been the prerogative of the all-powerful and the wealthiest families for generations tended to be abandoned by them because mass-produced imitations, even if flawed, deprived the originals of their symbolic value. Second, a growing proximity with the masses often generated an elitist fear of 'mobs'. In a context of the commercialisation of leisure, for instance, a desire rose for protected enclaves (first-class cabins or compartments, separate boxes at the theatre, etc.), with a view to preventing undesirable intrusion and to maintain distance. Admittedly, despite the fact that consumerism has undoubtedly democratising aspects, many avid consumers are condemned to window-shopping or at best to strolling through some prestigious stores. However, the very definition of what constitutes a luxury, and access to it, may quickly evolve from one generation to the next.[30] Furthermore, the progressive shift toward societies in which identities are increasingly supposed to be realised – not least through the capacity to acquire certain goods – and not merely fixed once for all, greatly alter representations.

Unsurprisingly, most of the major thinkers who took an interest in the question of social distinction at the turn of the twentieth century, during the 1920s and the post-World War II and 1960s economic booms, paid attention to the nodal theme of consumption. As we saw earlier, they attempted to offer interpretations subordinated to their overall schemes of interpretation, for example conspicuousness (Veblen), differentiation (Simmel), alienation (Marxists), status attainment (functionalists), taste and classifications (Bourdieu), etc. In many respects, although they have developed universalistic propositions, these models were typical products of their times. The paradox is that they are used retrospectively by many historians seeking a theoretical and conceptual apparatus.[31]

The new attitudes emphasised by analysts of postmodern realities (e.g. following Baudrillard's accounts, the consumption of signs instead of things, the fantasy world created by the shopping malls) suggest that the social imaginary of consumption is continuously on the move and that the prevailing theories of yesterday are not necessarily appropriate anymore. Yet the problem is that we are now dealing with a new orthodoxy which is far from able to provide convincing explanations for all what is taking place in the world today. As repeatedly hinted in the present volume, the cultural universes in which millions of 'status-seekers' live are not reducible to what is currently experienced in the 'West'.[32] Even among contemporary Euro-American societies, there are considerable differences from one country to the other. For example, the newly enriched 'Yuppies' of the mid-1980s, or the traders who later took advantage of some speculative bubbles, exhibit characteristics which cannot satisfactorily be reduced to either 'modern' Bourdieusian explanations or 'postmodern' interpretations.[33] Consumerism is not a universal behavioural code. More generally speaking, it is imperative to historicise elite distinction and analysis must be contextually sensitive.

8
Tradition, Fashion, Borrowing and Syncretism

Historian Paul Veyne claims that whatever predilection for the excellence they may chiefly cultivate, elites are sensitive to every means of distinction liable to 'mark them off from ordinary mankind'.[1] Yet, one may wonder to what extent they are open to novelty. Do elites from various parts of the world really show interest in any potential options, or do they mostly adhere to stable, well-proven formulas? There are several ways of approaching this topic. One consists of considering the diffusion of superiority signs from one society to another, which often requires thinking in terms of adoption/adaptation and, increasingly, in terms of globalisation/local social meanings. At a more basic level, however (not necessarily including inter-societal dimensions), the question raised is that of the attitudes of elites toward 'fashionability'.

Distinction through antiquity – distinction through novelty

The comparative study of the relations elites hold vis-à-vis innovation, as opposed to long-established codes of distinction, reveals a real diversity of cases and also many complexities. We may start with the well-documented assertion that fashion (understood as regular, ephemeral, changes in attire or other domains) was originally a Western, elitist phenomenon. This, of course, does not mean that evolutions were non-existent elsewhere, but only that the idea of a celebration of distinctiveness through recurrent modifications would have been largely meaningless and indeed shocking.[2] In many civilisations (including in 'pre-modern' Western Europe), what was sought instead was to perfect traditional canons deemed to express excellence. Spurning given canvases only makes sense in those cultural environments driven by a never-ending ambition to surpass previous stages.

Nonetheless, even among fashion-conscious societies, one meets elites who resolutely play the card of 'distinction through antiquity'. In a remote past, artefacts marking high status were often so intimately associated with their distinguished owners that they would typically follow them into the grave, but they could also pass through the hands of many people (heirs or conquerors) over several generations. Frequently, as various ethnological accounts illustrate, people inheriting or seizing such items were indeed hoping to win parts of the former owners' might. This was particularly significant in those contexts characterised by a lack of clear differentiation between persons and possessions (see, e.g. Simmel, 1978 [1900], p. 332), but still holds true in the contemporary world as Baudrillard (1996a [1968, p. 108]) reminds us. The desire to own ancient commodities may be accorded pre-eminent importance in so far as it serves to legitimise upper groups by anchoring their social worth in the past. Obviously, such a conservative code is especially frequent among 'old elites' eager to demonstrate through the 'patina' of their belongings (see McCracken, 1990, Chapter 2) their long-standing elite status. Nevertheless, it can also be found among 'new elites' who, rather than acquiring the latest products available on the market (that might betray their 'newness'), instead prefer to invest in ancient things. This strategy is manifest in the domain of architecture. For example, new elites might acquire an old mansion, build a house replicating styles of the past or even have a foreign palace entirely dismantled and then reassembled on their own land.[3]

Interpretations regarding these issues sometimes result in questionable causalities. Dogmatic assumptions lead all too easily to suggestions that the more established they are, the more systematically elites tend to favour timeless prestigious goods in order to validate their seniority, whereas the rage for novelty is seen as the mark of newcomers keen to distinguish themselves from former generations.[4] A comparative approach would caution against such simple assumptions. The relative esteem in which 'old' and 'new' commodities is held rests on a number of factors, including cultural representations or political stability.[5] By the eighteenth century, heirlooms could already be considered as a constraint in England, and some members of the highest aristocratic families did unscrupulously get rid of certain items, so as to be able to purchase more fashionable ones. Likewise, according to a French specialist of the history of furniture, fetishism vis-à-vis old pieces was usually absent during the *Ancien Régime* and, with a new style chasing away the previous one, a Henry II credence could very well end up in the chimney.[6] Reciprocally, as was already hinted, nouveaux riches can adopt old décors and passionately accumulate antiques. One wonders to what extent the latter also inherit the meaning of the ancient material artefacts with which they surround themselves. In this respect, psycho-sociologists interestingly show that some buyers continually empha-sise the qualities associated with the former owners whereas others are eager to 're-personalise' them. Needless to say, both logics provide a potential for social distinction. The contribution of socio-economists and specialists in marketing may also be instructive here. For example, with regard to contemporary buyers of two different sorts of distinction cars, Swann (2001, p. 63) explains that 'where distinction comes from novelty the elite will trade up to buy the newest models, and the second tier of consumers will suffice with last year's models' (Ferraris). 'Where greatest distinction comes from antiquity (Rolls Royces) the elite will seek the older, more distinguished model, while the nouveau riche will buy the newer models'. As a result, it is advisable to contrast the varying degrees of social prestige accorded to the 'old' and the 'new' depend-ing upon the actual perceptions of the elites under consideration, along with the bundle of meanings which gives them significance. It is important to underline the fact that many concrete situations prove ambiguous, which may reflect symbolic struggles between various seg-ments of the upper groups.

Let us now concentrate our attention more specifically upon the intricacies of the mechanisms of social distinction involving redefini-tions of the fashionable. The initial manifestations of a fashion system are usually related to the very first courts in Europe, at the end of the Middle Ages. Some commentators interpret this unprecedented craze for novelties partly in terms of a departure from tradition, within the framework of the singular Western process of 'modernisation' (see, e.g. Lipovetsky, 1994 [1987]). It also seems possible to attribute this new trend to a context of rising intra-elite competition, with individ-uals and courts increasingly vying with each other. A growing need for ostentation might have led prominent households to display new items with a view to continually reviving attention upon them, and a principle of emulation would explain the extension of the phenom-enon. It is difficult to understand the major causes and meanings at stake, but both sociological factors and deeper cultural ones should probably be taken into consideration. The combined functions of breaking monotony and of attracting interest are found in Flügel's (1930) famous 'shifting erogenous zones' theory of fashion. This early twentieth-century psychologist showed how constantly changing the rules regarding which parts of the body should be concealed, exposed or even accentuated, helped to renew captivation.[7]

With the incremental broadening of the social actors involved (made possible by the expansion of consumption and the enormous changes outlined in the previous chapter), students of distinction are on more familiar territory, in so far as fashion is predominantly analysed in terms of 'trickle-down' effects. We saw that Tarde, Veblen and Simmel, as well as American functionalists, posited similar theories according to which aspiring social groups tend to emulate the fashions of those groups more prestigious than they are, which drives the latter to continually adopt new insignia in order to differentiate themselves. As we observed above, such interpretations account rather convincingly for what was taking place in Europe or North America when the theories were elaborated (from the nineteenth century to the 1950s). However, a comparative perspective can help refine these reading grids. First, it is important to recall that some members of the upper groups remain largely immune to the idea of discarded markers, stubbornly keeping to 'correct' signs of superiority or high-quality possessions 'that will never go out of fashion'. Secondly, when ever-changing signs of social standing are concerned, the question arises as to whether we are talking of a quest for inherently superior things, minor improvements or novelty for novelty's sake. If continuous technological development provides opportunities to acquire up-to-the-minute equipment, merely subtle differences in styling or artificial obsolescence are often also involved (see Baudrillard, 1996a [1968]). Besides, in some cases, when there is no possibility of satisfactory newness or sophistication, (wo)men of fashion may have no other alternative than to resort to previous manners when being imitated.[8] Thirdly, if fashion evidently acquires its significance in contrast to the 'unfashionable', empirical studies reveal that strategies intended to demonstrate eminence in this way vary from society to society. For instance, it may make sense to distance oneself only a little from current fashions – distinction involving neither following trends immediately, nor too closely (this, of course, does not mean that they should be entirely ignored) – whereas in other places it is essential to be abreast of modish matters. The sensitive issue with which elites are faced is whether prescribing, adopting or skilfully playing with these temporal codes carries more status.

In any case, since at least the 1960s, it has been shown that fashion can no longer be reduced to interpretations in terms of 'class differentiation'.[9] Analysts of postmodernity readily emphasise the fact that the accelerated advent of new styles does not necessarily make the previous ones outdated (witness the importance of 'vintage' clothes) and they have good reasons to insist on the increasingly confused canons of fashionability. 'Trickle-down' logics have perhaps not entirely vanished everywhere, but many codes are ambivalent and obviously transcend social cleavages.[10]

Adoptions – adaptations

Research findings show that elites in 'traditional', more or less isolated, settings usually endeavoured to obtain (and, as we saw in Chapter 7, sometimes monopolise) the most impressive items available in their respective environments.[11] On the other hand, anthropologists suggest that 'exotic' valuables often conferred a special prestige; what appears to be involved is not only the fact that the latter contained an aura of exceptionality but also, most importantly, that they were related to the 'cosmological outside'.[12] The reading of case studies makes us realise that exposure to foreign contacts (notably through growing exchange or trade) and the subsequent intrusion of new goods and attitudes led to a wide range of reactions, ranging from deep suspicion to an irresistible attraction vis-à-vis anything external. In between, what could frequently be observed were processes of: *selection* (i.e. a marked reluctance to adopt certain items or habits while eagerly embracing others), *combinations* of ongoing signs of superiority with novel ones and *adaptation* of imports to local realities and meanings.[13]

The story of the diffusion of new means of distinction is, of course, not reducible to the peaceful circulation of products or styles. Foreign elements commonly gained ground through conquests and domination, either between neighbours or within the context of large-scale imperialism. More often than not, the codes of the victors defined the upper levels of the societies they colonised. Yet, there are great variations in the way in which interactions occurred. For instance, when Europeans expanded their commercial and colonial presence almost everywhere, they proved more or less inclined to inculcate their own ways. French and British colonial officers were certainly convinced of the superiority of their own civilisations, but whereas the former often wanted to transform the population they were controlling in the name of principles endowed with universal ambition, the latter typically thought that any endeavour to make natives 'British' was hopeless. If we look at different types of actors involved in the colonial process, dissimilarities are all the more obvious. It could make sense for missionaries or merchants to impose Western clothes in the name of decency or commercial interests. However, in the eyes of some settlers, the acquisition of imported items by traditional or new local elites – and notably consumerism for status – was perceived as potentially threatening to their own dominant position. From the native point of view, the intrusion of novel logics of distinction also prompted contrasted responses. Foreign goods were frequently adopted because they were simply superior in quality, in order to fight a complex of inferiority or merely because new needs had been initiated. The first generation educated in the missions south of the Sahara often adopted European-style items and behaviour. They became those first civil servants, doctors, lawyers and teachers enthusiastically elaborating their own identities in reference to that of the colonisers with whom they were collaborating.[14] Nevertheless, there was resistance as well, against the spread of what were perceived as harmful, alien influences – in some cases from the very beginning, but more commonly after a few generations, within a context of frustration and of rising nationalist feelings extolling a return to 'authenticity'.

To judge from numerous writings produced on this topic, it would be possible to characterise such encounters essentially in terms of colonial ascendancy and acculturation versus more or less active opposition and rejection (including boycotts and autos-da-fé of imported products). However, comparative perspectives reveal colonial situations in all their diversity and, for what is of particular concern here, clear differences concerning the relation of prestige to external symbols. World history is not without illustrations of conquerors being conquered, so to speak, by the more refined styles of life of their conquests. Despite their outstanding military or technological superiority, the invaders absorb some aspects of the culture of the colonised. In some cases, dominant countries indeed owed part of their sophistication to the inspiration of the people they once defeated.[15] It can also be emphasised that the forced 'Westernisation' of the apex of some societies, accompanied by the strict abolition of traditional items or practices deemed inferior, was sometimes the result of local rulers' will, and not of a foreign imposition.[16]

Relating the key manifestations of elite distinction to the question of the adoption of imported signs offers illuminating insights into the diversity of representations. Ethnological and historical monographs are replete with amazing instances of syncretism.[17] Borrowings and acclimatisation have been common occurrences, but significant misunderstandings were also involved. It was certainly possible for a Maharajah to purchase an impressive coach 'made in England', to adorn it with gold, silver and the most precious stones, and even to have it pulled by elephants, but it proved unthinkable to let the coachman sit above his master. Likewise, there was mutual incomprehension between European elites who wanted jewels to be as sparkling as possible (which could require substantial re-cutting) and Indian ones for whom size and weight were paramount. The symbolic world of grand eating is also symptomatic of noteworthy differences, with upper groups always being in search of novelties (as a major ingredient of their distinction) in certain contexts, whereas others feel revulsion for exotic tastes and remain attached to those meals that help them define their own status or class identity.[18] An interesting sub-theme is that of exporters, such as traders, diplomats or foreign artisans. It appears that in Western Europe, inter-dynastic marriages have played a key role in the diffusion of some products or habits. To take a single example, it is argued that the possible effect of superiority conveyed by a perfectly mastered immobility when giving an audience passed from the court of Spain to that of France in this way. It is of course the task of the comparativist to establish parallels; one may go as far back as the pharaohs, or think about the ritualised stillness of the Mikado, not to mention the imperturbability of dominant apes emphasised by ethologists.

Other relevant sub-themes include the topics of paragons and reference groups (to be discussed in the following chapter) and those of legitimacy and social consideration, which can prove quite complex. To return to the question of manners, in colonial settings distinction could involve constant references to the standards of the metropolis, including for those members of the most westernised sections of the native society who had the impression of representing a bastion of civilisation. Toward social inferiors, however, this could lead to either endlessly taking note of bad behaviour, or to ostentatiously turning a blind eye. Furthermore, particularly, in contexts characterised by a climate of relative uncertainty regarding the conventions of propriety, logics of distinction could be quite indeterminate.[19] Here, Eliasian or Bourdieusian reading grids are not of great help.

The advent of globalised patterns?

There is no doubt that the current process of globalisation widens horizons more than ever before. This involves the accelerated diffusion of products, but also a growing awareness of living standards and an increasing acuteness of cross-comparisons. Seen from a social distinction perspective, the extension of knowledge about other elites' marks of superiority is not an entirely new phenomenon and many authors justi-fiably make reference to previous, similar, trends (during the sixteenth or nineteenth centuries). In the 1950s, economist Ragnar Nurske (1958, pp. 58 ff.) did not hesitate to broaden the application of Duesenberry's concept of 'demonstration effect' (cf. Chapter 2 above) to the inter-national level, which may be related, or not, to a Veblenian approach in terms of conspicuousness (James, 1987). However, the current scale of circulation is of course unprecedented and there are several issues here. The first is to what extent the introduction of new patterns of distinction makes sense toward social subordinates within each given context. Because of globally extending media, people (from various lev-els) certainly become more familiar with foreign logics of standing, and notably with the lifestyles of the most advanced countries' elites, which are frequently overrepresented. Nevertheless, the question remains over how they are actually perceived, understood and appraised (see, e.g. Wilk, 1990). The second issue concerns intra-elite competition world-wide. There is a pervasive conviction that globalisation has conspired to create a sort of trans-national way of life and notably to dissemin-ate 'Western values'. That the same luxury shops can be found in all the major arcades or airport duty-free sections in thousands of cities is an example of this. Nevertheless, quite often, instead of drawing elites from various countries together, the attraction for certain goods associ-ated with success in other climes is liable to emphasise serious gaps, and even to render some elites ridiculous in the eyes of others when they use such goods inappropriately.[20]

One possible line of attack in dealing with this topic consists in resorting to the classic sociological differentiation between 'locals' and 'cosmopolitans' (Merton, 1949). Whereas the former confine their inter-ests to their community, the latter are ostensibly oriented to the world outside: they may reside somewhere but largely define themselves in reference to a wide range of external models. Obviously, ecumenical awareness is likely to be dependant upon the fact that one can afford to multiply experiences, to travel extensively or at least to show a cer-tain degree of curiosity with regard to the rest of the world; but what is implied is more than just greater resources or open-mindedness. It should be added that localism and cosmopolitanism are not necessarily exclusive. A Goffmanian approach keeping a close watch on concrete interactions might be appropriate here, in so far as social actors are apt often to prove themselves differently, according to the persons with whom they are momentarily in touch.[21] If, in some settings, a mere plastic bag referring to a foreign brand may carry more status than a locally produced handbag (as used to be the case in the USSR), it must be acknowledged that certain indigenous elements do not cease to be prestige. Indeed, some goods or attitudes have a durable distinguishing value that is peculiar to a specific milieu. What is at stake in such a situation is not a matter of choice between well-known global makes but of proudly asserting (allegedly) 'authentic' identities. Here, it may certainly be relevant to consider the spread of consumerism, and the possible desire to emulate elites from other places, in terms of (in)compatibilities with some traditional values or fundamental beliefs.[22] In this respect, however, it is indispensable to go beyond official principles and to take actual practices into account, including possible compromises with the dominant codes.[23]

In between strategies of 'accumulation of otherness'[24] and the fidelity to some habitual registers of distinction, most authors pay particular attention to the reinterpretation of imported status symbols in accordance with local views. The idea is that if some commodities indeed circulate widely, they are ultimately 'localised' in order to generate contextually relevant cultural meanings (Appadurai, e.g. 1986, 1995). Far from producing a general homogenisation, globalisation would therefore be mediated by many inflections. The abundant literature on consumption and cultural identities oscillates between ethnographic studies eager to show the limits of readings in terms of global hegemony, and others which posit that we should not lose sight of some common mechanisms.[25]

In any case, what is striking is the fact that despite the influence of trans-national actors (from international corporations to hybrid diasporas), the above-mentioned phenomenon of *selection* from exogenous possibilities is not seriously on the wane. People at the peak of societies, all over the world, may show interest in a variety of signs of superiority that perhaps might contribute to giving the impression that they belong to international high circles able to identify them as elites, beyond their respective origins. They may endeavour, especially, to obtain those products which have the reputation of being the finest.[26] However, this does not mean that absolutely everything will be judged acceptable. In this regard, it is fascinating to see, for instance, how Arab elites willingly resort to many Western status symbols but would reject the ones liable to threaten their own identity, or how wealthy Japanese acquire some foreign items without really making use of them.[27]

Besides, it should be emphasised that certain prized commodities, or services, play a crucial role in some societies and are therefore more valued than in others. One may think of education in prestigious establishments and exclusive club membership in England or in the United States, of elegant clothing in France and Italy, prestige cars in Germany, dwellings in Scandinavian countries, luxurious eating in China, etc. It appears that at the upper level, social actors particularly try to project a desirable image to others through these attributes.[28] One might be tempted to dismiss such aspects at once because they would amount to mere stereotypes. However, although prevailing stereotypes are crude simplifications of complex realities, they often contain an element of truth and researchers should compare them to realities that can be observed objectively. For instance, statistics prove that Scandinavians indeed spend much more on interior decoration than other Europeans (Löfgren, 1990, pp. 19 ff.) and a presentable, cosy, well-equipped home definitely occupies a central place in cross-perceptions.[29] To give a second example, in small Indonesian towns, conspicuous leisure is key: some distinguished persons, who otherwise may be very casually dressed, ostentatiously take tea at 10 a.m. when the bulk of the population is at work. This indirectly raises the issue of what is deemed not, or less, important – and opens a whole field for further study.

9
Beyond Reductionism

This last chapter pursues our discussion on variability by considering other key themes concerning the explanatory value of the general theories previously introduced. Among those dimensions which are important to an understanding of divergent manifestations of elite distinction, we would like to examine the relative value placed upon quantity and quality, as well as the complex matter of style in relation to dominant representations. The principal issue is, of course, not that of endless evaluations of the various thinkers, but to present evidence suggesting that more attention should be paid to diversity.

On profusion and sophistication

Some historians interested in social distinction with regard to food and drink have put forward a relevant division between (traditional) quantitative ostentation – feasting and the ability to satisfy the appetite of many guests – and a more modern emphasis on quality involving gastronomic and aesthetic aspects.[1] Although not all specialists are inclined to acknowledge such a linear evolution,[2] we are faced with a very fascinating subject from a comparative perspective. As we shall see, the question of profusion versus sophistication can be generalised to many other prestigious goods, but also to vicarious forms of distinction.

Since Hume [1752], if this topic is considered at all, it is often in a normative way; modern times are viewed as 'more civilised' and as attaching more importance to refinement. The significant question, for our purposes, is whether socially dominant actors tend to demonstrate their own eminence, and to judge that of others, by the number or the quality of what they possess. From an analytical point of view, it is pertinent to differentiate between various dimensions of quantitative superiority.

What may be taken into account is the number of properties (such as several estates), their impressive size (e.g. a stretched limousine) or visible accumulation. According to Baudrillard (1981 [1972, pp. 26–28]), (petit-)bourgeois distinction would most often entail redundancy and saturation, with a desire to underline what one owns (double curtains, multiple tablecloths, flowerpot holders, mats). What may be at stake is also variety or completeness.[3] Likewise, as Duesenberry (1949, Chapter 3) reminds us, quality may refer to various aspects, such as technical or aesthetic superiority.

In the following pages, we will return to the different manifestations of elite superiority presented in Part II and consider them in relation to these quantitative/qualitative expressions. This will allow us to point to the existence of several factors of complexity. Let us begin with adornment. Quantity here may refer either to the abundance of drapery used (the large number of flounces being shown, for example) or to the assortment of dress at one's disposal.[4] In certain contexts, what will mark superiority of position is not only being able to avoid wearing the same outfit on two consecutive days, or more than a few times in total, but also not to be dressed in anything that resembles clothing recently displayed by others in one's circle. Quality may be related to prestigious materials, exquisite cut, stylish accessories, etc. However, several of the dissimilarities emphasised in the previous chapters immediately come to mind. For instance, following fashion may, or may not, command social admiration. Fidelity to a certain style and even sometimes deliberately dressing down may carry more status than other attitudes. Given the extreme variability of the patterns of meanings involved, it proves quite difficult to provide credible generalisations. It would certainly be a mistake to look for any systematic homology between 'showy clothes' and nouveaux riches, or between discreet elegance and well-established elites. Admittedly, excesses in quantitative ostentation, far from enhancing one's image, may be interpreted in a Bourdieusian way as a fear of seeming to have too few and as betraying a complex. Instead of putting on all one's finery, it may be considered more judicious to sport just one or two extremely precious stones. This, however, returns to another theme mentioned earlier: that of meaningfulness – would the audience be competent enough to appreciate the value of a limited display? As far as clothing is concerned, many differences in quality are subtle and, particularly in the domain of jewellery, what is needed is indeed a tutored eye. In his work on the Chicago suburbs, Marcus Felson (1978) rightly asks whether clothing, cars and place of residence effectively communicate status when a large portion of the population cannot recognise the most prestigious makes or agree about how residential areas rank. With the increasing confusion of lifestyles emphasised by analysts of postmodernity, the ability to decipher symbolic hierarchies is even more problematic.

With regard to residences, quantitative aspects refer firstly to the number of houses one has. In the past, it was often symbolically crucial for rulers to own multiple castles in order to manifest their presence in various parts of their territory, or (as in the Middle East) to mark important political evolutions. In more modern contexts, what has usually been involved is ownership of at least one house in the city plus a 'cottage' in the country or a similarly pleasant resort and, for the 'ultra rich', mansions all over the world (see Packard, 1989). As already mentioned, quantitative intensification also concerns the size of the residences and what they contain. The accumulation of mirrors, carpets, curtains and swags or protective covers for chair legs may certainly be interpreted along Veblenian ('conspicuous consumption') or Baudrillardian ('redundancy of signs') lines. However, other readings are equally eligible.[5] Baudrillard himself (1981 [1972, p. 80]) admits that bareness (e.g. an empty wall) might be a sign of superiority; the question is whether austerity is a deliberate choice or imposed by a serious lack of resources. Thorough research into the topic indeed produces many intricate examples.[6] As for qualitative dimensions, they may include, *inter alia,* exclusive access to beautiful countryside, which can easily be analysed in terms of 'positional goods' competition.[7]

The study of vehicles as signs of distinction may be used to reveal other kinds of complexity. As we saw in Chapter 4, qualitative dimensions prove rather diverse and contradictory. From a quantitative perspective, aristocrats of the past could take pride in having many coaches and beautiful horses at their disposal, and what is involved in the present time is, of course, the possession of several cars. These will include perhaps a limousine for prestige and comfort, a sports vehicle for pleasure and display, an SUV for off-road driving, and a smaller city 'runabout'. Such a collection may be understood in terms of a search for distinct sensations (Edensor, 2004, p. 116) or as a desire to express various identities, symptomatic of postmodern consumption (Gartman, 2004, p. 192). Whatever the case, multiple ownership is likely to contribute to a blurring of image. From a theoretical point of view, it may be argued that when quantitative distinction involves elements that are not displayed simultaneously, the impression given by one (in this case a vehicle, but the same would apply for clothes or residences) might not be equivalent to that conveyed by others. Things become even more complicated when one takes into consideration the smaller vehicles possibly owned by other members of the family. A Mini may be the one and only car in the household, or it may be the fourth car in a Bentley-owning affluent family.[8] For neighbours and others who are well aware of the four-car garage and of what vehicles are contained in it, there will be no uncertainty, but in the eyes of strangers looking solely at the Mini, doubts might be raised. Commentators following a Bourdieusian approach will be tempted to say that what essentially counts, after all, is habitus and self-confidence, but this does not hold true everywhere. In order to add further relativism, one might evoke the intriguing case of elites who own several completely identical cars, as can sometimes be witnessed in Switzerland.

A comparative perspective – whether through direct observations or explorations within the widespread literature about various parts of the world and periods – introduces us to a wide array of representations about quantitative and qualitative display. To come back to culinary aspects, it is worth noting that in a country such as Nigeria, what is of enduring importance is quantity (with, for instance, piles of chicken, or hundreds of bottles of beer shared with followers), whereas research in the neighbouring Benin Republic shows that a local 'Big Man' may proudly display well-thought-out menus printed in advance and serve three types of Champagne with *petits fours* for dessert.[9] Within the domain of 'embodied signs of superiority' it is not difficult to emphasise heterogeneity as well. For example, a subtle perfume and a delicate use of cosmetics purporting to create a 'natural' look are probably expected in Paris and many other Western capital cities, but a face smothered in make-up undoubtedly makes sense in some places.[10]

As regards 'vicarious display', is it more impressive to keep an army of unqualified servants or to enjoy the service of a model valet (see Sombart, 1967 [1913], pp. 59, 91–92), to belong to as many social clubs as possible, or just to the most prestigious one, or to possess a few high-quality art-works or hundreds of lesser value?[11] Let us revisit here part of the subject of glamorous female company. From antiquity (where many rulers had hundreds of sexual partners at their disposal) to Kim Jong Il's 'joy brigades' in contemporary North Korea, polygyny has been practised in many civilisations, and regimes, throughout history. The 'harem' (or its equivalent) was of particular importance as a symbol of prestige and as an instrument of power. This quantitative dimension was designed not only to project an image of (supposed) exceptional virility and constantly renewed pleasure, but also to flaunt allegiance (many prominent households being eager to offer one of their daughters) and to produce countless descendants.[12] It is interesting to contrast the logics of distinction through 'hyper-sexuality' (one thinks of the mythical figure of Don Juan and his famous list kept by his servant) to more qualitative logics. In contexts where the lady's consent has increasingly become essential, what matters is to be able to seduce the most beautiful or most coveted women.[13] Simmel (1984 [1909], p. 150) emphasises the fact that whereas it is no longer possible 'to possess all the attractive women [...] flirtation is a remedy for this condition', a kind of substitute which can remain symbolically significant because 'the individual man *could* possess a large number of women' (emphasis added) and vice versa.

It would seem legitimate to conclude that what needs to be fully explored are the local modalities of appreciation of qualitative/quantitative distinction. Quantitative display may lose efficacy in certain cultural conditions, but not necessarily everywhere (see, e.g. Oushakine, 2000, about contemporary Russia). The same holds true in respect of two fundamental themes which lie at the heart of the study of social distinction: codes and styles.

On dominant codes and styles

In everyday language, as in scholarly analysis, the notion of style is rather confusing. Originally designating an instrument used by the ancients for writing on waxed tablets, it ambiguously refers to singularity as well as to shared forms of appearance. For instance, in the expression 'to live in style' distinctiveness is certainly denoted. However, it must be questioned whether we are talking of conformity to certain recognised standards, of a quest after particularity or of a mode of living implicating opulent and artful display. Some of the classics mentioned above – Simmel rather more than others – have struggled to disentangle the various dimensions implicated, not unequivocally at times.[14] Beyond lasting problems of definitional clarity, what can be emphasised from our comparative perspective is that in most traditional, holistic contexts, the idea of a range of styles rarely makes sense. In some others (e.g. some collectivist regimes), heterogeneity is strongly discouraged for ideological reasons. In many 'pre-modern' cases, freedom of style was a privilege of the elites. In more modern settings, we witness a tension between distinction expressed through the adoption of conventional goods, or adherence to certain norms enhancing one's sense of social significance, and attempts to be visible through originality or alternative styles.[15] In postmodern environments, according to some analysts, the issue is no longer blindly following existing models but being 'in harmony with oneself', which may involve practices of 'self-fashioning' and selections among a mixture of products and lifestyles corresponding to one's, allegedly distinct (and potentially changeable), individuality. Many sub-themes are implicitly present here: dominant representations, hegemonic models, reference groups, deviation from the norms, taste, tailoring, individuation, sub-cultural affiliations and manipulated or creative consumers, to name a few. As is immediately apparent, they are likely to be interpreted in vastly different ways between one theoretical framework and another. Before we discuss some of these sub-themes, it is appropriate to give a sense of the relativity of conceptions by returning yet again to our key manifestations.

Nowhere is the multi-faceted play between social differentiation, uniformity and originality more evident than in the domain of sartorial symbols. Status claims in attire might result in respecting dress codes scrupulously, perhaps overdressing for certain occasions; they might also involve insinuation through understatement, painstakingly following fashions, expressing defiance of conventional standards or even distinction by deliberate solecism, etc.[16] As we saw in Chapter 1, Simmel drew attention to the possible contradiction between communicating class membership (which frequently requires adherence to collective styles) and yearnings for personal visibility.[17] What elites principally have in mind must be investigated in empirical studies: a conformist demonstration of status orchestrated by tradition (or accepted fashionability), a desire for conspicuousness vis-à-vis fellow members of the upper groups, the display of individualised taste, etc. The danger here is that of dogmatic reductionism to one of the models of interpretations presented above: that is considering that it would always be about a Simmelean tension between representing the standards of one's group and the pretension of having a personal style; or attitudes being essentially dictated by concrete situations and interactions; or about systematically construing the selection of clothes as premeditated strategies; or in terms of wearers' habitus.[18] A comparative perspective is likely to point to the helpfulness, or the uselessness, of the various reading grids available according to the contexts studied. For instance, eccentricity may, or may not, make sense. It can be emphasised that, with the ambiguous exception of the nineteenth-century dandies who attempted to reveal the highest degree of individuality, image building through resorting to radical singularity is a rather exceptional phenomenon.[19] Originality often involves at best odd associations (e.g. adding some accessories that seem to contradict an overall impression) or miscellaneous touches of individuality combined with attire that reflects what each society considers acceptable. A key variable is to what extent we are dealing with tailor-made, designer apparel (with labels conspicuously affixed on the outside, or not) or more widespread ready-to-wear?

The study of residences as chief indicators of social positions leads to similar conclusions. If the pursuit of unusual styles and individualist competition is well represented, it is far from being a universal phenomenon. In the United Kingdom and North America, some upper-class people do not mind at all living in residential areas where houses are built according to single (high status) model. Quite on the contrary, it appears that such coherence brings a comforting impression to these groups.[20] Indeed, when a resident dares to show some external signs of individuality (painting an entrance door in yellow, or having an unconventional front lawn), s/he risks court action in so far as this is prone to disqualify the whole place from collective social status.[21] In the domain of vehicles, apart from a few possibilities of 'customising', concrete potentials for personal distinction are much more limited. Within a universe of standardised production, only some limited options are available. However, if we follow those psycho-sociologists who apprehend cars as 'self-extensions', there are strong grounds for thinking that owning strikingly unusual or embellished models plays a certain role as regards image management. On the other hand, one is struck by the discovery that social success may be symbolised by strongly mimetic attitudes.[22]

That the links between elite distinction, originality and conventionality are complex is also evident, for example, in the realm of physical appearance. Despite a general process of individualisation – strongly emphasised by historians working on the Western world – what can be observed is a durable tension between a desire to conform to canonical ideals of beauty and more individualistic styles. The latter may consist in going as far as deliberately accentuating uncommon features, or at least as using cosmetics in a singular fashion to suit one's face. In other words, self-confident attractiveness may be related to the fact that one conforms to certain beauty standards or to the proud affirmation of a divergent look. Likewise, regarding gesture, if some postures are powerfully codified, especially on the most formal occasions (one thinks, for instance, of 'audience restraint' during classical music concerts), it is also possible to make a statement through unorthodox body language under certain circumstances (see Douglas, 1970). We could offer many other illustrations. Once again, our intention is not to reason in terms of social/cultural contingency, and even less of parochial arbitrariness, but to lay emphasis on how elite dramaturgy may refer either to recognisable or 'extra-ordinary' modes of distinction.

A question inescapably raised here is that of who determines the standards of superiority and, for what concerns us more precisely, to what extent the elites of any given society are the ultimate arbiters of legitimate codes and styles. Admittedly, distinction characteristics often find their supreme expression at the higher echelons of the social ladder, and they clearly matter in the face of the respective attitudes of subordinate groups likely to compare more or less unfavourably. However, when reading some social theorists – notably Bourdieu's (1984 [1979]) analyses on taste or the early Baudrillard (1996a [1968]), who reasoned in terms of 'totalitarian codes of standing' – one is given the impression of having transposed to this symbolic domain the universalistic statement according to which 'the ideas of the ruling class are in every epoch the ruling ideas' (Marx and Engels, 1998 [1845]). From a comparative perspective, the view that indicators of prestige would always be defined by the 'dominant classes' and thus hegemonically serve as references for the whole of society is of course unacceptable. There are several ways to demonstrate this.

Firstly, hegemonic attempts (if observable at all) may prove more or less successful. As was already hinted when we discussed Tarde's model of imitation, subordinate groups do not always consider upper classes as exemplary. One may be proud of belonging to a social group which does not stand at the top rung of the ladder and keep up with symbolic conventions corresponding to that level.[23] Historically, there are certainly many examples of imposition of arbitrary elitist patterns, established with a view to fitting some (more or less enviable) traits embodied by an incumbent ruler, but they rather concerned intra-elite behaviour.[24] Even if, in some cultural settings, social actors quite evidently wish to see themselves as associated with the kind of people (and standards) they perceive as prevalent, reasoning exclusively in terms of dominant representations – akin to ideology – runs the risk of seriously simplifying empirical realities. As 'social identity theory' shows, for instance, low self-esteem may lead to following the model of the dominant 'out group', but it may also entail the formation of alternative, positive identities.[25] Another type of objection that may be put forward against the basic premise of upper-class hegemonic norms is the possible multiplicity of reference models. When several elites are competing, standards of superiority are potentially quite diverse for outside aspirants aiming to improve their status. As far as this bottom-up perspective is concerned, the concept of 'reference groups' remains useful for comparativists, provided they enquire extensively as to which model of behaviour, or consumption, groups are actually exposed (beyond that of the local upper class) from the nearest spheres to the remotest ones, directly or through the media, and how they concretely perceive these various paragons.

Furthermore, as was emphasised in several passages of this volume, the impact of the 'postmodern' pluralised culture, with its highly segmented worlds, has probably contributed to undermining the putative hegemony of elite models. It is not only that some contemporary societies would be characterised by 'self-identity bricolage' and become a collection of 'lifestyle enclaves' (Bellah et al., 1985) or fluid 'neo-tribes'.[26] What is emerging is a world in which everyone and every style is becoming increasingly respectable and where, paradoxically, even the most dominated desperately looking for consideration and dignity may become infatuated with the very signs that used to stigmatise them. When the latter are adopted by members of other strata, this may almost lead to a complete reversal of the former distinction processes. However, this is only one side of the coin. It might be more difficult than before 'to predict class position from cultural taste, or vice versa. But distinction is not yet extinguished' (Warde, 2002, p. 199). It is quite possible for a rapper to gain recognition and approval when performing his music, but to be rejected because of the very same look a few hours later under other circumstances (e.g. when being interviewed for a job). Elites are probably no longer the indisputable leaders for style but many scarce goods largely continue to serve as status symbols.

This explains why the literature on social distinction has remained so controversial – which is patently obvious in the field of taste, and especially that of cultural consumption.[27] Partly because these ambiguous evolutions are manifest within sectors such as that of music, and because the Bourdieusian scheme continues to focus attention – whether single-school-bound works aim at defending or rejecting it – we witness endless disputes. Peremptory pro- or anti-Bourdieusian positions have to be regarded as reductionist most of the time. However, fundamental disagreements have also contributed to the development of most relevant researches. One has in mind, notably, the stimulating reflections on 'omnivorous orientations', which have brought very interesting empirical data to bear on such debates. Has eclecticism replaced the opposition between highbrow and lowbrow culture, and to what extent does this reflect openness or a new criterion for expressing distinction?[28] As usual, a comparative perspective allows us to gain some helpful distance. Without pretending to examine these issues in any detail here, it is appropriate to recall that a differentiation between upper- and lower-class sub-cultures is more or less discernible from one society to the next. When considered in a dynamic fashion, the possible rejection by elites of certain norms, attitudes or tastes which used to be shared with the rest of a population is often the result of a gradual, and more or less accomplished project.[29] Equally, it is important to insist on the fact that in certain holistic environments those who stand at the top might be expected to epitomise the 'proper' standards of the whole society. Against the one-sided view implicit within the paradigm of domination, it is also possible to see this exemplarity in terms of constraints, as was suggested in Chapter 3.

Another way of underlining the complexity of 'legitimate' codes consists in stressing that the prevailing direction of taste formation is not systematically 'top-down'. Both Simmel and Sombart insisted that flamboyant *demi-mondaines* frequently had more influence on contemporary ideals of beauty than females from the upper circles. Likewise, famous stage actresses, and later film stars (who, remarkably, often had a lower class background fostering feelings of identification for large sectors of society) contributed to imposing new standards.[30] Moreover, paragons are not reducible to class logics only; they may concern prestigious capital cities in contrast with provincialism, among others. It might be objected that what is at stake is still a matter of domination. Nonetheless, the prestige of *'la Parisienne'* during the nineteenth century, for instance, was far from being exclusively related to members of the elite.

One of the most fascinating phenomena for students of elite distinction is that of 'trickle-up' processes, that is the adoption by the dominant social classes of items denoting lower-class membership. To take examples in the domain of dress, illustrations include folk costume, overalls, tank tops, rolled collars, tattoos or miniskirts borrowed by elites from peasants, factory workers, sailors, dockers and teenage girls in Soho. Various hypotheses have been proposed by semioticians working on fashion, such as convenience, trendiness and erotic display.[31] Proponents of the competing schools of thought have been anxious to offer explanations theoretically consistent with their respective analytical frameworks. From a postmodern viewpoint, these trends would be symptomatic of societies witnessing a deconstruction of symbolic hierarchies and the emergence of a constellation of complex meanings and playful identities. In contrast, according to Bourdieusian scholars, this process is by no means new (a classic example being Marie-Antoinette's *hameau*) and is routinely interpreted in terms of caprice or *encanaillement*,[32] that is a 'recreational' and temporary 'consumption of poverty' which would still pertain to a 'class distinguishing activity' (Halnon, 2002). Here, in other words, if the occurrence cannot be denied, the idea is that the above-mentioned clothes would be adopted only after having been diverted ironically from their original signification. To judge from high-quality rustic straw hats, expensive, torn, designer jeans prominently displaying prestigious labels (see, e.g. Davis, 1989), or 'Dr Marten's boots' adorned with coloured feathers, lace and pearl buttons, 'poor chic' remains ambiguous.

With these 'trickle-up' strategies (as well as with so many other aspects regarding elite distinction) we require inductive work aimed at deciphering contextually meaningful codes, not ubiquitous interpretations. Instead of attempting to account for all sorts of heterogeneous instances under the framework of one canonical theory, what is needed is a resort to models of interpretation in a judicious, non-dogmatic, way.

Conclusion

For all the efforts of a handful of pioneering scholars, the comparative analysis of elite distinction is still in its infancy. Empirical facts are seldom put side by side, and it is even less common to find works driven primarily by a comparative ambition.

The principal contribution of this book has been to confront the major theoretical frameworks with empirical evidence available across time and space. The conclusion seems evident. Researchers have no convincing grand theory to which they can systematically cling. As has been emphasised throughout, this does not mean, however, that the reading grids discussed above are irrelevant when it comes to explaining observable processes. It only means that they should be considered as more or less operational analytical tools, according to the contexts studied, and therefore should be applied appropriately.

It is hoped that this volume will stimulate reflection and encourage future research on a topic which needs more comparative investigations.

Notes

Introduction

1. This triple meaning can be found in various languages – the last one being more recent (from the nineteenth century).
2. Following, notably, the classic texts of Pareto, Mosca or Michels. On elites and elitism, see Field and Higley (1980).
3. On social distinction at the very bottom, see, e.g. MacEwen (1974, p. 212) about façades in Argentine shantytowns. From a comparative perspective, it may be argued that elite distinction is a widespread phenomenon, whereas social distinction (involving symbolic struggles at various levels) presupposes a strongly stratified society.
4. See notably Geertz (1973; 1993 [1983]) and his stress on meanings.
5. We have in mind what has been called in France 'Histoire des mentalités' and in the English world what is known as the 'New Cultural History' (see Hunt, 1989; Burke 1997; 2004). From a political science perspective, cf. also Chabal and Daloz (2006).
6. It is important to insist upon the fact that culture is here understood (following Geertz, 1973) not as values and norms but as that which enables individuals to be mutually intelligible. It is thus possible to belong to the same culture and to have radically different values – as is often the case in (post-)modern societies with a high degree of differentiation.

1 Classical Approaches to Social Emulation and Distinction

1. Plato (1941 [fourth century BC], Book II).
2. Aristotle (2002 [fourth century BC], Book IV/chapters 2 and 3).
3. Aristotle (1991 [fourth century BC], Book II/chapters X, XI and XVI respectively). One may connect such a view to his well-known warnings against oligarchy in contrast with the rule of the *aristoi* (i.e. the few best persons), never losing sight of the general interests of the city.
4. Demosthenes (1990 [363 BC]). Meidias was a wealthy and influential Athenian who had offended him.
5. This may be related to 'primitivist' theories of decline, most common in ancient thought: see Lovejoy and Boas (1980 [1935]). According to these, the first men were the best since they lived in a state of primeval equality; with the 'invention of property' and the 'discovery of gold', the ambition to have more possessions and distinction than one's neighbour would have unfortunately arisen. Lucretius', *De Rerum Natura*, V (1969 [first century BC]) or the *Annals* of Tacitus (2005 [second century AD]) contain typical presentations of this kind of evolutionist theory.
6. Cicero (1977 [63 BC]).

7. Epictetus, *Enchiridion* (1991 [second century AD], p. 39).
8. This does not apply to Epictetus; but Seneca or Sallust, for instance, sometimes fell prey to what they were stigmatising.
9. Swift (1808 [1708], p. 110).
10. On the history of the idea of luxury, and the above-mentioned eighteenth-century change, see, e.g. Berry (1994); Berg and Eger (2003).
11. Voltaire's, Hume's and Montesquieu's texts can easily be found on the Internet.
12. However, several prominent anthropologists from various generations have paid homage to Spencer's pioneering work: cf. Carneiro (1981). For a general presentation, see Low-Beer's (1969) or Andreski's (1971) readers.
13. To illustrate this point, Tarde insisted on the crucial role of 'Great Men', who make history, whereas Spencer, being far more deterministic, regarded them as inconsequential. An important caveat is in order. In this theoretical part, the concern is almost exclusively with divisions related to the analysis of (elite) distinction. The various disagreements between analysts belonging to different theoretical traditions will be alluded to here, but detailed considerations are obviously beyond the scope of this volume.
14. More precisely, at the very basis of his explanatory scheme stand some psychological principles such as belief/desire, invention and inter-psychological relations. These principles (or causes) produce effects: imitation, opposition and adaptation. On Tarde's grand theory, see for instance Clarke (1969) or the special issue of *Distinktion* (2004).
15. Following Dorfman's (1966 [1934]) voluminous biography, Riesman (1995 [1953]) was to insist upon this 'Norskie' dimension. According to later commentators, it should not be over-emphasised (see principally Edgell, 2001).
16. On this context, see Spindler (2002).
17. Chapters IX and X of *The Theory of the Leisure Class* are entitled respectively: 'The Conservation of Archaic Traits' and 'Modern Survivals of Prowess'.
18. Several other aspects could be considered here, for instance divergent views about the origins of property. On Veblen and Marxism, see Diggins (1978).
19. About Veblen's dissolute life, cf. Jorgensen and Jorgensen (1999), which is based on hitherto unpublished documents.
20. He would for instance mention 'certain Polynesian chiefs'; 'a certain king of France' (1994 [1899], pp. 27 and 28).
21. It should be mentioned here that Veblen was the author of 11 books, including important works on business, higher learning in America, engineers and the price system. These, however, are not particularly relevant to our present concern. On the intellectual legacy of Veblen, see Tilman (1992; 1996).
22. Here, an analytical link may obviously be proposed with Tarde's concept of imitation.
23. For a contradictory view, see Levine (1971).
24. Simmel is sometimes presented as a key analyst of modernity (see Frisby, 1992) but postmodernists appreciate his anti-positivism (Weinstein and Weinstein, 1993).
25. As several commentators have pointed out, one complication arises because the German word *stand* (plural *stände*), that Weber uses, may alternatively mean status, estate or prestige grouping. Likewise, the terms *vornehm, vornehmheit* express at the same time the ideas of quality, superiority

or nobleness, but also distinction from a moral, intellectual or cultural perspective – explaining some hesitation over translation.
26. On Sombart's life and scholarly work, the reader may refer to Backhaus (1996).
27. Cf. de Grazia (1996, pp. 19–21).
28. See, e.g. Mukerji (1993); Roberts (1998) and Appadurai (1986).

2 Major Subsequent Contributions

1. On the distinction between greed and craving for a particular kind of wealth, or between hedonism and miserliness, see Bologh (1979, pp. 75 ff.) on these dichotomies.
2. This may be related to one of the major Marxist objections to capitalism: that workers are alienated from what they have created. In his *History and Class Consciousness*, Lukacs (1971 [1923]) further developed this point. Contemporary Marxists consider that costly display by capitalists and top managers not only establishes their symbolic superiority over 'performers' but that the whole system functions as a ruse to induce the latter to work harder (cf., e.g. Resnick and Wolf, 1987, pp. 179–80).
3. For a critique of advertising in capitalist societies following a similar vein (and emphasising the importance of appearance and sexuality), see Haug (1986 [1971]).
4. See for instance Marcuse (1991 [1964], chapter 3). A very interesting piece, here, is Adorno's (1981 [1941]) view of (highbrow) culture as a means of transcending the 'drudgery of industrial life' and not just 'mere ostentation', as Veblen would have it. In one chapter, where he comments upon 'Veblen's Attack on Culture', Adorno goes as far as to write that 'Even the commodity fetishist who has succumbed to conspicuous consumption to the point of obsession participates in the truth-content of happiness' (p. 87).
5. For the sake of completeness, several other major currents of neo-Marxist thought could be mentioned here. We shall come across some more authors, such as Gramsci, Lefebvre and Williams.
6. Functionalist writings are prone to rely on this fundamental dichotomy, which is indeed debatable from a comparative perspective.
7. Noteworthy are the descriptive volume I (Warner and Lunt, 1941) of the 'Yankee City Series'; volume II (Warner and Lunt, 1942) on the status system; volume V (Warner, 1959) on symbolic behaviour; the study of a rural town named 'Jonesville' (Warner and collaborators, 1949), and the methodological opus entitled *Social Class in America* (Warner, Mecker and Eills, 1949).
8. Although, according to Blau and Duncan (1967, p. 5), he might well have never read Weber, Warner can be considered as implicitly Weberian in the sense that he was sceptical about the systematic primacy of economic factors (e.g. Warner, 1953, chapter 3). From the early vitriolic reviews of his work (by Mills for instance) to much more recent critical appraisals (see Goldman and Tickmayer, 1984), Warner was to be rejected continually on these grounds. He did, nonetheless, attempt to demonstrate the existence of *classes* in the United States.

9. Particularly the fundamental distinction between community and society (see Pfautz and Duncan, 1950).
10. See the 140 pages devoted to statistics in the second volume of the 'Yankee Studies Series', or the improbable discussions about 'the members of position 89' (Warner and Lunt, 1942).
11. Form and Stone (1957, p. 504).
12. Cf. his book with Neugarten (1971), where a new methodology related to an 'Index of Urban Status' is developed, or his *Social Standing in America* published with Rainwater (1978) which is dedicated to Warner and combines both qualitative and quantitative approaches.
13. The work of Duncan, who had been fairly critical of Warner's approaches at the beginning of his career, deserves particular mention here. See, e.g. his bestseller on the 'American Occupational Structure' and social mobility, co-authored with Blau (Blau and Duncan, 1967).
14. On Elias's life and work, see Mennell (1989) or van Krieken (1998) for a shorter introduction. Readers may also refer to the German scholar's own autobiography (1994).
15. For Elias, sociology meant the study of interdependent human beings and networks, forming and being shaped by social figurations. These figurations and processes are not the outcome of premeditated action but the product of intertwined socio-political dynamics that actors neither fully control nor comprehend (See Elias, 1978b [1970] and 1982 [1939]).
16. Some specialists of modern European history have notably demonstrated that Elias's interpretations of the French court society were outdated and, at times, wrong (see principally Duindam, 1995), relying as they did on the testimony of the Duke de Saint-Simon, a disappointed and biased aristocrat (Le Roy Ladurie, 1997), and exaggerating the capacity of the king to manipulate the political system for his own purposes. Louis XIV was, after all, as much the product as the architect of Versailles. Others have challenged the idea according to which civility would have originated in the court and passed down to the remainder of society. An alternative model consists in highlighting the importance of the civilised world of some Parisian salons, or that of the provincial academies, in contrast to the relatively depraved world of the court (Gordon, 1994).
17. On Goffman's theoretical ambiguities, see Gonos (1977). These debates are too wide ranging to be addressed here.
18. Bourdieu often accused other theorists (interactionnists and some Weberians) of subjectivism, or excessive objectivism (Durkheimians, old-fashioned structuralists), reductionist economism (Marxists) or excessive relativism (some anthropologists). It is fascinating to see how skilled Bourdieu became at systematically using the argument of each school against the other ones, thereby endeavouring to show the superiority of his own thought.
19. In summary, for Bourdieu, society consists of semi-autonomous fields in which actors draw on economic, cultural and social capital (connections) as a way of competing for supremacy and domination. Constructivist structuralism seeks to propose a sociology of representations depending on objective dimensions, but these representations also contribute to the construction of the social world. For the clearest introduction available on these themes, cf. Bourdieu (1989 [1987]).

20. In this respect he considers the 'middlebrow tastes' of the 'petty bourgeoisie', a class that would show 'cultural goodwill' but without the general ease in social situations characterising the upper classes. At the other extreme, one finds the 'popular taste' of the lower classes, largely determined by 'necessity'. This class analysis also emphasises the existence of intellectual and economic poles as well as the fact that social 'agents' tend to judge others in accordance with the respective composition of their capital.

21. A German scholar by training, Baudrillard was officially a sociologist but he was never fully accepted by academic circles in France. On the other hand, he became a well-recognised intellectual – especially in the United States – admired for the innovative character of his thought-provoking approaches.

22. We are mainly concerned here with writers who analyse objectively the nature and impact of changes found in 'postmodern societies' and not with the postmodernist epistemological movement aimed at challenging Western science and pre-eminence, or to lionise the cultures of the oppressed. For a nuanced view on postmodernity (with references to many authors), see Featherstone (1991).

23. The literature on the decline of material scarcity within post-industrial societies had previously brought forth such issues. See Blumberg (1974).

24. Belk (1988), Dittmar (1992), Cody and McLaughlin (1990), Johnson and Lennon (1999) include many references on these respective themes.

25. For a useful overview of this literature and its numerous refinements, see Suls and Wills (1991).

26. Fascinating experimental research was carried out in this respect: people were asked whether they would rather earn a higher amount of money proportionately inferior to that of their competitors, or a smaller one superior to that of their competitors. Strikingly, the comparative advantage was generally deemed more important than the amount of the actual sum given.

27. For instance, Coleman (the above-mentioned author who adapted Warner's model to large cities) eventually became a professor of marketing and wrote on 'The Continual Significance of Social Class' for this discipline (Coleman, 1983). On reference groups from a marketing theory perspective, see, e.g. Bearden and Etzel (1982).

3 Grand Theories: Limits and Merits

1. For instance, Simmel, who had written two reviews of Tarde's *Les lois de l'imitation*, was to quote him later. Goffman (1951, n3) declares that, to the best of his knowledge, 'the most general approach to the study of status symbols' is Spencer's (1893) work on 'ceremonial institutions' and he also gives a passing reference to Simmel. On their side, functionalists such as Form and Stone (1957) cite Spencer, Weber and Goffman.

2. Elias (1983 [1933], pp. 38 n5, 39 and 67).

3. In his book on the consumer society (1996b [1970, pp. 82–83]), he elaborates on trickle-down mechanisms but without indicating that he draws inspiration from anybody else, although Veblen's *Theory of the Leisure Class* is one of the titles in his bibliography. Likewise, if Mills used to say that

Veblen was the 'the best critic of America that America has produced' (see Horowitz, 2002, p. 107), he also indicated that he had eventually surpassed him with his analysis on *The Power Elite* (Mills, 1956). About Mills criticising Veblen, see Saram (1999, pp. 227–28).

4. We leave aside here the special case of disciples (such as Goffman as a student of Warner).

5. This is surprising, given that Warner's writings would be termed no more than 'a painstaking elaboration of Veblen's *Theory of the Leisure Class*' (Lipset and Bendix, 1951, n1). In fact, Warner was to finally refer to Veblen, but only in the very last volume of the 'Yankee Series' (Warner, 1959, implicitly p. 47, and explicitly p. 241).

6. Equally, one may wonder whether Elias's often cited reference to the episode of the Maréchal de Richelieu throwing a purse out of the window in order to explain his grandson that money is meant to be spent lavishly (Elias, 1983 [1933], p. 67) does not emanate from Sombart (1967 [1913], p. 88) who had used it years before. Actually, both authors quote the same French source (i.e. Taine's *Les origines de la France contemporaine*) but Elias, although providing a more detailed analysis, seems to ignore that the very same episode had already been commented upon in the (German!) sociological literature.

7. Consider for instance Weber's classic evocation of the parvenu rejected by the established status groups (Gerth and Mills, 1991 [1948], p. 192), Sombart's (1967 [1913]) comments on the *Turquarets* – an expression used to refer to vulgar upstarts, Elias's (1982 [1939]) descriptions of bourgeois gaining access to the aristocratic circles but being betrayed by their language, Warner's (1959, p. 46) reflections on the 'understatement of outward forms' demanded by old-family tradition versus 'the parvenu driven by his feelings of anxiety' and Bourdieu's (1984 [1979]) numerous deterministic interpretations in terms of habitus on this subject.

8. Cf. for instance Pinches (1999); Anthias (2001).

9. It is sufficient to give the example of the motorcar being rejected by some British aristocrats who were still very much attached to horse-driven carriages – a major emblem of their superior status for centuries (see Chapter 4).

10. Quoted by Tilman (1992, p. 223).

11. Veblen had indeed met Boas when he was teaching in Chicago. We shall have the opportunity to come back to the Kwakiutl *Potlatch* below.

12. The main exception is when they related superior chances of upward mobility, and low degree of deference between strata, with the stability of democracies: an important theme during the cold war period.

13. In the *Potlatch* system, there were reciprocal obligations between clans and not between individuals. It was the group as a whole, embodied in the person of the chief, that had to give and receive with 'dignity' or indulge in ostentatious 'consumption' (see, e.g. Codere, 1950). In the case of the courtly society, emphasis was placed upon competition between individual elites around the figure of the king, although maintaining the honour of one's household could also matter.

14. Only from the Middle Ages onward, most regrettably. Elias ignores antiquity as well as non-Western societies, which could be quite 'refined'. For criticisms directed at him on manners and civility from different points of view,

see Jaeger (1985), Kasson (1990) or Brambilla (1991). For a nuanced appraisal on the fact that twentieth-century dynamics – like informalisation or female emancipation processes – seem to run counter to Eliasian anticipated trends, see Wouters (e.g. 1977, 2004 and 2007).

15. For instance, what should the reader think of the following statement? 'Thus the higher one's place in the status pyramid, the smaller the number of persons with whom one can be familiar, the less time one spends backstage, and the more likely it is one will be required to be polite as well as decorous' (Goffman, 1958, pp. 81–82).

16. Another well-known exchange system studied by anthropologists, also meant to reinforce status.

17. On this point, see Gergen (1973). It must be acknowledged, however, that new generations of social-psychologists have developed comparative perspectives and are more conscious of cultural disparities when it comes, for instance, to 'power distance' or 'individualism-collectivism' dimensions (cf. many references in Smith and Bond, 1993).

18. It should be recalled that in the preface of the English version of *La Distinction*, Bourdieu did not hesitate to write, 'But I believe it possible to enter into the singularity of an object without renouncing the ambition of drawing out *universal propositions*' (italics added, Bourdieu, 1984, xi).

19. Authors paying heed to American exceptionalism accuse Bourdieu of excessively generalising from the French case. Cf. several contributions in Lamont and Fournier (1992), Halle (1993) and Erickson (1996) showing that higher-status people do not limit their tastes to the highbrow and indulge in many sorts of culture, not just the most elite forms. See also Holt (1997). We will address these debates in Chapter 9.

20. Suffice it to consider the singular realm of Japanese self-presentation and cross-perceptions (see for instance McVeigh, 2000, pp. 20 ff.), or a much less clear differentiation between human beings and objects than in the 'Western' universe.

21. One also finds attempts to rescue some authors who have been unduly criticised on certain aspects. See, e.g. Trigg (2001) on Veblen and Bourdieu.

22. A typical reproach from (neo-)structuralists. We know for instance that Bourdieu criticised scholars who paid too much attention to local meanings for their 'essentialism'. Indeed, the disagreement revolves around this question of meaning: according to the approach advocated here, it is precisely the study of what makes sense, or not, that is of interest from a comparative point of view.

23. Cf. for instance Bronner (1989) and Lears (1994).

24. In an interesting section of *La Distinction* (1979, pp. 271 ff.), Bourdieu considerably developed this theme, and used a fascinating oxymoron: '*l'ostentation de la discrétion*' (278).

25. An extreme example (reported by Leenhardt, 1947) is that of the Canaque chief who refused to wear the uniform distributed by the French colonial power: 'stripes, for me? ... What for? Is it not known that I am the chief?'.

26. This might not be systematically true, as we see in vim Bruke (2005) on the *Maria* elite in Yemen. Needless to say, the theme is appealing whether we consider ancient times or contemporary manifestations, especially in the Arab countries of the Persian Gulf.

27. Admittedly, these features are less pronounced when one considers today's nouveaux riches. Yet, even here, it is important to point out that few will ignore it and that the affirmation of a distinctive style of life is possible mainly outside their native country.
28. See, e.g. Robinson and Goodman (1996) and Pinches (1999).
29. In other words, it is important to avoid falling into the trap of sociologism. One might have in mind here, among others, Bourdieu's concept of habitus: reducing the perceptions and attitudes of 'agents' to their social position and background.

4   External Signs of Superiority

1. It is appropriate to recall that the word ostentation derives from the Latin verb *'ostentare'*: meaning to show with insistence.
2. Dubois (1936).
3. On luxury and necessity from a sociological perspective, see, e.g. Lunt and Livingstone (1992).
4. McKendrick, 'Introduction', in McKendrick, Brewer and Plumb (1982, p. 1). Cf. also Hine (1986).
5. Numerous social scientists rightfully criticise this mono-causal reading (e.g. Goode, 1978, pp. 63–64; Campbell, 1994). Several economists, thinking in terms of 'substantive' and 'symbolic' goods, could equally be cited here. Cf. also Douglas and Isherwood (1979).
6. In this respect, referring to the Veblenian perspective to illustrate his famous distinction between 'manifest' and 'latent' functions, Merton (1957, pp. 68–70) was to differentiate the 'excellence of the good' (manifest function) and the 'mark of higher status' (latent function). It must be admitted, however, that some items are effectively mere signs. The tie is a good illustration.
7. Consequently, both the Bourdieusian and the Veblenian reading grids (respectively in terms of 'ostentatious discretion' and 'conspicuous consumption') may prove applicable.
8. See, respectively, Sullivan and Gershuny (2004); O'Cass and McEwen (2004); Bearden and Etzel (1982).
9. Findings in anthropology and history about material cultures, but also in psycho-sociology about possessions as 'self-extensions' (cf. Dittmar, 1992, for a summary), shed doubts on the supposed universality of perceptions and behaviour.
10. On these aspects, see for instance Khalil (2002), although his typology in terms of 'prestige goods', 'pride goods', 'deference goods' and 'vanity goods' is questionable.
11. Some peoples who rarely wore garments nevertheless developed habits of self-adornment (such as Polynesian tattoos) and a vivid use of partial nudity could carry considerable status.
12. For example, in the middle of the nineteenth century, it became fashionable to wear a wealth of elaborate petticoats that could be glimpsed when the skirt was lifted to cross the street in Paris or London (see Steele, 1985, Chapter 10). Likewise, in his work on 'Pageantry and Power in Yoruba

Costuming', Drewal (1979) shows how the traditional *iro* (that is a loose, outer piece of clothing) requires constant retying, which allows quick looks at the (usually brightly coloured) undergarments. See also Murphy (1964).

13. To give just one illustration, black attire was favoured at the splendid Court of Burgundy because it was the best background to enhance items of jewellery, but also subsequently at the rather austere Spanish one; it was adopted by the seventeenth-century Protestant elite – being wary of garish, self-affirmative colours – and later by the (male) European bourgeoisie as a sign of gravity, differentiating themselves both from the extravagant aristocracy and from social inferiors. Nowadays, sombre, non-distracting colours are still favoured by many politicians and business people wishing to convey an impression of seriousness.

14. See Gandoulou (1989a and 1989b).

15. Resnick and Wolf (1987, p. 179). See also Haug (1986 [1971]) on seductive objects.

16. Think of the literal as well as the figurative sense of the word 'panache' or of the erectness and rigidity of the top hat.

17. The reader is referred to costume historians' works on the attire of elites. See for instance Ewing (1981) or Feltwell (1990). From a more analytical point of view, see Roche (1994 [1989]) or Burman and Turbin (2003), among many others.

18. To take the example of fur: ermine, sable and squirrel were usually monopolised by the highest levels. In England, where hierarchical dressing was essential, lynx and genet were the attribute of dukes, earls and barons.

19. Wolff (1950, pp. 338–44).

20. A relevant topic, e.g., is that of fans, with their elaborated languages.

21. See Rapoport (1982) or Duncan (1981).

22. In a passage of his book on manners in nineteenth-century urban America, Kasson (1990, p. 173) describes several types of 'ceremonial frames' along with the impressions of a visitor penetrating a large residence. Many of them would not be found outside Western cultures.

23. See also Scott (1995), particularly her Chapter 5, entitled 'A World of Distinction'.

24. Warner and Lunt (1941); Warner and collaborators (1949).

25. It should be noted that hugeness and comfort are at times symbolically related: for instance, the many impressive chimneys of Hampton Court Palace were a demonstration of exceptional wealth but they also indicated that many rooms could be warmed in the buildings.

26. Within the mansions of the upper echelons of the English aristocracy, one finds lavishly decorated 'state rooms' that were exclusively kept to accommodate a monarch or the highest officials of the country. The owner and his family therefore had to house themselves in the 'second best' apartments.

27. Cf. Daloz (2002, Chapter 5) on Nigeria. This would also hold true for some Kenyan or South African townships.

28. Cf., e.g. Seeley, Sim and Loosley (1956) about a Canadian case or Congalton (1969) on the status ranking of Sydney suburbs.

29. See, e.g. Borchert and Borchert (2002) about several American cities.

30. The pioneering work is that of F.S. Chapin (e.g. 1928) who tried to measure objectively people's socio-economic status through recording observation

of the equipment, condition (cleanliness and orderliness) and 'cultural expression' of this strategic room. See also, among others, J.A. Davis (1990 [1955]).

31. Consider for instance the case of the kitchen which, in many European countries, was a room that the master of the place would never enter. It later became a living place where well-to-do families could eat on a daily basis (but would never entertain guests). It can now be a large room featuring all the latest gadgets, and may be impressive enough to be opened to view. The status of intermediary places, such as balconies, is also ambiguous.

32. See, e.g. Csikszentmihalyi and Rochberg-Halton (1981).

33. We obviously have in mind, here, the extreme case of Versailles and the role of Le Nôtre who worked on this park over a period of 40 years, but also on several satellite ones, at the request of important members of the aristocracy vying with each other.

34. This tradition is dominated by the figure of 'Capability' Brown (see Turner, 1999 [1985]).

35. The canopy giving way to a roof, glass windows replacing curtains, bodies becoming lighter and therefore faster, etc.

36. On England, see, e.g. Stone (1967) and Watney (1961); on France, e.g. Baury (2002). Nineteenth-century novels are also full of interesting descriptions. Cf. for instance Zola's (1972 [1880]) *Nana*, on the hierarchy of cabriolets in Paris.

37. Particularly the *concours d'élégance*, that is: the parade of well-dressed women in beautiful cars. In the United Kingdom, petrol-fuelled cars were, justifiably, considered smelly and noisy, whereas in France it seems that elites were often more concerned with pollution problems caused by horses.

38. Miller (2001, p. 19) on Trinidad.

39. Such as tourism and the systematic discovery of one's country. On the distinctive style related to such activities at the beginning of the automobile era in the United Kingdom, see O'Connell's (1998) chapter 3 on 'The Right Crowd and No Crowding'.

40. This traditionally neglected topic has been tackled seriously by sociologists in the recent past. See, e.g. Urry (2004).

41. Conversely, especially in car-oriented cultures, not having a personal car, or not being able to drive, may contribute to a sense of social exclusion. This certainly explains why formerly materially deprived populations have been so eager to acquire vehicles and, as far as is possible, big, luxurious ones (cf. Gilroy, 2001, about Afro-Americans).

42. The intention was both to herald the arrival of dignitaries and to make sure that people would respectfully give way. See some illustrations from several continents in Spencer (1893, pp. 27–28).

43. Sometimes with strategies that, however, betray the social origin of the driver. One has in mind for instance the inclination to play extremely loud music while driving. See Bull (2004) on this willingness to be heard.

44. Giving interpretations on these attitudes is not as easy as it might look. 'Subduedness' and (false) modesty may be involved, but for the owner of a relatively small version the reverse could also be true, since observers may think that the car is actually a more prestigious and powerful model.

45. One thinks, e.g., of famous symbolic battles between Greek tycoons about who would have the world's most luxurious yacht.
46. The chromed, incredibly long American cars; the carefully crafted fit and finish of top British ones; the sturdiness and reliability of the German ones and the splendid lines of the ones produced in Italy. The marketing literature aimed at understanding the process of brand preference and image is full of sophisticated analyses in this respect. Studies evidently concern all social levels. See, e.g. Evans (1959) or Birdwell (1968).
47. Personalised registration plates frequently refer to the make of the car (LAMBO), its type (XJS) – for a Jaguar – or may claim supremacy (VIP or EL AJD). So-called 'vanity plates' are not the sole prerogative of elites. For example, in her work on Chicano car culture in New Mexico, Brenda Bright (1998) has a photograph of a registration plate reading '4U2SEE'.
48. Source: personal field research in Vilnius (April, 2008).
49. For instance, finishing what is on one's plate versus imperatively leaving remnants to indicate that one's hunger is amply satisfied; eating slowly with relish, or greedily, to demonstrate one's appreciation.
50. This thesis on appetite is defended by Mennell (1987) following an Eliasian argumentation. There are considerable controversies about food within social theory: between structuralists (notably some anthropologists) favouring the quest for a 'fundamental grammar', and authors much more sensitive to evolutions and cultural variability (principally historians). See for instance Douglas (1984), Goody (1982), Mennell (1985) and Rowley (2006).
51. From the stupendous receptions of the Babylonians or the Roman *'convivium'* to mediaeval celebrations designed to express relations of vassalage, to large banquets in republican France, the intention has often been to reaffirm a socio-political order: expressing loyalties, generosity and deference (Daloz, 1999).
52. See for instance Wiessner and Schiefenhövel (1996), Dietler and Hayden (2001), Strong (2002) or van der Veen (2003).
53. Figurative food, at times strategically allegorical, reached incredible heights during the Renaissance in Italy and at the beginning of the nineteenth century in France. It has also been essential within the Chinese cuisine tradition.
54. See Levenstein (1988, chapters 1 and 5).
55. In Bourdieu's book on Distinction (1984 [1979]), one finds interesting passages about the working-class way of eating (favouring 'filling' food – notably red meat for men) in contrast with classes aiming to exhibit their 'cultural capital'. From a sociology of consumption perspective, cf. Warde (1997).
56. See Warde, Martens and Olsen, 1999 on this debate.

5 Embodied Signs of Superiority

1. It should be recalled that within this scientific field studying animal behaviour, particular attention has been given to social communication among 'hierarchical species'. This had led to the formulation of large-scale theories useful for the understanding on non-verbal signals in challenging

situations. The main idea, for our concern, is that dominant individuals who carry themselves in an upright way display contempt for the risk of rank order contests, and thus are likely to be perceived as claiming some weight by others (see Knipe and Maclay, 1972). On status-related non-verbal cues, see also Ridgeway, Berger and LeRoy (1985).

2. The classic relativist statement is that of Mauss (1973 [1936]). From an anthropological perspective, see Hewes (1955) and especially Birdwhistell (1970). From a cultural history viewpoint, see Bremmer and Roodenburg (1991); Burke (1997a).

3. On his side, Castiglione (1974 [1528]) estimated that courtiers should never seem to be in a hurry, like servants, but not excessively slow either.

4. Including, of course, the question of taste, to be considered later in this work.

5. Dominant stance is perhaps, however, open to a certain amount of imitation. Mauss (1973 [1936]), who stresses the importance of learning, speaks of *'une imitation prestigieuse'* whereby children or adults endeavour to emulate the effective gestures of persons who have authority over them.

6. See for instance Firth (1970).

7. As in the case of the literary example cited by Goffman (1959, Introduction) of a holidaying Englishman on a summer beach who showily carries a Spanish translation of Homer and takes good care to avoid catching anyone's eye. Likewise, the lowering of the eyes may be an expected sign of submission but it may just as well be interpreted as revealing deceit.

8. Burke (1987a, p. 140) underlines that enormous ruffs made conspicuous not only wealth but also the 'sublime detachment' of elites who obviously had no need to bend. On the corset, see Steele (2001).

9. Vigarello, who has written extensively on posture, goes as far as differentiating the 'aristocratic bearing' (heads carried upright, haughty erectness and chest out) one (straight, as opposed to cambered, back). See for instance Vigarello (2004), pp. 83, 84 and 145.

10. Turbin (2003, p. 112) stresses that 'in the 1880s, collars of high-ranking men (including many employers) prevented a downward gaze, differentiating them from clerks, whose low collars allowed movements required for writing'. On clothing as inducing gesture, see also Perrot (1996 [1981, pp. 23–25]).

11. In her book entitled *Dressing the Elite*, Vincent (2003), relying on analyses by Hollander (1980), reminds us that 'comfort in clothing is not a physical condition, but a mental one. It does not arise from particular sensations of the body, but from having a particular self-image' (p. 47).

12. The most conventional critiques directed against Elias by scholars from various disciplines have taken aim at his Eurocentric bias and evolutionist views. From a different (structuralist) standpoint, Dürr (1998 [1988]), in his four volumes (published in German) on *The Myth of a Civilizing Process*, has strongly challenged the Eliasian thesis by contending that civility is an invariant present in all societies. Cf. also Mennell and Goudsblom (1997).

13. It is easier to take liberties with social inferiors, much less so with peers. It would be particularly daring to neglect rules of propriety in front of the superiors who have set them, or who are at least expected to act as

guarantors for them. Such considerations notwithstanding, elites often harbour a profoundly ambivalent attitude toward their own codes.

14. As some specialists have underlined, particularly with regard to North America. See Lamont's book (1992), *Money, Morals and Manners*. See also, Keller (1963).

15. Including, for instance, the exchange of compliments ostentatiously emphasising everyone else's qualities. See Sennett (1992 [1977], p. 61). In Bourdieusian terms, what is at stake is the display of the 'symbolic capital' of the whole group.

16. This is especially true between social equals, whereas those clearly inferior (children and servants) can always be reprimanded 'for their own good'.

17. This type of analysis is proposed, for instance, by some historians or sociologists working on the highest levels of French society. It is, importantly, argued that these elites were less affected than other social groups by the sharp decline of family values, and thus were able to pass on some highly distinctive habits – cultivated within exclusive clubs or society events – from generation to generation. Cf. Pinçon and Pinçon-Charlot (1989); Mension-Rigau (1990; 1997). With regard to an earlier period, see also Martin-Fugier (1990).

18. This thesis is noticeably contained within Bourdieu's (1984 [1979]) general analysis. See also Le Wita (1988).

19. Cf. Traube (1989). Interestingly, such attitudes are reminiscent of libertine aristocrat mentality, but also of the lower-class ethos of encouraging impulsive excesses against what are perceived as inhibited, 'uptight' stances.

20. This is not an entirely new development. Several of the authors mentioned in Chapter 1 – from Cicero, Pascal and Swift to Montesquieu, Diderot and, above all, Rousseau – may be seen as significant instigators.

21. One might even add bio-sociological factors, e.g. elites' higher ability to select 'beautiful' mates, genetic heritage, etc.

22. However, this may become a sign of distinction (particularly among some dominated classes), demonstrating that one has been working very hard. Such an attitude is reminiscent of the warrior taking pride in his scars.

23. Significantly, the word *'vilain'*, which used to designate a category of peasants under the European feudal system (villeins), still means 'ugly' in contemporay French.

24. An instructive illustration, in this respect, is that of hair. Some authors have endeavoured to show that long hair is systematically a sign of distinction, of saintliness or marginality, whereas short hair connotes submissiveness and social control (as in the case of soldiers, prisoners, monks and nuns). Yet, it is not a difficult task to provide counter-examples (see the chapter devoted to that topic in Firth, 1973). As early as Mesopotamia and pharaonic Egypt, one finds divergent attitudes: the Mesopotamian elites distinguished themselves by growing and sumptuously curling their hair whereas Egyptians shaved their heads entirely and wore wigs. See also Synnott (1987).

25. Detailed studies by art historians are of great value in this respect. See, for instance, Hollander (1988, chapter III).

26. As Spencer reminds us (1893, pp. 199–200), it was quite common for dignitaries (including men) to monopolise large shade-yielding parasols, or canopies – in Africa, South East Asia and Oceania – whereas commoners

were not allowed to protect themselves against the sun. In Indonesia, the *payung* (parasol) has been a major status symbol traditionally used by local chiefs to express hierarchy – ornamentation and colours differing according to rank – and later by Dutch colonial officers or senior indigenous administrators.

27. In this respect, the anthropological concept of 'big man' (see Chapter 7) needs also to be taken literally.

28. According to several chroniclers, Poppaea, Nero's second wife, mobilised about a hundred slaves for her morning toilette. Beau Brummell, the famous dandy, had three (specialised) hairdressers at his disposal.

29. In the media, in business or in the political sector, for instance, mainly because of the need for efficiency.

30. An interesting contribution, in this respect, is the study of imposing monuments such as Trajan's column in Rome, or the 'hall of mirrors' erected in praise of Louis XIV in Versailles. Not only are the symbolic repertoires of the carvings or paintings beyond most visitors' capacity to decipher, but they are often placed much too high to be clearly seen. Such structures have, nonetheless, been able to make especially strong visual impressions (Veyne, 1988; Sabatier, 1999).

31. A number of sociologists indeed see Latin as a dead language purposely instrumentalised by some upper groups as a sign of inclusion/exclusion. The use of some old Chinese characters may similarly carry an aura of prestige in some far-eastern languages.

32. Naturally, not all situations amount to oratorical duels. For instance, within 'light' conversation – so central for elite sociability in many contexts – discussions are deemed rather secondary. Yet this does not prevent endeavours at dazzling, or even outwitting, others with one's fluency. On conversation from the perspective of social history, see Burke (1993).

33. Japanese is a perfect example, with its very nuanced formulas stressing inferior and superior statuses when addressing others. See for instance Holmes (1992), pp. 271 ff.

34. For a synthetic introduction about 'language as a status symbol', see Burke (1987b).

35. Elites may also model their speech on that of a lower social group in order to sound more casual in certain situations.

6   Vicarious Display

1. See, e.g. Banton (1965), chapter eight.

2. We are touching here on several key sociological themes (such as social reproduction or the functional interest of individual merit for societies) but also on some symbolic aspects which fall within the scope of this book. One thinks, e.g., of grandiose funeral monuments which demonstrate a family's lasting claim to social superiority.

3. The debutante season (when young women make their official appearance in the elite adult society) provides occasions where exceptionally formal attire remains the rule. With regard to the United States, see Domhoff (1983, pp. 32–34); Thurgood Haynes (1998).

4. An extreme situation (although not infrequent in cases of upward or downward mobility from one generation to the other) is the one which sees fears of being any longer associated with some family members, largely for symbolic reasons.

5. It is fitting to recall that the concept of social capital lends itself to several definitions and uses. For Bourdieu, it refers to a certain amount of connections likely to be mobilised to assure or strengthen positions. Not being equally available to social agents, it therefore plays a crucial role (along with economic and cultural capital) in the production and the reproduction of inequality. In a more positive light (particularly in the conception of Robert Putnam), 'social capital' is rather viewed as a producer of civic participation and engagement.

6. In order to avoid any misunderstanding, it should be repeated that in many contemporary African or Asian societies, for instance, situations are rather ambivalent. They are no longer purely 'holistic', but they are not evolving into a recognisable 'individualistic' modernity either.

7. This obviously applies to court societies, but even in more modern settings some members of elites might refuse to speak to an unknown person before they have been formally introduced. What is involved is the guarantee given by a third party that the individuals who meet each other for the first time indeed belong to the same 'world' and can interact without any risk of undermining their own status.

8. Mills (1956, p. 74) emphasises that American society 'makes a fetish of competition [...]. It does not seem to matter what the man is the very best at; so long as he has won out in competition over all others, he is celebrated.' However, this is less true in some countries which obviously regard some 'trivial' activities as less legitimate. Another way to look at this question is to consider the issue of ethnicity or religious affiliation. Baltzell (1964) underlined the close-mindedness of White Anglo-Saxon Protestant elites.

9. The display of gifts received is also an important mode of public presentation of one's social bonds. See Lévi-Strauss (1969 [1949]), from an exchange perspective; Schwartz (1967) and Werbner (1996).

10. This has sometimes been related to a so-called 'French exception' (Ozouf, 1998 [1995]) contrasting, for instance, with gentlemen's British clubs. If husbands had to finance their wives' salons, and could certainly benefit from it (in terms of image or more concretely), it proves difficult to resort to a purely Veblenian 'instrumentalising' interpretation.

11. This frequently involves a two-level selection. At the first stage, one must be invited (thanks to a letter of recommendation, a previous encounter or a reputation). The next step is to be accepted as a regular visitor. On salons from an historical point of view, see Lilti (2005). See also Macknight (2005).

12. A most interesting case is that of the philanthropic club whose generosity to those in need may help to leaven the image of elite haughtiness. See Ostrower (1996).

13. See, e.g. Warner and Lunt, 1941 (chapter XVI); Warner and collaborators (1949); Coleman and Neugarten (1971); Domhoff (1983, pp. 28 ff.).

14. Henry Kissinger once declared that 'Power is a great aphrodisiac.' This may be understood in at least two ways: from a top-down perspective, as a

feeling of omnipotence for the powerful person; and from a bottom-up one, as an erotic fascination vis-à-vis prominent people.

15. For instance, against Lévi-Strauss's well-known thesis that incest is a universal taboo, not only is it possible to provide counter-examples (in pharaonic Egypt, Hellenistic Greece, Polynesia and sub-Saharan Africa), but it is significant to underline that incest has been used by rulers as a major way of distinguishing themselves, frequently in reference to incestuous gods within their own mythology.

16. In such a configuration, girls do know how to appear as desirable but not necessarily as attainable persons. Cf. Simmel's (1984 [1909]) sociological analysis of flirtation.

17. The libido must be considered in relation with the mentalities that shape the representations of the relations between the sexes. It is essential to unravel what makes sense to the actors concerned, whether extra-marital affairs regarded as fornication, or the post-1968 movement advocating paedophilia in order to 'liberate' children. Vigarello's book, *A History of Rape* (2000 [1998]) clearly makes us see an evolution of the social perception of nobles forcing themselves on subordinate females from an act almost taken for granted to something becoming unbearable.

18. A specialist of sexuality in the Middle Ages (Poly, 2003, p. 250) interestingly shows how, at a certain stage, some young nobles were hesitating between traditional strategies of self-affirmation and new courtly forms sublimating the sexual urge. A theme worthy of note here is that of gallantry.

19. It appears for instance that this did not make much sense in ancient Rome. By contrast, in the West Indies, to 'father many children by many wives' is 'the foundation of a man's reputation' (Wilson, p. 151).

20. Suffice it to mention here the case of what used to be called in French '*le cocu magnifique*', that is a deceived husband taking pride and advantage of his wife's affair with the king. As Molière metaphorically wrote in his play *Amphytrion*: 'sharing with Jupiter is not at all dishonourable', and it has proved, paradoxically, to be a source of distinction.

21. Historically, one has in mind, for instance, debauched lifestyle under Pope Alexander VI Borgia or under the seventeenth-century court of Charles II in England. As Stone (1977, p. 658) emphasised in the English case, there is a remarkable discrepancy between the aristocracy's obsession with lineage and arranged marriage – mainly because of concerns over property – and the fact that it was rather open towards sex ('seen as one of the supreme pleasures in life'). However, the 'double standard' of sexual morality often prevailed, i.e. married men could collect mistresses but wives were not supposed to have affairs. As has been well known since antiquity, what is mainly at stake is of course the issue of paternity.

22. See, e.g. Mansel (2000, Chapter 6).

23. It is arguable that for dominated people, to be 'loved' in this way is one of the few instances whereby they feel 'distinguished', even if by somebody from their own social class.

24. The situation appears to be particularly ambiguous when norms evolve, for instance as a result of colonisation. On the question of sex and manners in the West, see Wouters (2004).

25. As is well depicted in Zola's *Nana* (1972 [1880]) whose eponymous character was inspired by real courtesans leading an incredible life of luxury.
26. The following quotation is taken from her aforementioned novel *The House of Mirth* (1997 [1905]). 'Mrs Bart's worst reproach to her husband was to ask him if he expected her to "live like a pig"' (p. 27), and then she would order one or two dresses in Paris and call the jeweller (p. 29). It is however fair to state that there are other passages and characters which seem to corroborate Veblen's perspective. For instance (p. 155), 'I want my wife to make all the other women feel small.'
27. Similarly, in his article on 'The Big House Revisited', Kirkland (1976 [1956], pp. 54 ff.) opposes Veblen's interpretations as overgeneralised. According to him, external actors motivated by self-interest (architects) could also be largely responsible for exaggerated expenditure.
28. For example, investigations in Nigeria reveal logics which are far removed from those prevailing in Euro-American contexts. One may mention the case of female students who have a liaison with a middle-aged man, mainly in order to obtain things they cannot afford. When they are given a jewel, they typically redistribute it (to a friend, to their mother) as if it were more important to put the latter in the position of indebtedness to them than to enjoy the seductive distinction which the bodily accessory could convey to their own person (Daloz, 2002). See also Dinan (1983) about Ghana.
29. Something that is all too often forgotten is how much labour used to be required to handle everyday duties such as taking hot water upstairs, looking after fireplaces or horses, constantly cleaning oil lamps or chamber pots, not to mention doing laundry or gardening, in the absence of modern facilities and equipment.
30. This theme of freedom of choice in activities may lead to classical reflections in terms of the pursuit of leisure (understood as a privilege of the upper groups) against the background of work. However, one should move away from simple dichotomous views. From a comparative perspective, what is relevant is not only the socio-economic issue of labour relations (domestic servants used to 'sell' their masters the majority of their time) but also that of cultural representations: *otium* versus *negotium*, or Confucianist ethos versus Taoism, for instance.
31. See, e.g Horn (1975, p. 13) on Victorian England and Martin-Fugier (2004 [1979], p. 94) about France. A most significant attitude, noted by several authors, is an intensive use of the bell in very small apartments, where resorting to such a device would seem unjustified, except on purely symbolic grounds. Furthermore, a visibly submissive stance was of course expected from the maid in every circumstance. For a comparative view about the condition of domestic workers in Western societies, see Fauve-Chamoux and Wall (2005).
32. Lacing up a corset, or even getting on a horse when wearing a certain type of dress, for example.
33. Cf. Pascal (1976 [1670], n. 316–95). A good illustration is that of famous dishes elaborated by innovative cooks but being eventually designated by the name of their employer (e.g. beef Stroganoff).

34. For instance, Bouza (2004 [2000]) mentions the case of sixteenth-century Spanish courtiers who cultivated poor handwriting, thus demonstrating that they could afford a private secretary.
35. Spencer (1893, p. 98) reminds us that the word 'livery' is related to the fact that, in the Middle Ages, dresses were delivered by kings and nobles to their retainers because their households 'should appear with distinction'. Reciprocally, a poorly dressed servant was likely to undermine a household's reputation.
36. Laver (1969, pp. 79–83) gives a detailed account of servants' purposely 'discarded' costumes. See also Bell (1976). A significant modern development is that in many society parties or exclusive restaurants, the only persons wearing bow ties are the waiters.
37. About 'largesse', one may mention clothes handed down to the maids, e.g., or domestics being allowed to eat the remnants from their master's table. From an historical perspective, an interesting theme here is that of 'noble service' as a relatively advantageous position for landless sons or for some women of lower aristocratic rank. See, e.g. Mertes (1988). As for the phenomenon of dignity through identification, it should be noted that it has been addressed by Tarde (2003 [1899]) and earlier by Feuerbach (1957 [1841], p. 250).
38. Among the many reasons leading to the vanishing of servants, one may mention economic development and the rising availability of jobs perceived as more attractive (typist or shop assistant) for semi-qualified workers, a growing aversion for ostensibly servile positions and the development of 'household appliances'.
39. About the pillage of others' riches, it is fitting to recall that this is not only an attribute of a remote past (the plundering of Constantinople by Venetians and Crusaders in 1204, or that of many European cities by Napoleonic troops, constituting most famous episodes). Suffice it to think about some members of the Nazi elite endeavouring to grab artistic treasures from conquered countries during World War II.
40. This is well documented by ethnology as well as history. The question inevitably raised in this respect, however, is what is exactly meant by 'art' (inherently sacred or not, functional versus art for art's sake, etc.).
41. In this respect, books on art history describe the remarkable complicity between some rulers and painters (such as Titian, Holbein, Van Dyck, Velasquez or Le Brun) who served also as 'tutors' and advisers. About the seventeenth century, see for instance Brown (1995).
42. On the question of the visible or invisible character of collections – although from a slightly different perspective – see Pomian (1994 [1978]).
43. Some very sought-after cooks have for instance been able to negotiate profitable 'transfers', or to open lucrative restaurants. C.F. Worth, the designer who dominated Parisian fashion during the second half of the nineteenth century, could afford to treat his upper-class clients particularly condescendingly (making them wait for hours, smoking a cigar in their presence) in so far as they were too much dependent upon him for the achievement of their own distinction.
44. Which might, or might not, have to do with genuine appreciation.

7 The Historicity of Elite Distinction: Selected Themes

1. One has in mind, for instance, the splendour of the eighteenth dynasty in ancient Egypt; the pomp of some Hellenistic monarchs or Roman emperors; the pageantry of the Italian Renaissance, of Elizabethan England and of Versailles; the grandiosity of the Moghul or Ming eras; and the more contemporary lavish display of some American billionaires or Arab oil kings. Some monographs offer an interesting treatment of the question of elite distinction from an historical viewpoint (see, e.g. Clunas, 1991).

2. Admittedly, there is also a structuralist paradigm which considers that cultural features would merely be a superficial phenomenon masking deep invariants. At the heart of the discipline in fact lies an inherent tension between the intent to reaffirm the universal character of 'human nature' and to account for the relative plasticity of societies.

3. The anthropological model of the 'Big Man' who acquires (instead of inheriting) power was first proposed by Sahlins (1963) in his work on Melanesia. This generalisation was to be subsequently rejected by some anthropologists working on the same area (see Roscoe, 2000).

4. What has fascinated anthropologists, or archaeologists, for generations is more the circulation of prestigious goods than their possession or display. On the remarkable number of functions that they could perform, see, e.g. Brumfiel (1987) on the Aztec case. Cf. also Brumfiel and Fox (1994) from the perspective of political development.

5. Witchcraft may be involved here: whether it is instrumentalised as a social leveller compelling those who have enriched themselves to share their wealth with the community, or to demonstrate that a Big Man's sorcery is strong enough to render immune those under his protection to supernatural dangers and enemies. This is still a common process in some parts of the world (see, e.g. Geschiere 1997).

6. See for instance the special issue of the Journal *'Tiers Monde'* on *'L'économie ostentatoire'* (Poirier, 1968).

7. According to Sahlins (1976), the study of so-called 'primitive societies' exposes the limits of historical materialism. Hence, there is a dialogue of the deaf between advocates of the primacy of culture and adherents of an approach in terms of infrastructural constants and ideological mystifications. See Appadurai (1986); Parry and Bloch (1989).

8. Cf. Trubitt (2003). For a panorama of 'Precious Materials as Expressions of Status' and their meanings, see Clark (1986).

9. An interesting point regarding socio-cultural imaginary – alluded to by Mauss (1990 [1924]) about the *Potlatch* case – is the relation between fortune in the sense of luck and success, and in the sense of a great accumulation of wealth. On this theme, see also Douglas (1970).

10. Veyne's contribution can be cited here as a remarkable example of a work related to the questions occupying us in this volume. In his work on 'Bread and Circuses' in Hellenistic Greece and Rome (1976), he was able to show precisely why 'evergetism' (i.e. a gift to all the citizens of a city) had little to do with primitive forms of exchange described and analysed by anthropologists, nor with medieval charity, even though what was involved was asserting one's wealth and sublimating it through redistribution.

11. Historically, one may refer to some Puritan communities' admonitions to avoid ostentation in reference to the sins of pride and envy, or to subsistence economies with limited access to essential resources.

12. This was characteristically the position of mercantilists during the seventeenth century.

13. This idea of arbitrariness must, however, be nuanced in so far as some colours were more difficult to produce. Purple dye is the most obvious example.

14. In South Korea, because of the trade imbalance the government launched a 'frugality' campaign in the 1990s and a public debate emerged about 'excessive consumers'.

15. This question may be tackled from a rather abstract angle, as is often the case in political sociology (e.g. between 'state' and 'civil society'). The analysis becomes much more concrete when it is based on a study of the main actors involved.

16. On this topic, from a stratification point of view, see Scott (1996).

17. Significantly, the usual concepts referring to social standing and the ladder of honours began to be replaced by a vocabulary which still interpreted society as a hierarchical system but in a looser way.

18. Hence some major controversies and shifts in representations of sumptuousness. See Starobinski (2006 [1964]) and Shovlin (2000).

19. For a detailed account on the issue of luxury under the Stalin era, see Gronow (2003).

20. For example, Evans (2002) shows how some Buddhist gestures of respect as well as the 'royal language' suppressed by the communist regime in Laos – and replaced by more egalitarian handshakes and hugs between comrades – finally had to be restored.

21. For analytical and comparative reflections about political representatives and legitimacy in terms of eminence/proximity, see Daloz (2010).

22. Whereas some macro-models of deep mutations highlighted by historical sociology are admirable in their sophistication, the question is whether or not they are generally applicable. The concept of involution makes it possible to account for the logics of certain dynamics within their own local setting. On social distinction, cf. Daloz (2008, p. 315).

23. In this respect, contrast the systemic explanations of Gerth and Mills (1954), Balandier (1980) or Cohen (1981), on the theatrical dimensions of power, and the sceptical views offered by Firth (1973) or Geertz (1980).

24. In a well-known book, Pöllnitz (2004 [1734], p. 15) speaks of one of the major European aristocrats who thinks that greatness is more likely to obstruct pleasure than be conducive to it. The latter therefore introduces himself as a mere count, which was enough to ensure reception 'with distinction'.

25. Both of these have often been associated by historians with new mentalities and ways of life having first emerged in England and America (see, e.g. Perrot, 1995; Crowley, 2001).

26. Wearing extremely high stiletto heels is a good example.

27. Compare, for instance, Japan and the United States in this respect.

28. Cf. notably Braudel (1973 [1967]); Miller (1981); McKendrick, Brewer and Plumb (1982); Williams (1982); Mukerji (1983); Weatherhill (1988); McCracken (1990); Brewer and Porter (1993); Bermingham and Brewer (1995); Roche (2000 [1997]); Coquery (1998). As some commentators have

rightly emphasised, these enterprises focused on dissimilar phenomena and based their analysis on rather different theoretical frameworks. See Stearns (1997); Trentmann (2004).

29. Contrast Vichert's (1971) usage of the Veblenian reading grid and Weatherill's (1988) more sceptical views on emulation. See principally several contributions in Brewer and Porter (1993); Bermingham (1995, pp. 11–12) and Kwass (2003).

30. Consider for instance the current proliferation of low-cost flights which allow more and more people to travel by plane. This may drive wealthier customers to differentiate themselves by ostensibly enjoying elitist privileges (VIP lounges or an exclusive booking system). See Thurlow and Jaworski's (2006) well-informed study of airlines frequent-flyer programmes following (questionable) Bourdieusian perspectives.

31. It would be most interesting to investigate systematically how these historians apply the grand theories discussed above.

32. In order to complete our discussion on these matters, it can be emphasised that for many Latin American, African or Asian societies, the very term 'masses', often used in a dichotomised way with that of elites, is indeed questionable. We are perhaps dealing with situations of increasing intermixture of populations but very rarely with anonymous individuals entirely detached from any communal environment, be they reconstituted.

33. See, e.g. Dawson and Cavell (1986); Whimster (1992) Cf. also the essay by Brooks (2000).

8 Tradition, Fashion, Borrowing and Syncretism

1. See Veyne (1976, pp. 45 and 637).

2. On debates about the non-universalist character of fashion, and about reactions of incomprehension overseas, cf., e.g. Bell (1976) and Braudel (1973 [1967]).

3. See Crook (1999) on Victorian and Edwardian England. In France, at a time when many aristocrats were trying to modernise their old feudal fortresses, some bourgeois conversely endeavoured to give an ancient look to their residence (adding towers, high walls, etc.).

4. For a general reflection on social power and time, cf. Bourdieu (1984 [1979, p. 78]). See also Baudrillard (1996a [1968, pp. 105 ff., 210 ff.]) and (1981 [1972, pp. 28–30]).

5. For instance, in Buddhist contexts, because of belief in reincarnation, the relation to antiques is quite different to what it can be in the 'West' (e.g. Peleggi, 2004). As for the political dimension, in a context of endless competition between rival families in Rome during the Baroque era, 'each new pope was determined to outshine his predecessors and start afresh', whereas within well-established dynasties a king was likely to revere his ancestors' legacies and would feel 'no ambition to obliterate their memories' (Haskell, 1980, p. 188).

6. Rheims (1990, pp. 1077 and 1092).

7. See also Lowe (1984). Such interplay between dress and flesh should of course be related to what was said above about seductive attire and glamorous

company. Nonetheless, it must be underlined that in many places the same erotic conventions persist for generations.

8. Gloves are a good example. During the eighteenth century, in France, they were seldom worn in public (being perceived as connoting rusticity) and it was compulsory to take them off in the presence of peers. Later on, an inverted code of politeness prevailed and members of the elite were supposed to keep gloves on most of the time (except when eating). Being annoyed by the downward diffusion of this standard to the middle classes, some members of the highest circles had no other option than to give up such items (Rouvillois, 2006, pp. 72 ff.)

9. See the landmark articles by King (1973 [1963]), Burns (1966), Blumer (1969) and Horowitz (1975).

10. One of the key points is that the capacity incessantly to relinquish the old and adopt the new is no longer exclusively affordable by only the most affluent.

11. For instance, Pickenpaugh (1997) emphasises the fact that in Oceania, sub-Saharan Africa and lowland South America, necklaces made from the canines of the most powerful animals known (lions, leopards, jaguars, sperm whales, crocodiles, boars, etc.) were used as symbols of rank and power by elites. On local monopolies, see, e.g. Gluckman (1983 [1943]).

12. See Helms (1988 and 1993). Structuralists authors (like Lévi-Strauss or Baudrillard) have some grounds in showing that certain objects obtained from afar function as 'pure signs'. A recurrent illustration is that of the native who wears a watch as a status symbol without understanding its practical dimension.

13. For example, if the introduction of abstract currencies seriously disrupted traditional systems of exchange (see, e.g. Ekholm Friedman, 1977), coins could also be used as ornament.

14. Cf., e.g. Echeruo (1977) and Cole (1975). See also Martin (1995); Hendrickson (1996).

15. Examples comprise Romans bringing back home many commodities and customs which had delighted them in Greece or other colonies, medieval Crusaders developing a taste for the luxuries of near-eastern life or French lords being captivated by the amenities of the Italian Renaissance cities they had subjugated.

16. One thinks of Peter the Great ordering the Russian nobility to wear only Western dress and cut their beards (under penalty of taxation) or of Mustafa Kemal forbidding the fez in the 1920s.

17. For example, as far as clothing is concerned, the full regalia normally reserved for admirals of the British naval fleet (Caplan, 1970), or episcopal *capa magna*, were offered to some African chiefs. Engravings of the nineteenth century represent some of them wearing fascinating assortments: e.g. traditional grass skirts, with blazers, ties and top hats or bowlers.

18. The diversity of the provisions consumed could vividly express the more or less distant lands one was controlling. About curiosity vis-à-vis others' foods, one must admit that Western elites have often proved much more open than those from other civilisations.

19. This may result from, e.g., an opposition between colonists displaying a perfect civility as an outward badge of their respectability and some

immigrants eager to demonstrate a certain freedom from such traditional genteel codes. See Russel (2002) about nineteenth-century Australia. See also Ross (1999).

20. In Abidjan, according to European witnesses, air conditioning is sometimes put on to the maximum during parties, so that the rich female African guests may display their fur coats. Expatriates would of course make fun of such attitudes. For other illustrations, see Daloz (2003, Conclusion).

21. A significant case it that of the Nepalase elites studied by Lotter (forthcoming) who play the role of Asian fairy-tale princes(ses) when they are in London and of actors displaying the latest Western innovations when in Kathmandu.

22. Cf. Stearns (2001) and several contributions in Assouly (2005). It should be noted that some environments were most ambiguous: see Schama (1987) on the 'embarrassment of riches' in the seventeenth-century Netherlands.

23. Let us take the domain of lining as an illustration. At a time when a relative understatement was expected in men's attire (e.g. during a few decades of the nineteenth century in France), it was admissible to wear rather plain jackets or coats with the (non visible) inside made of luxurious materials. Similarly, in Japan, a precious kimono could be put under a simple one. Conversely, in the Muslim world where, according to the Islamic law, silk should not be worn (being perceived as reserved for heavenly pleasures), it remained forbidden to use it for undergarment – that is, against the skin – but wearing silk kaftans above cotton or other approved material was tolerated (Stanley, 2004, pp. 30–31).

24. The expression is borrowed from Friedman (1994, p. 113). See his anthropological interpretations of 'SAPE' (display of Parisian designer clothes) in Congo focusing on linkages to outside forces and signs of power, as well as his reflections on the limits of Veblenian and Bourdieusian lines of analysis.

25. See, for example many contributions in Miller (1995), Brewer and Trentmann (2006); Trentmann (2006).

26. From a marketing perspective, the usual question is of whether multi-nationals should have recourse to the image of the country of origin when advertising a brand, or adapt it to the targeted foreign market.

27. Moreover, misunderstandings are common occurrence. For example, some Scandinavian diplomats deplore the fact that at international summits 'the poorer the country, the more ostentatious its representatives'. Reciprocally, the conspicuously modest behaviour of the members of some Nordic non-governmental organisations appears to be incomprehensible in the eyes of sub-Saharan elites. It goes without saying that the role of the comparativist is to go beyond ethnocentric views and to make sense of the respective attitudes and cross-perceptions.

28. It is worth noting parenthetically that, from a methodological point of view, work on expatriated elites (cf., e.g. Wagner, 1998; Thompson and Tambyah, 1999; Beaverstock, 2002) – notably cross-national judgements on which goods or activities should be primary items of competitive display – proves most instructive.

29. In a self-ironical way, Norwegians employ the expression 'velstandsblemme' (literally meaning 'prosperity-blister') to refer to some new (but not always useful) items affluent people cannot help adding to their house.

9   Beyond Reductionism

1. See Braudel (1973 [1967]). One important idea, here, is that 'when the possibilities of quantitative consumption for the expression of social superiority had been exhausted, the qualitative possibilities were inexhaustible' (Mennell, 1987, p. 39). Several historians have also related this evolution to the rise of privacy; some elites feel less compelled to organise large symbolic demonstrations of their superiority in great halls and withdraw into separate dining rooms. We refer to our section on 'Processes of (In)Formalisation' in Chapter 7 above.
2. See Flandrin (1999 [1985, pp. 274 ff.]).
3. To be known to have an ostentatiously comprehensive collection of something (see Baudrillard, 1996a [1968, pp. 120 ff.] on this aspect).
4. Extreme examples include Empress Josephine who, by the time of her divorce from Napoleon, owned hundreds of cashmere shawls, as well as 876 dresses, and could order almost 1000 pairs of gloves per year (Mansel, 2005, p. 86) or, more recently, Imelda Marcos's 3000 pairs of shoes and 500 bras.
5. For instance, according to Kasson (1990, p. 175), what was mainly intended by the doubling-up of covers in nineteenth-century urban America was to confer an impression of smoothness.
6. To give two differing illustrations. Textile exuberance or the accumulation of curios usually means an accumulation of dust, and thus the necessity of constant cleaning and, most likely, servants, who are in themselves a sign of distinction. It is to know that in Norway an obligation of a few months' residence in any home per year is imposed, which considerably reduces the accumulation of second houses.
7. See Hirsch (1977, pp. 32 ff.). The capacity to control one's own environment is often essential. To take a literary example, in *The Great Gatsby* (Fitzgerald, 1950 [1925], p. 141), there is an anecdote about a brewer who proposes to pay the taxes of his neighbours for five years if the latter agree to thatch their roofs and therefore maintain the appearance of the vicinity in a traditional way. So said in passing, readers of F. Scott Fitzgerald, but also of Emile Zola, Henry James, Edith Wharton, John Galsworthy, Thomas Mann, Simon Raven, Chinua Achebe or Tom Wolfe, among many, many others, know that novels may prove to be full of remarkable observations about elite distinction. The inevitable question, however, is to what extent the social scientist can consider these works as reliable sources.
8. We are drawing here on Semon's (1979) comments about Felson's above-mentioned article.
9. Elites from this small French-speaking country often betray a complex of inferiority vis-à-vis their powerful neighbour, the self-dubbed 'Giant of Africa'. On the other hand, they would make fun of their Nigerian counterparts who put ice in their red wine (Daloz, 1999).
10. For a sophisticated study on women's cosmetic and status competition, see Chao and Schor (1998).
11. Weber reminds us that, in Rome, whenever the financial situation of a family improved, one of its first priorities was to acquire new slaves. Equally, during the eighteenth century, rich families in England employed as large a staff as they could afford. However, qualification or modishness (a gorgeously

decked little black boy, for instance, or a foreign nurse) could also play a certain role in the past. It goes without saying that the most prosperous elites do not really have to make a choice between quantity and quality.

12. For example, according to some sources, the Moroccan emperor Moulay Ismail had about 1000 children! In Swaziland, the present king (who was born in 1968) has already many wives and descendants.

13. For instance, eighteenth-century libertine literature significantly abounds with military metaphors. There the challenge is to conquer those women who seem the least accessible.

14. For example, when Bourdieu in the original French version of his book on distinction [1979] extensively speaks of *'styles de vie'*, it is often unclear whether he rather means 'styles of life' (in a Weberian sense, i.e. related to fixed statuses) or 'lifestyles' (related to choice in consumer societies). For general reflections on lifestyles and social theory, see, e.g. Featherstone (1987) and Chaney (1996); on the concept of style, see Eckert and Do (2006).

15. For an enlightening discussion of these developments, see Ewen (1988). See also Ewen and Ewen (1992).

16. For a semiotic reflection on (non-)uniformity, with numerous illustrations, see Joseph (1986). See also, for instance, Brooks (1981).

17. From a psycho-sociological perspective, see also Lemaine (1974).

18. Many researchers tend to reason in a deductive way, with hypotheses related and then tested in accordance with a favourite analytical mould. Less common are attempts to use case studies in order to assess the limits of some theoretical frameworks. For a critique of Simmel, based on a Swedish investigation on personal and collective styles, see Sellerberg (1994).

19. When we consider famous British and French dandies, such as Brummell, Disraeli, Barbey d'Aurevilly, Baudelaire or d'Orsay, it proves difficult to generalise. If the desire to demonstrate uniqueness appears ever present, is absolute distinctiveness related to a kind of 'neo-aristocracy' within a context of rising egalitarianism and mass society or to an 'existential revolt' displaying contempt for every convention?

20. Packard in his descriptive essay on 'Status Seekers' (1960) mentions that this standardisation is actually a selling point for estate agents in the United States who insist on the social/spatial homogeneity of the neighbourhood.

21. See Mangham and Overingon (1987, p. 132). Cf. also Whyte (1956).

22. For instance, in Nigeria, the present author once witnessed how a rising 'Big Man' strove to acquire the very same car (model, colour and interior) as his major rival, so that everyone (especially followers from both sides) might draw a parallel.

23. For instance, under the *Ancien Régime*, the French minor provincial aristocracy was to build up a model emphasising moral rigour, while denouncing the court's decadence. Sceptical views have also been expressed by historians working on the perceptions of the upper class by some middle-ranking elements in Great Britain (see Nenadic's study, 1994, among many others). Within British neo-Marxism, equally, one finds reflections on working-class resistance (see, e.g. Williams, 1982, pp. 217 ff.) or spectacular youth subcultures (Hebdige, 1979) combining a Gramscian understanding of symbolic domination and oppositional styles.

24. Famous illustrations include the espousal of the *vertugado* (farthingale with hoops) consecutively to a fashion initiated by Juana of Portugal who originally wanted to cover up an unwanted pregnancy and the adoption of red dyes, and later – when the queen began to loose her hair – of wigs, by ladies in Elizabeth I's entourage. Likewise, Louis XIV, who went bald early, was to appoint many royal wigmakers and the court followed suit.

25. See several contributions in Tajfel (1978). Cf. also Meyer's (2000) views about 'Taste Formation in Pluralistic Societies' from a rather Eliasian point of view.

26. For a discussion of this concept introduced by Maffesoli and Bauman, see Lury (1996, pp. 250 ff.). See also Warde (1997, Chapter 1).

27. Markers of social superiority and classifications in this field should of course be related to what was said earlier about cultural competence (Chapter 6). On this theme, see for instance DiMaggio and Useem (1978); Levine (1988); Katz-Gerro (2002) and the special issue (I/3, 2008) of the new *Journal of Cultural Economy* (edited by Warde).

28. Cf. the seminal contributions by Peterson (1992); Peterson and Kern (1996); Bryson (1996 and 1997) and Holt (1998). For a panorama of how debates stand at present (with references to many other authors), see the special issue of *Poetics*, edited by Ollivier, van Eijck and Warde (2008). See also Bennett et al. (2009).

29. See Burke's (1988 [1978], pp. 270 ff.) analysis of 'the withdrawal of the upper classes' from 'popular culture' in Early modern Europe.

30. In their aforementioned article, Barber and Lobel (1952) show how American women from various (sub-)classes were respectively influenced by Windsor, Paris and Hollywood. Needless to say, film stars have often been 'fabricated'. As for the question as to whether they may themselves be considered as belonging to the elite or not, this depends on each society's perceptions. Cf. Chapter 6, n 8.

31. See, e.g., several contributions in Solomon (1985).

32. Passeron (in Grignon and Passeron, 1989, p. 60). NB: the French verb *s'encanailler* may be translated into English as 'to mix with the riffraff', with a strong connotation of looking for pleasures forbidden in respectable spheres.

Works Cited

ADORNO, Theodor (1974 [1951]) *Minima Moralia* (London: NLB).

ADORNO, Theodor (1981 [1941]) 'Veblen's Attack on Culture', in *Prisms* (Cambridge MA: MIT Press).

ADORNO, Theodor and HORKHEIMER, Max (1979 [1944]) *Dialectic of Enlightenment* (London and New York: Verso).

ALEXANDER, Jeffrey C. (2003) *The Meanings of Social Life: A Cultural Sociology* (New York: Oxford U.P.).

ALMANEY, Adnan J. and AHWAN, A. (1982) *Communicating with the Arabs* (Prospect Heights IL: Waweland Press).

ANDRESKI, Stanislav (ed.) (1971) *Herbert Spencer: Structure, Function and Evolution* (London: Michael Joseph).

ANTHIAS, Floya (2001) 'The Material and the Symbolic in Theorizing Social Stratification: Issues of Gender, Ethnicity and Class', *British Journal of Sociology*, 52/3, 367–390.

APPADURAI, Arjun (1986) 'Introduction: Commodities and the Politics of Value', in APPADURAI, Arjun (ed.) *The Social Life of Things: Commodities in Cultural Perspectives* (Cambridge: Cambridge U.P.).

APPADURAI, Arjun (1995) 'The Production of Locality', in FARDON, Richard (ed.) *Counterworks: Managing the Diversity of Knowledge* (London: Routledge).

ARISTOTLE (1991 [4th Century BC]) *On Rhetoric: A Theory of Civic Discourse* (translated and edited by George A. KENNEDY; Oxford: Oxford U.P.).

ARISTOTLE (2002 [4th Century BC]) *Nichomachean Ethics* (translated and edited by Roger CRISP; Cambridge: Cambridge U.P.).

ASSOULY, Olivier (ed.) (2005) *Le luxe: Essais sur la fabrique de l'ostentation* (Paris: Institut français de la mode/Regard).

BACKHAUS, Jürgen (1996) *Werner Sombart (1863–1941) 3 volumes* (Marburg: Metropolis).

BALANDIER, Georges (1980) *Le pouvoir sur scènes* (Paris: Balland).

BALTZELL, E. Digby (1964) *The Protestant Establishment: Aristocracy and Caste in America* (Glencoe: The Free Press).

BANTON, Michael (1965) *Roles: An Introduction to the Study of Social Relations* (New York: Basic Books).

BARBER, Bernard and LOBEL, Lyle (1952) 'Fashion in Women's Clothes and the American Social System', *Social Forces*, 31/2, 124–131.

BAUDRILLARD, Jean (1981) *For a Critique of the Political Economy of the Sign* (St Louis: Telos Press); original version in French: [1972] *Pour une critique de l'économie politique du signe* (Paris: Gallimard).

BAUDRILLARD, Jean (1994) *Simulacra and Simulations* (Ann Arbor: The University of Michigan Press); original version in French: [1981] *Simulacres et simulations* (Paris: Galilée).

BAUDRILLARD, Jean (1996a) *The System of Objects* (London: Verso); original version in French: [1968] *Le système des objets* (Paris: Gallimard).

BAUDRILLARD, Jean (1996b) *The Consumer Society: Myths and Structures* (Thousand Oaks: Sage); original version in French: [1970] *La société de consommation* (Paris: Denoël).

BAUMAN, Zygmunt (1992) *Intimations of Post Modernity* (London: Sage).

BAURY, Roger (2002) 'L'ubiquité nobiliaire aux XVIIè et XVIIIè siècles', in PONTET, Josette, FIGEAC, Michel, BOISSON, Marie (eds) *La Noblesse de la fin du XVIè siècle au début du XXè siècle, un modèle social ? Tome 1* (Anglet: Atlantica).

BEARDEN, William O. and ETZEL, Michael J. (1982) 'Reference Group Influence on Product and Brand Purchase Decision', *The Journal of Consumer Research*, 9/2, 183–194.

BEAVERSTOCK, Jonathan V. (2002) 'Transnational Elites in Global Cities: British Expatriates in Singapore's Financial District', *Geoforum*, 33/4, 525–538.

BELK, Russel W. (1988) 'Possessions and the Extended Self', *The Journal of Consumer Research*, 15/2, 139–168.

BELL, Quentin (1976) *On Human Finery*, 2nd edn (London: The Hogarth Press).

BELLAH, Robert, MADSEN, Richard, SULLIVAN, William, SWIDELER, Ann and TIPTON, Steven (1985) *Habits of the Heart: Individualism and Commitment in American Life* (New York: Harper & Row).

BENNETT, Tony, SAVAGE, Mike, SILVA, Elizabeth, WARDE, Alan, GAYO-CAL, Modesto and WRIGHT, David (eds) (2008) *Culture, Class, Distinction* (London: Routledge).

BERG, Maxine and EGER, Elizabeth (eds) (2003) *Luxury in the Eighteenth Century: Debates, Desires and Delectable Goods* (Basingstoke and New York: Palgrave).

BERMINGHAM, Ann (1995) 'Introduction', in BERMINGHAM, Ann and BREWER, John (1995) (eds) *The Consumption of Culture 1600–1800: Image, Object, Text* (London: Routledge).

BERMINGHAM, Ann and BREWER, John (1995) (eds) *The Consumption of Culture 1600–1800: Image, Object, Text* (London: Routledge).

BERRY, Christopher J. (1994) *The Idea of Luxury: A Conceptual and Historical Investigation* (Cambridge: Cambridge U.P.).

BIRDWELL, Al. E. (1968) 'A Study of the Influence of Image Congruence on Consumer Choice', *Journal of Business*, 41/1, 76–88.

BIRDWHISTELL, Ray L. (1970) *Kinesics and Context: Essays on Body-Motion Communication* (Philadelphia: University of Pennsylvania Press).

BLACK, Paula and SHARMA, Ursula (2001) 'Men are Real, Women are "Made Up": Beauty Therapy and the Construction of Feminity', *The Sociological Review*, 49/1, 100–116.

BLAU, Peter and DUNCAN, Otis Dudley (1967) *The American Occupational Structure* (New York: Wiley).

BLUMBERG, Paul (1974) 'The Decline and Fall of the Status Symbol: Some Thoughts on Status in Post-Industrial Society', *Social Problems*, 21/4, 480–494.

BLUMER, Herbert (1969) 'Fashion: From Class Differentiation to Collective Selection', *Sociological Quaterly*, 10/3, 275–291.

BOLOGH, Roslyn (1979) *Dialectical Phenomenology: Marx's Method* (Boston and London: Routledge & Kegan Paul).

BOLTANSKI, Luc (1975) 'Les usages sociaux de l'automobile: concurrence pour l'espace et accidents', *Actes de la recherche en sciences sociales*, 1/2, 25–49.

BORCHERT, James and BORCHERT, Susan (2002) 'Downtown, Uptown, Out of Town: Diverging Patterns of Upper-Class Residential Landscapes in Buffalo, Pittsburg, and Cleveland, 1885–1935', *Social Science History*, 26/2, 311–346.

BOURDIEU, Pierre (1977) 'Remarques provisoires sur la perception sociale du corps', *Actes de la recherche en sciences sociales,* 14, 51–54.

BOURDIEU, Pierre (1984) *Distinction: A Social Critique of the Judgement of Taste* (London: Routledge); original version in French: [1979] *La distinction: critique sociale du jugement* (Paris: Minuit).

BOURDIEU, Pierre (1989) 'Social Space and Symbolic Power', *Sociological Theory,* 7/1, 14–25; original version in French: [1987] 'Espace social et pouvoir symbolique', in *Choses dites* (Paris: Minuit).

BOURDIEU, Pierre (1994) 'Espace social et espace symbolique', in *Raisons Pratiques: Sur la théorie de l'action'* (Paris: Le Seuil).

BOURDIEU, Pierre (2001) *Masculine Domination* (Cambridge: Polity); original version in French: [1998] *La domination masculine* (Paris: Le Seuil).

BOUZA, Fernando (2004 [2000]) *Communication, Knowledge, and Memory in Early Modern Spain* (Philadelphia: University of Pennsylvania Press).

BRAMBILLA, Elena (1991) 'Modèle et méthode dans la "société de cour" de Norbert Elias', in ROMAGNOLI, Daniela (ed.) *La ville et la Cour: les bonnes et les mauvaises manières* (Paris: Fayard).

BRAUDEL, Fernand (1973) *Capitalism and Material Life 1400–1800* (London: Weidenfeld & Nicolson); original version in French: [1967] *Civilisation matérielle, économie et capitalisme, XVè – XVIIIè siècles, 1. Les structures du quotidien* (Paris: Armand Colin).

BREMMER, Jan and ROODENBURG, Herman (eds) (1991) *A Cultural History of Gesture* (Cambridge: Polity).

BREWER, John and PORTER, Roy (eds) (1993) *Consumption and the World of Goods* (London and New York: Routledge).

BREWER, John and TRENTMANN, Frank (eds) (2006) *Consuming Cultures, Global Perspectives: Historical Trajectories, Transnational Exchanges* (Oxford: Berg).

BRIGHT, Brenda (1988) '"Heart like a Car": Hispano/Chicano Culture in Northern New Mexico', *American Ethnologist,* 25/4, 583–609.

BRONNER, Simon J. (ed.) (1989) *Consuming Visions: Accumulation and Display of Goods in America, 1880–1920* (New York: Norton).

BROOKS, David (2000) *Bobos in Paradise: The New Upper Class and How They Got There* (New York: Touchstone).

BROOKS, John (1981) *Showing Off in America: From Conspicuous Consumption to Parody Display* (Boston: Little Brown).

BROWN, Jonathan (1995) *Kings and Connoisseurs: Collecting Art in Seventeenth-Century Europe* (New Haven: Princeton U.P.).

BRUMFIEL, Elizabeth M. (1987) 'Elite and Utilitarian Crafts in the Aztec State', in BRUMFIEL, Elizabeth M. and EARLE, Timothy K. (eds) *Specialization, Exchange, and Complex Societies* (Cambridge: Cambridge U.P.).

BRUMFIEL, Elizabeth M. and FOX, John W. (eds) (1994) *Factional Competition and Political Development in the New World* (Cambridge: Cambridge U.P.).

BRYSON, Bethany (1996) '"Anything but Heavy Metal": Symbolic Exclusion and Musical Dislikes', *American Sociological Review,* 61/5, 884–899.

BRYSON, Bethany (1997) 'What about the Omnivores? Music Dislikes and Group-Based Identity Construction among Americans with Low Levels of Education', *Poetics,* 25/2–3, 141–156.

BULL, Michael (2004) 'Automobility and the Power of Sound', *Theory, Culture and Society,* 21/4–5, 243–259.

BURKE, Peter (1987a) *The Historical Anthropology of Early Modern Italy: Essays on Perception and Communication* (Cambridge: Cambridge U.P.).

BURKE, Peter (1987b) 'Introduction', in BURKE, Peter and PORTER, Roy (eds) *The Social History of Language* (Cambridge: Cambridge U.P.).

BURKE, Peter (1988 [1978]) *Popular Culture in Early Modern Europe* (London: Wildwood House).

BURKE, Peter (1993) *The Art of Conversation* (Cambridge: Cambridge U.P.).

BURKE, Peter (1995) *The Fortunes of the Courtier: European Reception of Castiglione's 'Cortegiano'* (Cambridge: Polity).

BURKE, Peter (1997) *Varieties of Cultural History* (Cambridge: Cambridge U.P.).

BURKE, Peter (2004) *What is Cultural History?* (Cambridge: Polity).

BURMAN, Barbara and TURBIN, Carole (eds) (2003) *Material Strategies: Dress and Gender in Historical Perspective* (Oxford: Blackwell).

BURNS, Tom (1966) 'The Study of Consummer Behaviour: A Sociological View', *European Journal of Sociology*, 7, 313–329.

CAMPBELL, Colin (1987) *The Romantic Ethic and the Spirit of Modern Consumerism* (Oxford: Blackwell).

CAMPBELL, Colin (1994) 'Capitalism, Consumption and the Problem of Motives: Some Issues in the Understanding of Conduct as Illusrated by an Examination of the Treatment of Motive and Meaning in the Work of Weber and Veblen', in FRIEDMAN, Jonathan (ed.) *Consumption and Identity* (Chur: Harwood Academic Press).

CAMPBELL, Colin (1995) 'Conspicuous Confusion? A Critique of Veblen's Theory of Conspicuous Consumption', *Sociological Theory*, 13/1, 37–47.

CANNADINE, David (1994) *Aspects of Aristocracy: Grandeur and Decline in Modern Britain* (New Haven: Yale U.P.).

CAPLAN, Gerald L. (1970) *The Elites of Barotseland 1878–1969: A Political History of Zambia's Western Province* (London: Hurst).

CARNEIRO, Robert L. (1981) 'Herbert Spencer as an Anthropologist', *The Journal of Libertarian Studies*, V/2, 153–210.

CASTIGLIONE, Baldassare (1974 [1528]) *The Book of the Courtier* (translated by Sir Thomas HOBY, London: J.M. Dent & Sons).

CHABAL, Patrick and DALOZ, Jean-Pascal (2006) *Culture Troubles: Politics and the Interpretation of Meaning* (London: Hurst Publ. and Chicago: The University of Chicago Press).

CHANEY, David (1996) *Lifestyles* (London: Routledge).

CHAO, Angela and SCHOR, Juliet B. (1998) 'Empirical Tests of Status Consumption: Evidence from Women's Cosmetics', *Journal of Economic Psychology*, 19, 107–131.

CHAPIN, F. Stuart (1928) 'A Quantitative Scale for Rating the Home and Social Environment of Middle Class Families in an Urban Community', *Journal of Educational Psychology*, 19/2, 99–111.

CICERO, Marcus Tullius (1977 [63 BC]) 'In Catilinam I-IV', in *Speeches (Selections)* (translated by Coll MacDONALD; London: Heinemann).

CLARK, Fiona (1982) *Hats* (London: Batsford).

CLARK, Grahame (1986) *Symbols of Excellence: Precious Materials as Expressions of Status* (Cambridge: Cambridge U.P.).

CLARKE, Terry N. (1969) *Gabriel Tarde: On Communication and Social Influence – Selected Papers* (Chicago: The University of Chicago Press).

CLUNAS, Craig (1991) *Superfluous Things: Material Culture and Social Status in Early Modern China*, 2nd edn (Honolulu: University of Hawai'i Press).

CODERE, Helen (1950) *Fighting with Property: A Study of Kwakiutl Potlatching and Warfare 1792–1930* (New York: J.J. Augustin).

CODY, Michael J. and McLAUGLHIN, Margaret L. (eds) (1990) *The Psychology of Tactical Communication* (Clevedon and Philadelphia: Multilingual Matters).

COHEN, Abner (1981) *The Politics of Elite Culture: Exploration in the Dramaturgy of Power in a Modern Society* (Los Angeles: University of California Press).

COLE, Patrick (1975) *Modern and Traditional Elites in the Politics of Lagos* (Cambridge: Cambridge U.P.).

COLEMAN, Richard P. (1983) 'The Continual Significance of Social Class to Marketing', *The Journal of Consumer Research*, 10/3, 265–280.

COLEMAN, Richard P. and NEUGARTEN, Bernice L. (1971) *Social Status in the City* (San Francisco: Jossey Bass).

COLEMAN, Richard P. and RAINWATER, Lee (1978) *Social Standing in America: New Dimensions of Class* (New York: Basic Books).

COLLINS, Randall (1975) *Conflict Sociology* (New York: Academic Press).

CONGALTON, Athol Alexander (1969) *Status and Prestige in Australia* (Melbourne: Cheshire).

COQUERY, Natacha (1998) *L'hôtel aristocratique au XVIIIè siècle* (Paris: Publications de la Sorbonne).

CROOK, Joseph Mordaunt (1999) *The Rise of the Nouveaux Riches: Style and Status in Victorian and Edwardian Architecture* (John Murray: London).

CROWLEY, John (2001) *The Invention of Comfort: Sensibilities and Design in Early Modern Britain and Early America* (Baltimore: Johns Hopkins U.P.).

CSIKSZENTMIHALYI, Mihaly and ROCHBERG-HALTON, Eugene (1981) *The Meanings of Things: Domestic Symbols and the Self* (Cambridge: Cambridge U.P.).

DALOZ, Jean-Pascal (1989) 'De l'importance des calendriers', *Politique Africaine*, 34, 109–111.

DALOZ, Jean-Pascal (1990) 'Voitures et prestige au Nigeria', *Politique Africaine*, 38, 148–153.

DALOZ, Jean-Pascal (1999) 'Pouvoir politique et ostentation: aspects culinaires', *Revue internationale de Politique comparée*, 6/2, 337–350.

DALOZ, Jean-Pascal (2002) *Elites et représentations politiques: la culture de l'échange inégal au Nigeria* (Pessac: Presses Universitaires de Bordeaux).

DALOZ, Jean-Pascal (2003) 'Ostentation in Comparative Perspective: Culture and Elite Legitimation' *Comparative Social Research*, 21, 29–62.

DALOZ, Jean-Pascal (2007a) 'Elite Distinction: Grand Theory and Comparative Perspectives', *Comparative Sociology* , 6/1–2, 27–74.

DALOZ, Jean-Pascal (2007b) 'Political Elites and Conspicuous Modesty: Norway, Sweden, Finland in Comparative Perspective' *Comparative Social Research*, 23, 171–210.

DALOZ, Jean-Pascal (2008) 'Towards the Cultural Contextualisation of Social Distinction', *Journal of Cultural Economy*, 1/3, 305–320.

DALOZ, Jean-Pascal (2010) 'How Political Representatives Gain Legitimacy: Symbolic Perspectives', *International Social Science Journal*, 196, forthcoming.

DARIAN, Jean C. (1998) 'Parents-Child Decision-Making in Children's Clothing Stores', *International Journal of Retail & Distribution Management*, 26/11, 421–428.

DAVIS, Fred (1989) 'Of Maids' Uniforms and Blue Jeans: The Drama of Status Ambivalences in Clothing and Fashion', *Qualitiative Sociology*, 12/4, 337–355.

DAVIS, James A. (1990 [1955]) *Living Rooms as Symbols of Status: A Study in Social Judgement* (New York: Garland).

DAWSON, Scott and CAVELL, Jill (1986) 'Status Recognition in the 1980s: Invidious Distinction Revisited', *Advances in Consumer Research*, 14, 487–491.

DE GRAZZIA, Victoria (1996) 'Introduction Part I: Changing Consumption Regimes', in DE GRAZZIA, Victoria with FURLOUGH, Ellen (eds) *The Sex of Things: Gender and Consumption in Historical Perspective* (Berkeley: University of California Press).

DEMOSTHENES (1990 [363 BC]) *Against Meidias (Oration 21)* (edited with introduction, translation, and commentary by Douglas M. MacDOWELL; Oxford: Clarendon Press).

DIETLER, Michael and HAYDEN, Brian (eds) (2001) *Feasts: Archeological and Ethnographic Perspectives on Food, Politics, and Power* (Washington: Smithsonian Inst.).

DIGGINS, John P. (1978) *The Bard of Savagery: Thorstein Veblen and Modern Social Theory* (New York: Seabury Press).

DiMAGGIO, Paul and USEEM, Michael (1978) 'Social Class and Arts Consumption: The Origins and Consequences of Class Differences in Exposure to the Arts in America', *Theory and Society*, 5/2, 141–161.

DINAN, Carmel (1983) 'Suggar Daddies and Gold Diggers: The White-Collar Single Women in Accra', in OPPONG, Christine (ed.) *Female and Male in West Africa* (London: George Allen & Unwin).

Distinktion – Scandinavian Journal of Social Theory (2004), 9, Special Issue on Gabriel Tarde.

DITTMAR, Helga (1992) *The Social Psychology of Material Possessions: To Have is to Be* (New York: Saint Martin's Press).

DOGAN, Mattei (ed.) (2003) *Elite Configurations at the Apex of Power* (Leiden and Boston: Brill).

DOMHOFF, William G. (1983) *Who Rules America Now? A View for the '80s* (Englewood Cliffs NJ: Prentice-Hall).

DORFMAN, Joseph (1966 [1934]) *Thorstein Veblen and His America* (New York: August M. Kelley Publ.).

DOUGLAS, Mary (1970) *Natural Symbols: Explorations in Cosmology* (New York: Pantheon).

DOUGLAS, Mary (ed.) (1984) *Food and the Social Order: Studies of Food and Festivities in Three American Communities* (New York: Russell Sage Foundation).

DOUGLAS, Mary and ISHERWOOD, Baron (1979) *The World of Goods: Towards an Anthropology of Consumption* (New York: Basic Books).

DREWAL, Henry John (1979) 'Pageantry and Power in Yoruba Costuming', in CORDWELL, Justine M. and SCHWARZ, Ronald A. (eds) *The Fabrics of Culture: The Anthropology of Clothing and Adornment* (La Haye: Mouton).

DUBOIS, Cora (1936) 'The Wealth Concept as an Integrative Factor in Tolowa Tutini Culture', in LOWIE, Robert (ed.) *Essays Presented to A. L. Kroeber* (Berkeley: University of California Press).

DUESENBERRY, James (1949) *Income, Saving and the Theory of Consumer Behavior* (Cambridge MA: Harvard U.P.).

DUINDAM, Jeroen (1995) *Myths of Power: Norbert Elias and the Early Modern European Court* (Amsterdam: Amsterdam U.P.).

DUNCAN, James S. (1981) 'From Container of Women to Status Symbol: The Impact of Social Structure on the Meaning of the House', in DUNCAN, James S. (ed.) *Housing and Identity: Cross Cultural Perspectives* (London: Croom Helm).

DÜRR, Hans Peter (1998) *Nudité et pudeur: Le mythe du processus de civilisation* (Paris: Editions de la Maison des sciences de l'Homme): the first of the 4 volumes published in German [1988].

ECHERUO, Michael J.C. (1977) *Victorian Lagos: Aspects of Nineteenth-Century Lagos Life* (London: Macmillan).

ECKERT, Claudia M. and DO, Ellen Yi-Luen (eds) (2006) Special Issue on 'Understanding, Representing and Reasoning about Style', *Artificial Intelligence for Engineering Designs, Analysis and Manufacturing,* 20.

EDENSOR, Tim (2004) 'Automobility and National Identity: Representation, Geography and Driving Practive', *Theory, Culture and Society,* 21/4–5,61–79.

EDGELL, Stephen (2001) *Veblen in Perspective: His Life and Thought* (Armonk NY: M.E. Sharpe).

EKHOLM FRIEDMAN, Kajsa (1977) 'External Exchange and the Transformation of Central African Social Systems', in FRIEDMAN, Jonathan and ROWLANDS, Michael (eds) *The Evolution of Social Systems* (London: Duckworth).

ELIAS, Norbert (1978a [1939]) *The Civilizing Process, vol. I: The History of Manners* (Oxford: Blackwell).

ELIAS, Norbert (1978b [1970]) *What is Sociology?* (London: Hutchinson).

ELIAS, Norbert (1982 [1939]) *The Civilizing Process, vol. II: State Formation and Civilization* (Oxford: Blackwell).

ELIAS, Norbert (1983 [1933]) *The Court Society* (Oxford: Blackwell).

ELSTER, Jon (1983) *Sour Grapes: Studies in the Subversion of Rationality* (Cambridge: Cambridge U.P.).

ENGELS, Friedrich (1940 [1884]) *The Origin of the Family, Private Property and the State* (London: Lawrence & Wishart).

EPICTETUS (1991 [2nd Century AD]) *Enchiridion* (translated by George LONG; New York: Prometheus Books).

ERICKSON, Bonnie H. (1996) 'Culture, Class and Connections', *American Journal of Sociology,* 102/1, 217–251.

EVANS, Franklin B. (1959) 'Psychological and Objective Factors in the Prediction of Brand Choice: Ford versus Chevrolet', *Journal of Business,* 32/4, 340–369.

EVANS, Grant (2002) 'Revolution and Royal Style: Problems of Post Socialist Legitimacy in Laos', in SHORE, Chris and NUGENT, Stephen (eds) *Elite Cultures: Anthropological Perspectives* (London: Routledge).

EWEN, Stuart (1988) *All Consuming Images: The Politics of Style in Contemporary Culture* (New York: Basic Books).

EWEN, Stuart and EWEN, Elizabeth (1992) *Channels of Desire: Mass Images and the Shaping of American Consciousness* (Minneapolis: University of Minnesota Press).

EWING, Elizabeth (1981) *Fur in Dress* (London: B.T. Batsford).

FALLERS, Lloyd A. (1961 [1954]) 'Fashion: A note on the "trickle-effect"', in LIPSET, Seymour and SMELSER, Neil (eds) *Sociology: Progress of a Decade* (Englewood Cliffs NJ: Prentice Hall).

FAUVE-CHAMOUX, Antoinette and WALL, Richard (eds) (2005) Special issue on 'Domestic Servants in Comparative Perspective', *History of the Family*, 10.

FEATHERSTONE, Mike (1987) 'Lifestyle and Consummer Culture', *Theory, Culture and Society*, 4/1, 55–70.

FEATHERSTONE, Mike (1991) *Consumer Culture and Post Modernism* (London: Sage).

FELSON, Marcus (1978) 'Invidious Distinctions Among Cars, Clothes and Suburbs', *The Public Opinion Quaterly*, 42/1, 49–58.

FELTWELL, John (1990) *The History of Silk* (London: Allan Sutton).

FESTINGER, Leon (1954) 'A Theory of Social Comparison Processes', *Human Relations*, 7, 117–140.

FEUERBACH, Ludwig (1957 [1841]) *The Essence of Christianity* (New York: Harper).

FIELD, G. Lowell and HIGLEY, John (1980) *Elitism* (London: Routledge).

FINKELSTEIN, Joanne (1989) *Dining Out: A Sociology of Modern Manners* (Cambridge: Polity).

FINKELSTEIN, Joanne (1991) *The Fashioned Self* (Cambridge: Polity).

FIRTH, Raymond (1970) 'Postures and Gestures of Respect', in POUILLON, Jean, MARANDA, Pierre (eds) *Echanges et Communications: Mélanges offerts à Claude Lévi-Strauss, vol. 1* (The Hague: Mouton).

FIRTH, Raymond (1973) *Symbols: Public and Private* (London: George Allen & Unwin).

FITZGERALD, F. Scott (1950 [1925]) *The Great Gatsby* ((Harmondsworth: Penguin).

FLANDRIN, Jean-Louis (1999) 'Distinction through Taste', in CHARTIER, Roger (ed.) *A History of Private Life (vol. 3) Passions of the Renaissance* (Cambridge MA: Harvard U.P.); original version in French: [1985] 'La distinction par le goût', in CHARTIER, Roger (ed.) *Histoire de la vie privée (vol. 3) De la Renaissance aux Lumières* (Paris: Le Seuil).

FLÜGEL, John Carl (1930) *The Psychology of Clothes* (London: The Hogarth Press).

FORM, William H. and STONE, Gregory P. (1957) 'Urbanism, Anonymity, and Status Symbolism' *American Journal of Sociology*, 62, 504–514.

FRANK, Robert H. (1985) 'The Demand for Unobservable and Other Nonpositional Goods', *American Economic Review*, 75/1, 101–116.

FRIEDMAN, Jonathan (1994) *Cultural Identity & Global Process* (London: Sage).

FRISBY, David (1992) *Simmel and Since: Essays on Georg Simmel's Social Theory* (London and New York: Routledge).

GALBRAITH, John Kenneth (1958) *The Affluent Society* (Boston: Houghton Mifflin).

GANDOULOU, Justin-Daniel (1989a) *Au cœur de la sape: Mœurs et aventures des Congolais à Paris* (Paris: L'Harmattan).

GANDOULOU, Justin-Daniel (1989b) *Dandies à Bacongo: le culte de l'élégance dans la société congolaise contemporaine* (Paris: L'Harmattan).

GANS, Herbert (1999 [1974]) *Popular Culture and High Culture: An Analysis and Evalutation of Taste*, 2nd edn (New York: Basic Books).

GARTMAN, David (2004) 'Three Ages of the Automobile: The Cultural Logic of the Car' *Theory, Culture and Society*, 21/4–5,169–195.

GEERTZ, Clifford (1973) *The Interpretation of Cultures: Selected Essays* (New York: Basic Books).

GEERTZ, Clifford (1980) *Negara: The Theatre State in Nineteenth Century Bali* (Princeton: Princeton U.P.).

GEERTZ, Clifford (1993 [1983]) *Local Knowledge: Further Essays in Interpretive Anthropology* (London: Fontana Press).

GERGEN, Kenneth J. (1973) 'Social Psychology as History', *Journal of Personality and Social Psychology*, 26/2, 309–320.

GERTH, Hans H. and MILLS, C. Wright (1954) *Character and Social Structure: The Psychology of Social Institutions* (London: Routledge & Kegan Paul).

GERTH, Hans H. and MILLS, C. Wright (1991 [1948]) *From Max Weber: Essays in Sociology* (London: Routledge).

GESCHIERE, Peter (1997) *The Modernity of Witchcraft: Politics and the Occult in Postcolonial Africa* (Charlottesville VA: University of Virginia Press).

GILROY, Paul (2001) 'Driving While Black', in MILLER, Daniel (ed.) *Car Cultures* (Oxford: Berg).

GILSENAN, Michael (1976) 'Lying, Honor and Contradiction', in KAPFERER, Bruce (ed.) *Transaction and Meaning* (Philadelphia: Institute for the Study of Human Issues).

GLUCKMAN, Max (1983 [1943]) 'Essays on Lozi Land and Royal Property', in DALTON, George (ed.) *Research in Economic Anthropology, vol. III* (Greenwhich, Conn: JAI Press).

GOFFMAN, Erving (1951) 'Symbols of Class Status', *British Journal of Sociology*, 2, 294–304.

GOFFMAN, Erving (1959) *The Presentation of Self in Everyday Life* (Garden City NJ: Anchor Books). Preliminary version (1958) (Edimburgh: University of Edimburgh).

GOFFMAN, Erving (1961) *Encounters* (Indianapolis: Bobbs-Merrill).

GOFFMAN, Erving (1963a) *Stigma: Notes on the Management of Spoiled Identity* (Englewood Cliffs NJ: Prentice Hall).

GOFFMAN, Erving (1963b) *Behaviour in Public Places: Notes on the Social Organization of Gatherings* (New York: The Free Press).

GOFFMAN, Erving (1967) *Interaction Ritual: Essays on Face-to-Face Behavior* (Garden City NJ: Anchor Books).

GOFFMAN, Erving (1970 [1969]) *Strategic Interaction* (Oxford: Blackwell).

GOFFMAN, Erving (1971) *Relations in Public: Micro studies of the Public Order* (New York: Basic Books).

GOFFMAN, Erving (1974) *Frame Analysis: Essays on the Organization of Experience* (New York: Harper and Row).

GOLDMAN, Robert and TICKAMYER, Ann (1984) 'Status Attainment and the Commodity Form: Stratification in Historical Perspective', *American Sociological Review*, 49/2, 196–209.

GONOS, George (1977) 'Situation versus Frame: The "Interactionist" and the "Structuralist" Analysis of Everyday Life', *American Sociological Review*, 42/6, 854–867.

GOODE, William J. (1959) 'The Theoretical Importance of Love', *American Sociological Review*, 24/1, 38–47.

GOODE, William J. (1978) *The Celebration of Heroes: Prestige as a Social Control System* (Berkeley: University of California Press).

GOODY, Jack (1982) *Cooking, Cuisine and Class: A Study in Comparative Sociology* (Cambridge: Cambridge U.P.).

GOODY, Jack (1996) *The East in the West* (Cambridge: Cambridge U.P.).

GORDON, Daniel (1994) *Citizens without Sovereignty: Equality and Sociability in French Thought, 1670–1789* (Princeton: Princeton U.P.).

GRACIAN, Baltasar (2005 [1647]) *The Art of Worldly Wisdom* (translated by Joseph JACOBS; Mineola NY: Dover Publications).

GRIGNON, Claude and PASSERON, Jean-Claude (1989) *Le savant et le populaire: Misérabilisme et populisme en sociologie et en littérature* (Paris: EHESS – Gallimard – Le Seuil).

GRONOW, Jukka (1997) *The Sociology of Taste* (London: Routledge).

GRONOW, Jukka (2003) *Caviar with Champagne: Common Luxury and the Ideals of the Good Life in Stalin's Russia* (Oxford: Berg).

GRUNDMANN, Reiner and STEHR, Nico (2001) 'Why is Werner Sombart Not Part of the Core of Classical Sociology?', *Journal of Classical Sociology*, 1/2, 257–287.

GUNN, Fenja (1973) *The Artificial Face: A History of Cosmetics* (Newton Abbot: David & Charles).

HALL, Edward T. (1966) *The Hidden Dimension* (New York: Doubleday).

HALLE, David (1993) *Inside Culture: Art and Class in the American Home* (Chicago: The University of Chicago Press).

HALNON, Karen Bettez (2002) 'Poor Chic: The Rational Consumption of Poverty', *Current Sociology*, 50/4, 501–516.

HASKELL, Francis (1980) *Patrons and Power: Art and Society in Baroque Italy* (New Haven: Yale U.P.).

HAUG, Wolfang Fritz (1986 [1971]) *Critique of Commodity Aesthetics* (Cambridge: Polity).

HEBDIGE, Dick (1979) *Subculture: The Meaning of Style* (London: Routledge).

HEINICH, Nathalie (2005) *L'élite artiste: excellence et singularité en régime démocratique* (Paris: Gallimard).

HELLMAN, Mimi (1999) 'Furniture, Sociability and the Work of Leisure in Eighteenth-Century France', *Eighteenth-Century Studies*, 32/4, 415–445.

HELMS, Mary W. (1988) *Ulysses' Sails: An Ethnographic Odyssey of Power, Knowledge and Geographical Distance* (Princeton: Princeton U.P.).

HELMS, Mary W. (1993) *Craft and the Kingly Ideal: Art, Trade and Power* (Austin: University of Texas Press).

HENDRICKSON, Hildi (ed.) (1996) *Clothing and Difference: Embodied Identities in Post-Colonial Africa* (Durham: Duke U.P.).

HEWES, Gordon W. (1955) 'World Distribution of Certain Postural Habits, Part 1', *American Anthropologist*, 57/2, 231–244.

HILL MAHER, Kristen (2004) 'Borders and Social Distinction in the Global Suburb', *American Quaterly*, 56/3, 781–806.

HINE, Thomas (1986) *Populuxe* (New York: Alfred A. Knopf).

HIRSCH, Fred (1977) *Social Limits to Growth* (London: Routledge & Kegan Paul).

HIRSCHMAN, Elizabeth C. and HOLBROOK, Morris B. (eds) (1981) *Symbolic Consumer Behavior* (Ann Arbor: Association for Consumer Research).

HOLLANDER, Anne (1980) *Seing Through Clothes* (New York: Viking Press).

HOLLINGSHEAD, August B. (1949) *Elmstown's Youth: The Impact of Social Classes on Adolescents* (New York: Wiley).

HOLMES, Janet (1992) *An Introduction to Sociolinguistics* (London: Longman).

HOLT, Douglas B. (1997) 'Distinction in America? Recovering Bourdieu's Theory of Tastes from its Critics', *Poetics*, 25/2–3, 93–120.

HOLT, Douglas B. (1998) 'Does Cultural Capital Structure American Consumption?' *Journal of Consumer Research*, 25/1, 1–25.

HORN, Pamela (1975) *The Rise and Fall of the Victorian Servant* (Dublin: Gill and Macmillan).

HOROWITZ, Irving Louis (ed.) (2002) *Veblen's Century: A Collective Portrait* (New Brunswick: Transaction Publishers).

HOROWITZ, R. Tamar (1975) 'From Elite Fashion to Mass Fashion', *Archives Européennes de Sociologie*, 16/2, 283–295.

HORWOOD, Catherine (2005) *Keeping Up Appearances: Fashion and Class between the Wars* (Stroud: Sutton Publishing).

HUGUES, Diane Owen (1983) 'Sumptuary Laws and Social Relations in Renaissance Italy', in BOSSY, John (ed.) *Disputes and Settlements: Law and Human Relations in the West* (Cambridge: Cambridge U.P.).

HUGUES, Diane Owen (1986) 'Distinguishing Signs: Ear-Rings, Jews and Fransciscan Rhetoric in the Italian Renaissance City', *Past & Present*, 112, 3–59.

HUNT, Alan (1996) *Governance of the Consuming Passions: A History of Sumptuary Law* (New York: Saint Martin's Press).

HUNT, Lynn (ed.) (1989) *The New Cultural History* (Berkeley and Los Angeles: University of California Press).

HUNT, Lynn (1990 [1987]) 'The Unstable Boundaries of the French Revolution', in PERROT, Michèle (ed.) *A History of Private Life (vol. 4) From the Fires of Revolution to the Great War* (Cambridge MA: Harvard U.P.).

HUPPERT, George (1977) *Les Bourgeois Gentilshommes: An Essay on the Definition of Elites in Renaissance France* (Chicago: The University of Chicago Press).

JAEGER, C. Stephen (1985) *The Origins of Courtliness: Civilizing Trends and the Formation of Courtly Ideals, 939–1210* (Philadelphia: University of Pennsylvania Press).

JAMES, Jeffrey (1987) 'Positional Goods, Conspicuous Consumption, and the International Demonstration Effect Reconsidered', *World Development*, 15/4, 449–462.

JOHNSON, Kim K.P. and LENNON, Sharon J. (eds) (1999) *Appearence and Power* (Oxford: Berg).

JORGENSEN, Elizabeth Watkins and JORGENSEN, Henry Irvin (1999) *Thorstein Veblen: Victorian Firebrand* (Armonk NY: M.E. Sharpe).

JOSEPH, Nathan (1986) *Uniforms and Nonuniforms: Communication through Clothing* (New York: Greenwood Press).

KANTOROWICZ, Ernst (1957) *The King's Two Bodies: A Study in Medieval Theology* (Princeton: Princeton U.P.).

KASSON, John F. (1990) *Rudeness and Civility: Manners in Nineteenth-Century Urban America* (New York: Hill & Wang).

KATZ-GERRO, Tally (2002) 'Highbrow Cultural Consumption and Class Distinction in Italy, Israel, West Germany, Sweden, and the United States' *Social Forces*, 81/1, 207–229.

KELLER, Suzanne (1963) *Beyond the Rulling Class: Strategic Elites in Modern Societies* (New York: Random House).

KHALIL, Elias L. (2000) 'Symbolic Products: Prestige, Pride and Identity Goods', *Theory and Decision*, 49, 53–77.

KING, Charles W. (1973 [1963]) 'A Rebuttal to the "Trickle Down" Theory', in WILLS, Gordon and MIDGLEY, David (eds) *Fashion Marketing: An Anthology of Viewpoints and Perspectives* (London: George Allen & Unwin).

KIRKLAND, Edward Chase (1976) 'The Big House Revisited', in BREWER, Thomas B. (ed.) *The Robber Barons: Saints or Sinners?* (New York: Holt, Rinehart & Winston).

KNIPE, Humphry and MACLAY, George (1972) *The Dominant Man: The Mystique of Personality and Prestige* (London: Souvenir Press).

KWASS, Michael (2003) 'Ordering the World of Goods: Consumer Revolution and the Classification of Objects in Eigthteenth-Century France', *Representations*, 82, 87–116.

LAMONT, Michèle (1992) *Money, Morals, and Manners: The Culture of the French and the American Upper-Middle Class* (Chicago: The University of Chicago Press).

LAMONT, Michèle and FOURNIER, Marcel (eds) (1992) *Cultivating Differencies: Symbolic Boundaries and the Making of Inequality* (Chicago: The University of Chicago Press).

LAMONT, Michèle and LAREAU, Annette (1988) 'Cultural Capital: Allusions, Gaps and Glissandos in Recent Theoretical Developments', *Sociological Theory*, 6, 153–168.

LAVER, James (1969) *Modesty in Dress: An Inquiry into the Fundamentals of Fashion* (London: Heinemann).

LEARS, Jackson (1994) *Fables of Abundance: A Cultural History of Advertizing in America* (New York: Basic Books).

LEENHARDT, Maurice (1947) *Do Kamo, la personne et le mythe dans le monde mélanésien* (Paris: Gallimard).

LEFEBVRE, Henri (1971) *Everyday Life in the Modern World* (London: Allen Lane – The Penguin Press); original version in French: [1968] *La vie quotidienne dans le monde moderne* (Paris: Gallimard).

LEIBENSTEIN, Harvey (1950) 'Bandwagon, Snob and Veblen Effects in the Theory of Consumers Demand', *Quaterly Journal of Economics*, 64, 183–207.

LEMAINE, Gérard (1974) 'Social Differentiation and Social Originality', *European Journal of Social Psychology*, 4/1, 17–52.

LENSKI, Gehrard E. (1966) *Power and Privilege: A Theory of Social Stratification* (Chapel Hill: University of North Carolina Press).

LE ROY LADURIE, Emmanuel (1997) *Saint-Simon ou le système de la cour* (Paris: Fayard).

LEVENSTEIN, Harvey (1988) *Revolution at the Table: The Transformation of the American Diet* (New York: Oxford U.P.).

LEVINE, Donald N. (ed.) (1971) *Georg Simmel: On Individual and Social Forms* (Chicago: University of Chicago Press).

LEVINE, Lawrence W. (1988) *Highbrow/Lowbrow: The Emergence of Cultural Hierarchy in America* (Cambridge MA: Harvard U.P.).

LÉVI-STRAUSS, Claude (1969) *The Elementary Structures of Kinship* (Boston: Beacon Press); original version in French (1967 [1949]) *Les structures élémentaires de la parenté*, 2nd edn (Paris: Mouton).

LE WITA, Béatrix (1988) *Ni vue ni connue: Approche ethnographique de la culture bourgeoise* (Paris: Maison des Sciences de l'Homme).

LILTI, Antoine (2005) *Le monde des salons: sociabilité et mondanité à Paris au XVIIIè siècle* (Paris: Fayard).

LINDER, Staffan Burendam (1970) *The Harried Leisure Class* (New York: Columbia U.P.).

LIPOVETSKY, Gilles (1994) *The Empire of Fashion: Dressing Modern Democracy* (Princeton: Princeton U.P.); original version in French: [1987] *L'empire de l'éphèmère: la mode et son destin dans les sociétés modernes* (Gallimard: Paris).

LIPSET, Seymour M. and BENDIX, Reinhard (1951) 'Social Status and Social Stucture: A Reexamination of Data and Interpretations', *British Journal of Sociology*, II/1, 150–168 and II/3, 230–254.

LÖFGREN, Orvar (1990) 'Consuming Interests', *Culture & History*, 7, 7–36.

LOFLAND, Lyn H. (1973) *A World of Strangers: Order and Action in Urban Public Space* (New York: Basic books).

LONGHURST, Brian, BAGNALL, Gaynor and SAVAGE, Mike (2001) 'Ordinary Consumption and Personal Identity: Radio and the Middle Classes in the North West of England', in GRONOW, Jukka and WARDE, Alan (eds) *Ordinary Consumption* (London: Routledge).

LOTTER, Stephanie (forthcoming) 'Distinctly Different Everywhere: The Politics of Appearance amongst Rana Elites Inside and Outside Nepal'.

LOVEJOY, Arthur and BOAS, George (1980 [1935]) *Primitivism and Related Ideas in Antiquity* (New York: Octagon Books).

LOW-BEER, Ann (ed.) (1969) *Herbert Spencer* (London: Collier Macmillan).

LOWE, Elizabeth D. (1984) 'Aesthetic Rules in Women's Apparel: Empirical Fact or Fantaisy', *Journal of Consumer Studies and Home Economics*, 8, 169–181.

LUCRETIUS (1969 [1st century BC]) *On the Nature of Things* (translated by Martin Ferguson SMITH; London: Sphere).

LUKACS, Georg (1971 [1923]) *History and Class Consciousness: Studies in Marxist Dialectics* (London: Merlin Press).

LUNT, Peter K. and LIVINGSTONE, Sonia M. (1992) *Mass Consumption and Personal Identity* (Buckingham: Open U.P.).

LURY, Celia (1996) *Consumer Culture* (Cambridge: Polity).

LYND, Robert and LYND, Helen Merrell (1929) *Middletown: A Study in American Culture* (New York: Harcourt, Brace and Co).

LYND, Robert and LYND, Helen Merrell (1937) *Middletown in Transition* (New York: Harcourt, Brace and Co).

MacEWEN, Alison M. (1974) 'Differentiation among the Urban Poor: An Argentine Story', in de KADT, Emanuel and WILLIAMS, Gavin (eds) *Sociology and Development* (San Diego: Tavistock).

MacHIAVELLI, Niccolo (1995 [1532]) *The Prince* (edited and translated by David WOOTTON; Indianapolis: Hackett Publ.).

MacKNIGHT, Elizabeth C. (2005) 'Cake and Conversation: The Women's Jour in Parisian High Society, 1880–1914', *French History*, 19/3, 342–363.

MANDEVILLE, Bernard (1962 [1714]) *The Fable of the Bees, or Private Vices, Public Benefits* (edited by Irwin PRIMER; New York: Capricorn Books).

MANGHAM, Iain and OVERINGTON, Michael A. (1987) *Organizations as Theatre: A Social Psychology of Dramatic Appearances* (Chichester: John Wiley & Sons).

MANSEL, Philip (2000) *Sultans in Splendor: Monarchs of the Middle East 1869–1945*, 2nd edn (London: Parkway Publ.).

MANSEL, Philip (2005) *Dressed to Rule: Royal and Court Costume from Louis XIV to Elizabeth II* (New Haven and London: Yale U.P.).

MARCUSE, Herbert (1991 [1964]) *One-Dimensional Man: Studies in the Ideology of Advanced Industrial Society* (London: Routledge).

MARTIN, Phyllis M. (1995) *Leisure and Society in Colonial Brazzaville* (Cambridge: Cambridge U.P.).

MARTIN-FUGIER, Anne (1990) *La vie élégante ou la formation du Tout-Paris, 1815–1848* (Paris: Fayard).

MARTIN-FUGIER, Anne (2004 [1979]) *La place des bonnes: la domesticité féminine à Paris en 1900* (Paris: Perrin).

MARX, Karl (1932 [1849]) *Wage-Labour and Capital* (Moscow: Progress Publishers).

MARX, Karl (2006 [1867]) *Capital: A Critique of Political Economy, vol. 1* (Harmondsworth: Penguin).

MARX, Karl and ENGELS, Friedrich (1998 [1845]) *The Communist Manifesto* (London: Verso).

MASON, Roger S. (1981) *Conspicuous Consumption: A Study of Exceptional Consumer Behaviour* (Westmead: Gower).

MAUSS, Marcel (1973) 'The Techniques of the Body', *Economy and Society*, 2/1, 70–88; original version in French: [1936] 'Les techniques du corps', in MAUSS, Marcel (1950) *Sociologie et anthropologie* (Paris: Presses Universitaires de France).

MAUSS, Marcel (1990) *The Gift: Forms and Functions of Exchange in Archaic Societies* (London: Routledge); original version in French: [1924] 'Essai sur le don: forme et raison de l'échange dans les sociétés archaïques', in MAUSS, Marcel (1950) *Sociologie et anthropologie* (Paris: Presses Universitaires de France).

MAZA, Sarah C. (1983) *Servants and Masters in Eighteenth-Century France* (Princeton: Princeton U.P.).

McCRACKEN, Grant (1990) *Culture and Consumption: New Approaches to the Symbolic Character of Consumer Goods and Activities* (Bloomington: Indiana U.P.).

McINTYRE, Richard (1992) 'Consumption in Contemporary Capitalism: Beyond Marx and Veblen', *Review of Social Economy*, 50/1, 40–60.

McKENDRICK, Neil, BREWER, John and PLUMB, J.H. (eds) (1982) *The Birth of a Consumer Society: The Commercialization of Eigtheenth-Century England* (London: Europa publications).

McVEIGH, Brian J. (2000) *Wearing Ideology: State, Schooling and Self-Presentation in Japan* (Oxford: Berg).

MENNELL, Stephen (1985) *All Manners of Food: Eating and Taste in England and France from the Middle Ages to the Present* (Oxford: Blackwell).

MENNELL, Stephen (1987) 'On the Civilizing of Appetite', *Theory, Culture and Society*, 4/2–3, 373–403.

MENNELL, Stephen (1989) *Norbert Elias: Civilization and the Human Self-Image* (Oxford: Blackwell).

MENNELL, Stephen and GOUDSBLOM, Johan (1997) 'Civilizing Process – Myth or Reality? A Comment on Duerr's Critique of Elias', *Comparative Studies in Society and History*, 39/4, 729–733.

MENSION-RIGAU, Eric (1990) *L'enfance au château: L'éducation familiale des élites françaises au XXè siècle* (Paris: Rivages).

MENSION-RIGAU, Eric (1997) *Aristocrates et grands bourgeois: éducation, traditions, valeurs* (Paris: Perrin).

MERTES, Kate (1988) *The English Noble Household 1250–1600: Good Governance and Political Rule* (Oxford: Blackwell).

MERTON, Robert (1949) 'Patterns of Influence: A Study of Interpersonal Influence and of Communications Behavior in a Local Community', in LAZARFELD, Paul A. and STANTON, Frank N. (eds) *Communication Research 1948–1949* (New York: Harper).

MERTON, Robert (1957) *Social Theory and Social Structure*, revised and enlarged edn (Glencoe: The Free Press).

MEYER, Heinz-Dieter (2000) 'Taste Formation in Pluralistic Societies: The Role of Rhetorics and Institutions', *International Sociology*, 15/1, 33–56.

MILLER, Daniel (ed.) (1995) *Worlds Apart: Modernity through the Prism of the Local* (London: Routledge).

MILLER, Daniel (2001) 'Driven Societies', in MILLER, Daniel (ed.) *Car Cultures* (Oxford: Berg).

MILLER, Michael B. (1981) *The Bon Marché: Bourgeois Culture and the Department Store, 1869–1920* (London: George Allen & Unwin).

MILLS, C. Wright (1956) *The Power Elite* (New York: Oxford U.P.).

MUKERJI, Chandra (1983) *From Graven Images: Patterns of Modern Materialism* (New York: Columbia U.P.).

MUKERJI, Chandra (1993) 'Reading and Writing with Nature: A Materialist Approach to French Formal Gardens', in BREWER, John and PORTER, Roy (eds) *Consumption and the World of Goods* (London and New York: Routledge).

MURPHY, Raymond (1988) *Social Closure: The Theory of Monopolization and Exclusion* (Oxford: Clarendon Press).

MURPHY, Robert F. (1964) 'Social Distance and the Veil', *American Anthropologist*, 66, 1257–1274.

NENADIC, Stana (1994) 'Middle-Rank Consummers and Domestic Culture in Edinburgh and Glasgow, 1720–1840', *Past and Present*, 145, 122–156.

NURSKE, Ragnar (1958) *Problems of Capital Formation in Under-Developed Countries* (Oxford: Blackwell).

O'CASS, Aron and McEWEN, Hmily (2004) 'Exploring Consumer Status and Conspicuous Consumption', *Journal of Consumer Behaviour*, 4/1, 25–39.

O'CONNELL, Sean (1998) *The Car and British Society: Class, Gender and Motoring, 1896–1939* (Manchester: Manchester U.P.).

OLLIVIER, Michèle, van EIJCK, Koen and WARDE, Alan (eds) Special Issue on 'Models of Omnivorous Cultural Consumption: New Directions in Research', *Poetics*, 36/2–3.

OSTROWER, Francie (1996) *Why the Wealthy Give: The Culture of Elite Philanthropy* (Princeton: Princeton U.P.).

OUSHAKINE, Serguei Alex (2000) 'The Quantity of Style: Imaginary Consumption in the New Russia', *Theory, Culture and Society*, 97–120.

OZOUF, Mona (1998) *Women's Words: Essay on French Singularity* (Chicago: The University Press of Chicago); original version in French: [1995] *Les mots des femmes: essai sur la singularité française* (Paris: Fayard).

PACKARD, Vance (1960) *The Status Seekers* (London: Longman).

PACKARD, Vance (1989) *The Ultra Rich* (Boston: Little Brown).

PARRY, Jonathan and BLOCH, Maurice (eds) (1989) *Money and the Morality of Exchange* (Cambridge: Cambridge U.P.).

PASCAL, Blaise (1976 [1670]) *Pensées* (Paris: Garnier Flammarion).

PELEGGI, Maurizio (2004) 'Royal Antiquarianism, European Orientalism and the Production of Archælogical Knowledge in Modern Siam', in RAVI,

Srilata, RUTTEN Mario and GOH, Beng-Lan (eds) *Asia in Europe, Europe in Asia* (Singapore: ISEAS Publications).

PERROT, Philippe (1995) *Le luxe: une richesse entre faste et confort, XVIIIe-XIXe siècle* (Paris: Le Seuil).

PERROT, Philippe (1996) *Fashioning the Bourgeoisie: A History of Clothing in the Nineteenth Century* (Princeton: Princeton U.P.); original version in French: [1981] *Les dessus et les dessous de la bourgeoisie: une histoire du vêtement au XIXè siècle* (Paris: Fayard).

PETERSON, Richard A. (1992) 'Understanding Audience Segmentation: From Elite and Mass to Omnivore and Univore', *Poetics*, 21/4, 243–258.

PETERSON, Richard A. and KERN, Roger M. (1996) 'Changing Highbrow Taste: From Snob to Omnivore', *American Sociological Review*, 61/5, 900–907.

PFAUTZ, Harold and DUNCAN, Otis Dudley (1950) 'A Critical Evaluation of Warner's Work in Community Stratification', *American Sociological Review*, 15, 205–215.

PICKENPAUGH, Thomas E. (1997) 'Symbols of Rank, Leadership, and Power in Traditional Cultures', *International Journal of Osteoarchaeology*, 7, 522–541.

PINCHES, Michael (ed.) (1999) *Culture and Privilege in Capitalist Asia* (London and New York: Routledge).

PINÇON, Michel and PINÇON-CHARLOT, Monique (1989) *Dans les beaux quartiers* (Paris: Le Seuil).

PLATO (1941 [circa 380 BC]) *The Republic* (translated and edited by Francis MacDONALD CORNFORD; London: Oxford U.P.).

POIRIER, Jean (ed.) (1968) Special Issue on 'L'économie ostentatoire: Etudes sur l'économie du prestige et du don', *Tiers Monde*, IX.

PÖLLNITZ, Monsieur de (2004 [1734]) *La Saxe galante* (Paris: Mercure de France).

POLY, Jean-Pierre (2003) *Le chemin des amours barbares: Genèse médiévale de la sexualité européenne* (Paris: Perrin).

POMIAN, Krzystof (1994 [1978]) 'The Collection between the Visible and Invisible', in PEARCE, Susan M. (ed.) *Interpreting Objects and Collections* (London: Routledge).

RAPOPORT, Amos (1982) *The Meaning of the Built Environment* (Beverly Hills: Sage).

RAPPAPORT, Erika (2000) *Shopping for Pleasure: Women in the Making of London's West End* (Princeton: Princeton U.P.).

RESNICK, Stephan A. and WOLF, Richard D. (1987) *Knowledge and Class: A Marxian Critique of Political Economy* (Chicago: The University of Chicago Press).

RHEIMS, Maurice (1990) 'Histoire du mobilier', in POIRIER, Jean (ed.) *Histoire des mœurs I, vol. 2* (Paris: Gallimard).

RIBEIRO, Aileen (2002) *Dress in Eighteenth-Century Europe, 1715–1789*, 2nd edn (New Haven: Yale U.P.).

RIDGEWAY, Cecilia, BERGER, Joseph and SMITH, LeRoy (1985) 'Nonverbal Cues and Status: An Expectation State Approach', *American Journal of Sociology*, 90/5, 955–978.

RIESMAN, David (1995 [1953]) *Thorstein Veblen* (New Brunswick: Transaction Publishers).

RIESMAN, David, in collaboration with DENEY, Reuel and GLAZER, Nathan (1950) *The Lonely Crowd: A Study of the Changing American Character* (New Haven: Yale U.P.).

ROBERTS, Mary Louise (1998) 'Review Essay: Gender, Consumption, and Commodity Culture', *American Historical Review*, 103/3, 817–844.

ROBINSON, Richard and GOODMAN, David S.G. (eds) (1996) *The New Rich in Asia: Mobile Phones, McDonald's and Middle-Class Revolution*. (London and New York: Routledge).

ROCHE, Daniel (1994) *The Culture of Clothing: Dress and Fahsion in the Ancien Regime* (Cambridge: Cambridge U.P.); original version in French: [1989] *La culture des apparences: une histoire du vêtement, XVIIè-XVIIIè siècle* (Paris: Fayard).

ROCHE, Daniel (2000) *An History of Everyday Things: The Birth of Consumption in France, 1600–1800* (Cambridge: Cambridge U.P.); original version in French: [1997] *Histoire des choses banales: naissance de la consommation XVIIè-XIXè siècle* (Paris: Fayard).

ROJEK, Chris (2000) 'Leisure and the Rich Today: Veblen's Thesis after a Century', *Leisure Studies*, 19/1, 1–15.

ROSCOE, Paul (2000) 'New Guinea Leadership as Ethnographic Analogy: A Critical Review', *Journal of Archaeological Method and Theory*, 7/2, 79–126.

ROSS, Robert (1999) *Status and Respectability in the Cape Colony 1750–1870: A Tragedy of Manners* (Cambridge: Cambridge U.P.).

ROTH, Guenther and WITTICH, Claus (eds) (1978 [1968]) *Max Weber – Economy and Society: An Outline of Interpretive Sociology*, 2 vols (Berkeley and Los Angeles: University of California Press).

ROUSSEAU, Jean-Jacques (1992) *Discourse on the Sciences and Arts (first discourse) and Polemics* (edited by MASTERS, Roger D. and KELLY, Christopher; Hanover NH: University Press of New England). French version: (2004 [1750]) *Discours sur les sciences et les arts* (Paris: LGF).

ROUSSEAU, Jean-Jacques (2003) *Emile – or Treatise in Education* (translated by William H. PAYNE; Amhurst: Prometheus Books). French version: (1995 [1762]) *Emile ou De l'éducation* (Paris: Gallimard).

ROUVILLOIS, Frédéric (2006) *Histoire de la politesse de 1789 à nos jours* (Paris: Flammarion).

ROWLANDS, Michael (1994) 'The Material Culture of Success: Ideals and Life Cycles in Cameroon', in FRIEDMAN, Jonathan (ed.) *Consumption and Identity* (Chur: Harwood Academic Press).

ROWLEY, Anthony (2006) *Une histoire mondiale de la table: stratégies de bouche* (Paris: Odile Jacob).

RUSSEL, Penny (2002) 'The Brash Colonial: Class and Comportment in Nineteenth-Century Australia', *Transactions of the Royal Historical Society*, 12, 431–453.

SABATIER, Gérard (1999) *Versailles ou la figure du roi* (Paris: Albin Michel).

SAHLINS, Marshall D. (1963) 'Poor Man, Rich Man, Big Man, Chief: Political Types in Melanesia and Polynesia', *Comparative Studies in Society and History*, 5/3, 285–303.

SAHLINS, Marshall D. (1976) *Culture and Practical Reason* (Chicago: The University of Chicago Press).

SARAM, P.A. (1999) 'The Vanishing Subtitle in Veblen's *Leisure Class*', *International Journal of Politics, Culture and Society*, 13/2, 225–240.

SCHAMA, Simon (1987) *The Embarrassment of Riches: An Interpretation of Dutch Culture in the Golden Age* (London: Collins).

SCHWARTZ, Barry (1967) 'The Social Psychology of the Gift', *American Journal of Sociology*, 73/1, 1–11.

SCOTT, John (1996) *Stratification and Power: Structures of Class, Status and Command* (Cambridge: Polity).

SCOTT, Katie (1995) *The Rococo Interior: Decoration and Social Spaces in Early Eighteenth-Century Paris* (New Haven: Yale U.P.).

SEELEY, John R., SIM, R.A. and LOOSLEY, Elizabeth W (1956) *Crestwood Heights: A Study of the Culture of Suburban Life* (New York: Basic Books).

SELLERBERG, Ann-Mari (1994) *A Blend of Contradictions: Georg Simmel in Theory and Practice* (New Brunswick: Transaction Publishers).

SEMON, Thomas T. (1979) 'On Felson's "Invidious Distinctions"', *Public Opinion Quaterly*, 43/1, 119–120.

SENNETT, Richard (1992 [1977]) *The Fall of Public Man* (New York and London: W.V. Norton and Company).

SHIBUTANI, Tamotsu (1955) 'Reference Groups as Perspectives', *The American Journal of Sociology*, 60/6, 562–569.

SHOVLIN, John (2000) 'The Cultural Politics of Luxury in Eigtheenth-Century France', *French Historical Studies*, 23/4, 577–606.

SIMMEL, Georg (1957 [1904]) 'Fashion', *The American Journal of Sociology*, LXII/6, 541–558.

SIMMEL, Georg (1978 [1900]) *Philosophy of Money* (London: Routledge).

SIMMEL, Georg (1984 [1909]) *On Women, Sexuality and Love* (ed. by OAKES, Guy; New Haven: Yale U.P.).

SLATER, Don (1997) *Consumer Culture and Modernity* (Cambridge: Polity).

SMITH, Peter B. and BOND, Michael Harris (1993) *Social Psychology Across Cultures: Analysis and Perspectives* (New York: Harvester Wheatsheaf).

SOLOMON, Michael R. (ed.) (1985) *The Psychology of Fashion* (Lexington MA: Lexington books).

SOMBART, Werner (1967 [1913]) *Luxury and Capitalism* (Ann Arbor: The University of Michigan Press).

SPENCER, Herbert (1893) *The Principles of Sociology vol. II/part IV Ceremonial Institutions* (London: Williams & Norgate).

SPINDLER, Michael (2002) *Veblen and Modern America: Revolutionary Iconoclast* (London: Pluto Press).

STANLEY, Tim (2004) *Palace and Mosque* (London: V & A Publications).

STAROBINSKI, Jean (2006 [1964]) *L'invention de la liberté, 1700–1789,* 2nd edn (Paris: Gallimard).

STEARNS, Peter (1997) 'Stages in Consumerism: Recent Work on the Issues of Periodization', *Journal of Modern History*, 69, 102–117.

STEARNS, Peter (2001) *Consumerism in World History: The Global Transformation of Desire* (London: Routledge).

STEELE, Valerie (1985) *Fashion and Eroticism: Ideals of Feminine Beauty from the Victorian Era to the Jazz Age* (New York: Oxford U.P.).

STEELE, Valerie (2001) *The Corset: A Cultural History* (New Haven: Yale U.P.).

STONE, Lawrence (1967) *The Crisis of the Aristocracy 1558–1641* (New York: Oxford U.P.).

STONE, Lawrence (1977) *Family, Sex and Marriage, 1500–1800* (New York: Harper & Row).

STRONG, Roy C. (2002) *Feast: A History of Grand Eating* (London: Jonathan Cape).

SULLIVAN, Oriel and GERSHUNY, Jonathan (2004) 'Inconspicuous Consumption: Work-Rich, Time-Poor in the Liberal Market Economy', *Journal of Consumer Culture*, 4/1, 79–100.

SULS, Jerry and WILLS, Thomas Ashby (eds) (1991) *Social Comparison: Contemporary Theory and Research* (Hillsade NJ: Lawrence Erlbaum).

SWANN, G.M. Peter (2001) 'The Demand for Distinction and the Evolution of the Prestige Car', *Journal of Evolutionary Economics*, 11, 59–75.

SWIFT, Jonathan (1808 [1708]) *Works - Vol. III* (London: J. Nichols and Son).

SYNNOTT, Anthony (1987) 'Shame and Glory: A Sociology of Hair', *The British Journal of Sociology*, 38/3, 381–413.

TACITUS, Cornelius (2005 [2nd Century AD]) *Annals, Books 1–6* (Cambridge: Cambridge U.P.).

TAJFEL, Henri (ed.) (1978) *Differentiation between Social Groups: Studies in the Social Psychology of Intergroup Relations* (London: Academic Press).

TAJFEL, Henri (ed.) (1984) *The Social Dimension: European Developments in Social Psychology, 2 vol.* (Cambridge: Cambridge U.P. and Paris: éditions de la Maison des Sciences de l'Homme).

TARDE, Gabriel de (1962) *The Laws of Imitation* (Gloucester: P. Smith); French version: *Les lois de l'imitation* (1993 [1890] Paris: Kimé).

TARDE, Gabriel de (2003 [1899]) *Les transformations du pouvoir* (Paris: Les empêcheurs de tourner en rond - Le Seuil).

TASCHEN, Angelika (ed.) (2008) *Aesthetic Surgery* (Köln: Taschen).

TAUBER, Edward M. (1972) 'Why Do People Shop?', *Journal of Marketing*, 36/4, 46–59.

THOMPSON, Craig J. and TAMBYAH, Siok Kuan (1999) 'Trying to be Cosmopolitan', *The Journal of Consumer Research*, 26/3, 214–241.

THOMPSON, Edward P. (1991) *Customs in Common* (London: Merlin Press).

THURGOOD HAYNES, Michaele (1998) *Dressing up Debutantes: Peagantry and Glitz in Texas* (Oxford: Berg).

THURLOW, Crispin and JAWORSKI, Adam (2006) 'The Alchemy of the Upwardly Mobile: Symbolic Capital and the Stylization of Elites in Frequent-Flyer Programmes', *Discourse and Society*, 17/1, 99–135.

TILMAN, Rick (1992) *Thorstein Veblen and His Critics, 1891–1963: Conservative, Liberal and Radical Perspectives* (Princeton: Princeton U.P.).

TILMAN, Rick (1996) *The Intellectual Legacy of Thorstein Veblen: Unresolved Issues* (London: Greenwood Press).

TRAUBE, Elizabeth G. (1989) 'Secrets of Success in Postmodern Society', *Cultural Anthropology*, 4/3, 273–300.

TRENTMANN, Frank (2004) 'Beyond Consumerism: New Historical Perspectives on Consumption', *Journal of Contemporary History*, 39/3, 373–401.

TRENTMANN, Frank (ed.) (2006) *The Making of the Consumer: Knowledge, Power and Identity in the Modern World* (Oxford: Berg).

TRIGG, Andrew B. (2001) 'Veblen, Bourdieu and Conspicuous Consumption', *Journal of Economic Issues*, 35/1, 99–115.

TRUBITT, Mary Beth D. (2003) 'The Production and Exchange of Marine Shell Prestige Goods', *Journal of Archaelogical Research*, 11/3, 243–277.

TURBIN, Carole (2003) 'Fashioning the American Man: The Arrow Collar Man, 1907–1931', in BURMAN, Barbara and TURBIN, Carole (eds) *Material Strategies: Dress and Gender in Historical Perspective* (Oxford: Blackwell).

TURNER, Bryan and EDMUNDS, June (2002) 'The Distate of Taste: Bourdieu, Cultural Capital and the Australian Postwar Elite', *Journal of Consumer Culture*, 2/2, 219–240.

TURNER, Roger (1999 [1985]) *Capability Brown and the Eighteenth-Century English Landscape* (Chichester: Phillimore).

URRY, John (2004) 'The System of Automobility', *Theory, Culture and Society*, 21/4–5, 25–39.

van DER VEEN, Marijke (2003) (ed.) Special issue on 'When is Food a Luxury?', *World Archaeology*, 34/3.

van KRIEKEN, Robert (1998) *Norbert Elias* (London and New York: Routledge).

VEBLEN, Thorstein (1994 [1899]) *The Theory of the Leisure Class* (New York: Dover Publications).

VEYNE, Paul (1976) *Le pain et le cirque: Sociologie historique d'un pluralisme politique* (Paris: Le Seuil).

VEYNE, Paul (1988) 'Conduites sans croyances et œuvres d'art sans spectateurs', *Diogène*, 143, 3–22.

VICHERT, Gordon (1971) 'The Theory of Conspicuous Consumption in the 18th Century', in HUGUES, Peter and WILLIAMS, David (eds) *The Varied Pattern: Studies in the 18th Century* (Toronto: M. Hakkert).

VIGARELLO, Georges (2000) *A History of Rape: Sexual Violence in France from the 16th to the 20th Century* (Cambridge: Polity); original version in French: [1998] *Histoire du viol, XVIe-XXe siècle* (Paris: Le Seuil).

VIGARELLO, Georges (2004) *Histoire de la beauté: le corps et l'art d'embellir de la Renaissance à nos jours* (Paris: Le Seuil).

vom BRUKE, Gabriele (2005) 'The imagined "Consumer Democracy" and Elite (Re)Production in Yemen', *Journal of the Royal Anthropological Institute* (N.S.), 11, 255–275.

VINCENT, Susan (2003) *Dressing the Elite: Clothes in Early Modern Britain* (Oxford: Berg).

WAGNER, Anne-Catherine (1998) *Les nouvelles élites de la mondialisation: une immigration dorée en France* (Paris: Presses Universitaires de France).

WARDE, Alan (1997) *Consumption, Food and Taste: Culinary Antinomies and Commodity Culture* (London: Sage).

WARDE, Alan (2002) 'Production, Consumption and "Cultural Economy"', in DU GAY, Paul and PRYKE, Michael (eds) *Cultural Economy: Cultural Analysis and Commercial Life* (London: Sage).

WARDE, Alan (ed.) (2008) Special Issue on 'Cultural Consumption, Classification and Power', *Journal of Cultural Economy*, 1/3.

WARDE, Alan, MARTENS, Lydia and OLSEN, Wendy (1999) 'Consumption and the Problem of Variety: Cultural Omnivorousness, Social Distinction and Dining Out', *Sociology*, 33/1, 105–127.

WARDE, Alan and MARTENS, Lydia (2000) *Eating Out: Social Differentiation, Consumption and Pleasure* (Cambridge: Cambridge U.P.).

WARNER, W. Lloyd (1953) *American Life: Dream and Reality* (Chicago: The University of Chicago Press).

WARNER, W. Lloyd (1959) *The Living and the Dead: A Study of the Symbolic Life of Americans* (New Haven: Yale U.P.).

WARNER, W. Lloyd and LUNT, Paul S. (1941) *The Social Life of a Community* (New Haven: Yale U.P.).

WARNER, W. Lloyd and LUNT, Paul S. (1942) *The Status System of a Modern Community* (New Haven: Yale U.P.).

WARNER, W. Lloyd, MECKER, Marchia and KENNETH, Eills (1949) *Social Class in America: A Manual of Procedure for the Measurement of Social Status* (Chicago: Science Research Associates).

WARNER, W. Lloyd and Collaborators (1949) *Democracy in Jonesville: A Study of Quality and Inequality* (New York: Harper & Brothers).

WATNEY, Marylian (1961) *The Elegant Carriage* (London: J. A. Allen).

WEATHERHILL, Lorna (1988) *Consumer Behaviour and Material Culture in Britain, 1660–1760* (London: Routledge).

WEBER, Max (1951 [1915]) *The Religion of China: Taoism and Confucianism* (New York: The Free Press).

WEINSTEIN, Deena and WEINSTEIN, Michael A. (1993) *Postmodern(ized) Simmel* (London and New York: Routledge).

WERBNER, Pnina (1996) 'The Enigma of Christmas: Symbolic Violence, Compliant Subjects and the Flow of English Kinship', in EDGELL, Stephen, HETHERINGTON, Kevin and WARDE, Alan (eds) *Consumption Matters: The Production and Experience of Consumption* (Oxford: Blackwell).

WHARTON, Edith (1997 [1905]) *The House of Mirth* (Ware: Wordsworth).

WHIMSTER, Sam (1992) 'Yuppie: A Keyword of the 1980s', in BUDD, Leslie and WHIMSTER, Sam (eds) *Global Finance & Urban Living: A Study of Metropolitan Change* (London: Routledge).

WHYTE, William H. (1956) *The Organization Man* (Garden City NJ: Doubleday Anchor Books).

WIESSNER, Polly (1996) 'Levelling the Hunter: Constraints on the Status Quest in Foraging Societies', in WIESSNER, Polly and SCHIEFENHÖVEL, Wulf (eds) *Food and the Status Quest: An Interdisciplinary Perspective* (Providence RI: Bergham Books).

WIESSNER, Polly and SCHIEFENHÖVEL, Wulf (eds) (1996) *Food and the Status Quest: An Interdisciplinary Perspective* (Providence RI: Bergham Books).

WILK, Richard (1990) 'Consumer Goods as Dialogue about Development', *Culture & History*, 7, 79–100.

WILLIAMS, Raymond (1982) *The Sociology of Culture* (New York: Schocken books).

WILLIAMS, Rosalind H. (1982) *Dream Worlds: Mass Consumption in Late Nineteenth Century France* (Berkeley: University of California Press).

WILLS, Thomas Ashby (1981) 'Downward Comparisons Principles in Social Psychology', *Psychological Bulletin*, 90/2, 245–271.

WILSON, Peter J. (1973) *Crab Antics: The Social Anthropology of English Speaking Negro Societies of the Caribean* (New Haven: Yale U.P.).

WOLFF, Kurt H. (ed.) (1950) *The Sociology of Georg Simmel* (Glencoe: The Free Press).

WOOD, Joanne V. (1989) 'Theory and Research Concerning Social Comparisons of Personal Attributes', *Psychological Bulletin*, 106/2, 231–248.

WOUTERS, Cas (1977) 'Informalisation in the Civilising Process', in GLEICHMANN, Peter Reinhart *et al.* (eds) *Human Figurations: Essays for Norbert Elias* (Amsterdam: Amsterdams Sociologisch Tijdschrift).

WOUTERS, Cas (2004) *Sex and Manners: Female Emancipation in the West 1890–2000* (London: Sage).

WOUTERS, Cas (2007) *Informalization: Manners and Emotions since 1890* (Los Angeles: Sage).

WRIGLEY, Richard (2002) *The Politics of Appearances: Representation of Dress in Revolutionary France* (Oxford: Berg).

ZOLA, Emile (1972) *Nana* (London: Penguin Classics); original version in French: [1880] (Paris: Charpentier).

Name Index

Subject Index